Enduring respect for Dr. Tav
and early praise for *Inside*

"[Tawfik] Hamid is a great scholar whose knowledge of terrorism is extremely valuable. There is no doubt about his firsthand experience and depth of knowledge. He is truly a treasure."

—Lt. Gen. Claude M. "Mick" Kicklighter, U.S. Army (retired)

"I have had the distinct pleasure of knowing Dr. Hamid for quite some time and through some rather dark and challenging days. He is clearly one of the most courageous men I have ever known. He has stood up fearlessly to the tsunami of Islamic extremism to share his tolerant vision of the immediate need for Islam's reformation – to truly become a religion of peace. He has risked himself and his family to fanatic, horrific violence for this "crime."

If there is to be hope for a beginning to a better world, and for future generations to be spared endless religious war with massive casualties, then Dr. Hamid is the answer – the personification, the embodiment – of that hope. Should we ignore him and others like him, and not support their message to the fullest extent, then we shall reap the whirlwind. I am eminently proud, and greatly honored, to call this man my friend. I am grateful to, and blessed by, the Good Lord to think of him as my brother."

—Dr. Robert Katz, Executive Director, The Intelligence Summit SM

"Dr. Tawfik Hamid has a compelling personal story. He's had a front-row seat to radical Islam and has firsthand knowledge of the dangers posed by the growing global *jihad* movement. His is a voice that must be heard."

—Van D. Hipp, Jr., Chairman, American Defense International, Inc.

"*Inside Jihad* is a powerful source book by a former insider who explains how Islamic jihadists use their strict interpretation of the Quran and the *hadiths* to recruit new members and indoctrinate them into a culture of hate. Today, as many as 25,000 foreigners have traveled to the Middle East to join up with ISIS, al-Qaeda and other terror groups. But Dr. Hamid's book demonstrates how the same holy texts can be used to counter the jihadist message. It is a must-read for scholars, and lawmakers and policy-makers during this critical period."

—Cecily Hilleary, Reporter, Middle East Monitor, Voice of America

"The world is on fire. The West must awaken to the reality of the threats it currently faces. The spread of violent Islamic *jihad* in the 21st century is one of the greatest threats to world peace since the rise of violent fascism, Nazism and communism in the 20th century. Many people denied the reality of the threats of these isms, which resulted in the deaths of millions around the world before, during and after World War II and the Cold War. History is repeating itself with the rise of Islamic *jihad* and ISIS. Many in the U.S. government, media, academia and the public are in denial about this threat.

"Dr. Hamid's well-researched, well-written and clearly presented information in *Inside Jihad* is mandatory reading for everyone who wants to understand the reality of the threats the world faces. You must know your enemy to defeat your enemy, and Dr. Hamid knows the enemy as only a former jihadist could know. The CI Centre uses this book for all of our courses on terrorism. Every serious educator in this field would be wise to do the same. Eventually the Western world will have to face the truth of violent *jihad*, just as it was forced to face and defeat fascism and Nazism."

—David G. Major, retired FBI executive,
founder of the Centre for Counterintelligence and Security Studies

"When he writes about jihadism, Tawfik Hamid knows whereof he speaks. Having experienced radicalization himself, before quitting in time this danger-ous path, he has been able to identify the key elements that are used by radical Islamists to attract young men to their ranks. *Inside Jihad* is an illuminating read for anyone willing to understand a phenomenon that constitutes a huge threat to our modern world."

—Laure Mandeville, Chief U.S. Correspondent, *Le Figaro*

"Dr. Tawfik Hamid is uniquely qualified by background, culture, and faith to speak cogently on the issue of radical Islam and how it is used as a tool by those seeking power. An Egyptian, Dr. Hamid grew up knowing the allure of radical-ism in his country and the effects it has had, not only in Egypt but also through-out the Islamic world. Using a rational, critical examination of jihadism and its emotional forces, Dr. Hamid has developed powerful strategies to address – and hopefully defeat – the use of the Islamic faith as a weapon."

—Jeff Young, Senior Analyst/Investigative Correspondent,
Voice of America TV

Inside Jihad

Inside Jihad

Dr. Tawfik Hamid

UPDATED EDITION

MOUNTAIN LAKE PRESS
Mountain Lake Park, Maryland

NOTE FROM THE AUTHOR

I did not use traditional translations of the Quran, because many do not convey a precise understanding of the verses. Instead, I translated the Quranic text from Arabic (my mother tongue) into English in a way that conveys how the verses are understood and interpreted by most Islamic scholars. In addition, because there are no formal rules for transliterating Arabic into English, I used the most common spellings found in Google searches. I hope by doing so I have made it easier for readers who wish to delve more deeply into the background of the names and concepts discussed in the text.

Inside Jihad
How Radical Islam Works; Why It Should Terrify Us; How to Defeat It

Copyright © 2015 Dr. Tawfik Hamid – All Rights Reserved
ISBN: 978-0-9908089-1-6
Library of Congress Control No. 2014945085

Published in the United States of America
By Mountain Lake Press

Design by Michael Hentges

Cover photo: Medyan Dairieh/ZUMA Wire

Printed in the United States of America

To the soul of my father, Mohamed Abdelhamid, M.D.,
to my dear wife, Maha, to my son, Mada,
and to my daughter, Mariam

Contents

Foreword

As we watch the most recent news and video reports of the acts of barbarism conducted by ISIS, we in the civilized world are shocked, sickened and confounded by a threat that appears to be growing out of control. Any rational person wants to know how such evil could exist in the modern world. Who are these people? What motivates them? Is there something in Islamic culture that prompts such behavior? Can these atrocities be stopped?

For the past several years, like many I've wondered about these and other essential questions regarding the growth of radical Islam. America's foreign policy and military solutions appear inadequate in stemming the rising tide of ISIS and related organizations. Moreover, ISIS leaders publicly state their intent to spread influence throughout the world in pursuit of imposing Sharia law under an Islamic Caliphate. Their primary means of advancement is death and destruction of any person, group or institution that attempts to resist.

One assumes that "moderate Muslims" are waiting in the wings to rise up, denounce the videotaped beheadings of group after group of Christian and Muslim victims, and demonstrate their revulsion en masse. And yet few, if any, such counter actions seem to occur within Islam.

Is the world headed toward a protracted war of civilizations? What happens if Islamic radicals, who promote suicide bombings, beheadings, unspeakable oppression of women and annihilation of ancient religious sites, acquire access to nuclear weapons?

At this critical 21st-century moment, I consider it vital for elected officials, law enforcement, pastors, business leaders, scholars, teachers, community leaders and parents to become educated – fast and with sufficient depth – about what drives radical Islamists. To that end, this book is an essential resource.

Having just completed *Inside Jihad* by Dr. Tawfik Hamid, my orientation has shifted from a limited understanding to clarity. He provides a roadmap for the West that is accessible, concise, current and sufficiently thorough to enhance any serious reader's frame of reference.

Dr. Hamid brings a unique perspective to the challenge of diagnosing radical Islam and prescribing a solution to this modern-day scourge. The combination of his Egyptian and family roots, fluency in Arabic and English, and his medical training and expertise in cognitive psychology, coupled with his in-depth exposure to Islam with profound knowledge of the Quran and related teachings, has equipped him to guide the reader with a most reliable hand.

Inside Jihad begins with the author's personal experience, as a medical student in Cairo, of being recruited by a radical Islamist group. As in his earlier works, Dr. Hamid explains the psychological phases and tactics by which terrorists are transformed into killers without conscience. Make no mistake, the clash of civilizations being played out in the media through gruesome images begins with an internal change occurring in the hearts and minds of those recruited. Dr. Hamid makes a compelling contribution to our understanding of the psychic cancer that drives such inhumane behavior. His training as a physician and psychologist, along with his own experience of entering and exiting the world of radical Islam, provide deep insights that would otherwise be unattainable.

Dr. Hamid continues with an overview of the myths and misconceptions about Islamism that exposes the fallacies of the most popular analyses so often bandied about by media pundits. In contrast to them, his well-researched and documented analysis is articulated with the care of a physician, the insight of a psychologist and the depth of a scholar.

In the final two chapters, the good doctor examines the quest for Islamic reformation and provides an outline for a strategic plan to defeat radical Islam. Dr. Hamid penetrates the source material in the Quran and Islamic hadiths that drive the dark, murderous behavior of ISIS, al-Qaeda and others, and he provides a lucid alternative that is bound to make a difference.

As demonstrated by the popularity of the author's own website, which casts a new interpretive light on the Quran for young Muslims who seek an alternative to the fearful, rage-filled juggernaut of Islamism, Dr. Hamid has won widespread support because he has dared to take the fight to the source. In this great war of ideas that brings terror closer and closer to home, *Inside Jihad* is a vital contribution. Anyone who cherishes freedom, faith and family will benefit from engaging its pages.

In short, Dr. Hamid provides a concise yet thorough critique of Islamic and Western societies alike. The foggy notions perpetuated by America's politically correct dominant media and policy cultures are dissipated with radiant sunlight through the analysis and thoughtful leadership Dr. Hamid delivers. I urge all concerned with how to overcome the threat of radical Islam to give *Inside Jihad* a well-deserved read.

Thomas P. McDevitt
Chairman, *The Washington Times*

Introduction to the Updated Edition

In the time since I first published this book seven years ago, the world has become a far more dangerous place – in many ways just as I predicted. The response of the West generally, and the United States in particular, continues relatively unchanged and futile. We have spent trillions of dollars fighting the War on Terrorism with almost no perceptible positive results. In fact, the problem is spreading and getting worse. Islamism is on the rise. Organizations such as ISIS in the Levant (so far) and Boko Haram in Nigeria have expanded their territory and are committing ever more terrible acts ever more regularly. Radical Islam has become an undeniable threat to the world.

We are confronted today with this seemingly intractable scourge. Some tragic souls have experienced it in person; most encounter the spectacle on their video screens. We are haunted by images of 9/11, of the Bali nightclubs, of the subways in Madrid and London, and of the school children in Beslan and Nigeria. We witness daily misery in myriad locations. Radical Islamists are now regularly recording their horrific deeds – beheading innocent people, burning people alive in cages – and posting macabre videos of the atrocities on the Internet to billions of people.

All of this has led decent people to ask questions and seek answers:

What kind of people could commit these horrors?
What is their purpose?
What is propelling this unspeakable behavior, and who is to blame?
What can we do about it?

In response, a wave of books is emerging about Islam and Islamic terror, many of which have helped to raise awareness. Not long ago, words such as "Sharia" and "Wahhabism" would have been met with blank stares. Now, these and other related terms have become more familiar. Nevertheless, there remains profound confusion about Islamism. Many non-Muslims seem mystified by the ideological cancer that has infected the body of the approximately 1.5 billion adherents to Islam.

Critics have leveled the charge at me that I am anti-Islam because I dare even to raise questions about the state of the faith. Nothing is further from the truth. I am a Muslim, and I consider much in Islam to be beautiful and worthwhile. But the way Islam is taught today in most communities is perverted and destructive. Radical Islam could only have arisen in an environment that prepared the ground for its evil seeds to sprout. I am convinced, therefore, that Islam desperately needs a reformation – or, at least, an extensive reinterpretation – and that such change is entirely possible. I have been working intensely toward this goal, and elsewhere in these pages I will outline the key elements of an Islamic reformation that I hope will be transformative.

The history of the 20th century bestowed upon us the carnage of two World Wars, the unspeakable horrors of the Nazi concentration camps, the equally horrific Soviet labor camps and the Chinese "Re-education through labor" camps. The century also produced genocide and ethnic cleansing in places as disparate as Cambodia, Rwanda and Bosnia. And the last century of the second millennium also saw the rise of Islamic terrorism. If the world has gained anything from those experiences, we would expect it to be the capacity to diagnose ideological and societal illnesses, to confront them and defeat them. Sad, but that expectation leads to disappointment. In our new century, events such as the ongoing genocide in the Darfur region of western Sudan testify to a persistent record of inaction, indifference and misdirected blame; of cowardice, apathy and feigned ignorance.

So, too, is the case with *jihad*.

In writing this book, I hope to offer my personal experiences – which included intimate involvement with radical Islam – in an attempt to clarify the problem of Islamic terrorism and propose ways to neutralize it.

Yes, the subject matter is complex, and I know how time can be limited for most readers, what with television, books, radio and newspapers all competing with blogs, email, texting and social media to monopolize our spare moments as never before. But understanding radical Islam is essential, perhaps to our very survival. So I have produced a text of modest length in the hope that as busy as you are you will find the time to read it.

If you would like to probe this topic a little more deeply, I have provided additional material in the back of the book to help you. There is a Glossary of important terms and notable individuals mentioned in the text, as well as a Recommended Books list and three appendices containing valuable background. I hope you will find it all useful.

Tawfik Hamid
May 2015

A Brief Overview of Islam

This book is not about Islam – it is about Islamism and how to combat it. Nevertheless, you cannot confront the problem of Islamism without a basic understanding of the Muslim faith. Within these pages, you will encounter various Arabic words and Islamic concepts, so you must gain some familiarity with them to make sense of my arguments.

For basic definitions, please see the Glossary on page 188.

Obviously, I can't provide a complete and detailed exposition of Islam. For that role, I will recommend some excellent books later on. Indeed, many commonly available encyclopedias provide adequate coverage of Islam if you lack the time or inclination to examine the subject in depth. You might already be knowledgeable about Islam; if so, I commend your commitment to understanding. Here, I will cover only the main structural components of the religion and those terms that are critical to my arguments.

The word Islam means "submission" to God, or Allah. It is a monotheistic faith that originated in the early 7th century with Prophet Muhammad. Its primary text is the Quran, which Muslims believe is the literal Word of God transmitted to the Prophet by the archangel Gabriel. The revelation of the Quran to Muhammad is marked by Islam's holiest month, Ramadan.

Muhammad was born in the Arabian Peninsula, an area holy to Muslims. They call it, in Arabic, the Hejaz. The region encompasses the holy cities of Mecca and Medina, two cities visited every year by millions of Muslims as part of their obligatory pilgrimage, known as the *hajj*.

Initially, Prophet Muhammad faced persecution for his new faith. As time passed, he was able to gather adherents and control the city of Medina, where he established his authority. From there, he fought battles against the armies of Mecca with mixed results. Eventually, by employing a strategy of constriction and direct assault, Muhammad overcame the city with little struggle. During that time, a quarrel arose between the Jews of Medina and Muhammad's followers, which led to the quick destruction of the Jewish community. This destruction, in combination with further conversions and conquest, enabled Muhammad to consolidate power.

By the time of his death, in 632, Muhammad ruled the entire Hejaz. After his death, Muslims selected a prince, or caliph, to lead an Islamic government called the Caliphate. Historians distinguish between several caliphates, which were headquartered in various cities and were the source of some conflicts, particularly the conflict between the Sunni and Shia sects of Islam, which continues to this day.

Under the first caliphs – and remarkably, in less than 150 years – Islam exploded across the Middle East, North Africa and parts of Europe in what is known as the Islamic Conquests. In that short span of time, many native languages and religions disappeared; they were swallowed up by Arabic and Islam.

Because he was considered the final prophet, the man chosen to reveal God's last message to humanity, and because of his success, most Muslims consider the Sunnah – the words and deeds of Muhammad – to be the foundational component of Islam. Muhammad's exploits are recorded in chronicles known as *hadith*, a word employed in both the singular and plural sense, although *hadiths* is the popular term among English speakers.

The Quran is divided into 114 chapters, called *suwar* and more commonly as the singular, *sura*, and the anglicized plural, *suras*, which contain 6,236 poetic verses, or *ayat*. The Word of God was revealed to Muhammad not at once but over a period of time. The earlier *suras* typically covered spiritual and ethical matters, while the later *suras* focused on the regulation of society; for example, marital relations, criminal punishment and war.[1] The Quran does not cover every aspect of Islamic life, so many Muslims look to the Sunnah, the source of Sharia law as recorded in the *hadiths*, for guidance when the Quran is silent.

The *hadiths* constitute a very large body of oral tradition, propagated and expanded for hundreds of years, until at last they were assembled and recorded during the Abbasid Caliphate, beginning in the mid-8th century. At the time, it was discovered that many *hadiths* were contradictory or dubious, so efforts were made to classify them in terms of their accuracy and, by extension, importance. The Arabic word for "accurate" is *sahih*, and the two collections of *hadiths* considered most accurate, and which are most renowned, are *Sahih al-Bukhari* and *Sahih Muslim*. The former was written before the year 870 by Imam Bukhari and contains 7,275 *hadiths*; the latter was written sometime before 875 by Imam Muslim and contains 9,200 *hadiths*.

Although Islam has a number of sects and systems of belief, Muslims typically are required to obey the so-called Five Pillars. The first pillar, called *shahada*, is the basic testament of every Muslim: "I testify that there is none worthy of worship except God and I testify that Muhammad is the Messenger of God." The testament is uttered upon conversion to Islam, and any Muslim who disputes it is considered an apostate. Islam does not practice baptism as Christianity does, nor does it have any other important initiation ritual.

The second pillar, *salah*, is the obligation to pray, typically five times each day. Notably, the Quran says nothing about the five prayer sessions, merely:

> *And establish regular prayers at the two ends of the day and at the approaches of the night: For those things that are good remove those that are evil: Be that the word of remembrance to those who remember (their Lord).* [11:114]

The injunction to pray five times a day, as opposed to another number, is derived from the *hadiths*. Indeed, some sects pray three times a day, while some Sufi Muslims do not believe ritualistic prayer is even necessary.

The third pillar, *zakah*, involves obligatory charity. Every Muslim must assist less-fortunate Muslims, based on his or her capacity to do so. There are various subsidiary types of *zakah*, the details of which are not important to this discussion.

The fourth pillar is called *sawm*, which means "to fast." Fasting is typically performed for repentance, as part of a ritual, or to commune with God. Muslims are required to fast during the month of Ramadan.

The fifth and final pillar is the *hajj*, which I mentioned earlier. Once in every Muslim's life, he or she must travel to Mecca and worship, if circumstances permit. The *hajj* takes up the entire Islamic month of Dhu al-Hijjah.

You might be surprised to learn that the Five Pillars are never mentioned explicitly in the Quran. The notion is based on a well-known saying of Prophet Muhammad. Nevertheless, it is a core concept; for many, it is the most familiar component of Islam.

Islamic law, or Sharia, is central to Islamic life today. Sharia has a long tradition and involves every aspect of daily existence. It is both a legal system and code of conduct that covers a vast array of issues, from criminal law to government matters to everyday problems. Sharia concerns itself with marriage, punishment, inheritance and banking; also worship, charity and civil cases. Scholars of Sharia, known as *ulema*, are responsible for interpreting Islamic law and applying it to new situations. Sharia takes for its basis the Quran, the Sunnah, the actions of Muhammad's disciples, the *fiqh* (or jurisprudence) and various *tafsir* (explanations) of the Quran. Sharia is considered by Muslims to be divine law; more important, it is considered by many to be the only law that should, ultimately, be respected.

As we shall see, Sharia plays perhaps the most critical role in Islamism.

NOTE

1. Interesting, but the *suras* are not necessarily arranged chronologically; lower-numbered *suras* were sometimes written later. For example, Sura 2 was written during the Medina period (late stages of revelation), while Sura 114 – the last *sura* in the Quran – was written in the very early stages of Islam, in the Mecca period. Thus, when we speak of "earlier *suras*," we mean earlier in time, not earlier in number.

Inside Jihad

CHAPTER I

The Making of an Islamic Terrorist

Childhood

Islamism didn't find very fruitful ground in Egypt under President Gamal Abdel Nasser – it didn't fit into his secular ideology of pan-Arab socialism. Nasser aligned himself with the Soviets, accepting their military aid and advisers. Although Nasser was a sworn enemy of the United States, he saw militant Islam as the larger menace. During the period when he held power (1956-1970), he cracked down on Islamist incitement and violence.[2] He strictly curtailed travel to and from traditionally Islamic nations, such as Saudi Arabia, because he feared their Wahhabi sect would propagate a militant brand of Islam known as Salafism.

It was at the time of his regime that I was born, in 1961, to a secular Muslim family in Cairo. My mother was a French teacher whose political views were generally liberal. In her youth she attended a French-speaking elementary school and an Arabic-speaking high school. She was exceptionally intelligent; after placing fourth highest in the University of Egypt's entrance examinations, she took her degree there in French literature. My father, an orthopedic surgeon, was so secular that, privately, he was an atheist. He placed great value on critical thinking and logical analysis. He wanted us to be comfortable with reality and not seek to augment it with fantasy. He believed that what he regarded as superstition, which stemmed from insularity, was a source of many problems in the world. He felt it incumbent upon himself to broaden our exposure to "life." Accordingly, when I was about eight years old, my father took my brother and me to a cadaver room at the medical school to show us "death" – to show us, in other words, that death is not a romantic or mysterious affair but a scientific one.

Perhaps, but I had recurring nightmares for years.

Although my father might have worshipped science and logic, he was also in every respect a warm and upright man. He raised us with the value of tolerance, teaching us to respect all religious beliefs, including those of Christians and Jews. Our own practice of Islam was negligible – it was limited to a cultural observance of the Ramadan fast and its corresponding feast. In more traditional Islamic families, boys start learning how to pray at age seven and are strongly encouraged to pray regularly and go to the mosque at age 10. I did not habitually visit the mosque until my latter teenage years.

In 1970, Anwar Sadat succeeded Nasser and relaxed his predecessor's travel restrictions. My father was well regarded in the medical community, so he seized the opportunity to work abroad regularly, particularly in Algeria, Saudi Arabia and Libya – often for extensive periods of time. During his long absences I busied myself with poetry, chess and playing with my friends, some of whom were Christian. I loved my father, but because he was away so much of the time, my uncle Kamal – a famous actor and director in Egyptian cinema – became my role model.

Kamal had graduated from La Sorbonne in Paris as a theatrical director. He used to collaborate often with my mother; she would translate French dramatic works into Arabic and then help him produce them for the stage. I enjoyed attending the rehearsals.

Often, he would show up at my school to watch me in class. The students and teachers knew him and paid me extra respect. When my uncle and I would walk down the street, passersby would salute him, ask him for his autograph and invite us to meals. He was not only charismatic and successful but also generous with time and money. Many families would invite him over for the holiday feasts, and when he arrived he typically would give each child the equivalent of US$100. He liked listening to me recite poems. He helped me with handwriting and public speaking, working with me on a regular basis to improve both.

Egypt's Revival of Islam

In the early 1970s, we Egyptians increasingly heard the phrase "Revival of Islam." This happened for several reasons. During and after the OPEC oil embargo against America and its allies – an offshoot of the 1973 war between Israel and Egypt and Syria – the price of petroleum skyrocketed, leading to astronomical profits for the OPEC member-nations, especially Saudi Arabia. I remember the price per barrel jumping from US$12 to $42. We heard about the Saudis getting rich from news reports and saw Egyptians return from employment there flush with cash. In Egypt, doctors, engineers, financiers and similar professionals might earn the equivalent of $30 per month. But in Saudi Arabia the same positions would often net them more than $1,000. As a result, the gap in the Arab world between rich and poor increased, strengthening the sense of inadequacy that Egyptians felt.

Infusions of foreign cash had the secondary effect of increasing inflation. Prices rose, and basic necessities became more expensive. In response, a growing percentage of the Egyptian skilled labor force felt compelled to work in Saudi Arabia. A cycle developed that created, in essence, an unhealthy dependency on the Saudis for propping up the Egyptian economy. In return, the Saudis gained additional leverage over Egyptian politics. In the 1940s, it was the Saudis who were struggling economically. Egyptians contributed money to help maintain the Kiswah, the magnificent fabric cover of the Kaaba, the holiest building in Islam. Money flowed eastward from Egypt to Saudi Arabia. By the 1970s, the situation had reversed. OPEC nations became a source of marvel throughout the Arab world, not only from the perspective of wealth but also from pride at Arab resistance to the United States. Because the Saudis practiced Salafism and implemented Sharia law throughout the kingdom, many believed the Saudis were being rewarded by Allah with wealth and respect in recognition of their strict devotion.

Sadat himself never pursued Nasser's socialist, anti-American agenda. Subsequent to the 1973 war, he actually sent the Soviet military advisers home. When he ascended to power, Sadat sought immediately to limit the influence of the Nasserists, and he did so by releasing their enemies: the Islamists that Nasser had imprisoned. Because most of Egypt's mosques were strictly controlled by the government, Sadat underestimated the threat the Islamists would pose if they could freely preach in their enclaves. In addition, the release of imprisoned Islamists might have reflected a genuine desire on Sadat's part to ease restrictions on speech and religion.

Sadat also began to pursue rapprochement with the United States. He did so by utilizing the government-controlled mosques to disseminate messages of peace with America and Israel. In response, the Islamists whom Sadat had released earlier began to accuse him of being un-Islamic, even an infidel. They asserted that a good Muslim should never accept a civil-service post, for example, because such a post assisted an un-Islamic regime. Sadat was forced to respond to the attacks on his reputation. He would occasionally refer to himself as "Muhammad" (his real first name) Sadat, and to show good faith he further eased the suppression of radical, unregulated mosques.

The newly freed Islamists were hardly appeased by Sadat's Islamic façade. As might be expected, the radical incitement began to permeate more mainstream establishments. Sadat was still able to inhibit Islamist violence, but he failed to combat their incitement at prayers. Mainstream mosques encountered a similar dilemma. Previously, these establishments had focused on the Five Pillars and little else. They were not especially interested in doctrinal complexity. Islamists began to preach from their isolated pulpits that the conventional mosques fostered a diluted Islam and that their members were weak Muslims. Day in and day out, they would carry on about Sharia and the Caliphate. Mainstream institutions, too, were forced to defend their reputations against these allegations by making a public show of their Islamic devotion. And so the Revival got underway.

It started mildly enough and has never really ceased. It developed in various institutions at various times and at various rates, but it constituted, on the whole, a perceptible collective shift. At first there was an awakened pride in Islam, followed by an insistence on a return to ritual, e.g., regular mosque attendance and quintuplicate daily prayers. Earlier, in the 1950s and 1960s, it was rare for an employee to interrupt his work to pray. If he did so, it was perceived as bizarre and often treated with scorn. By the 1970s, it became much more common, and even fellow employees who opted not to pray would express approval of their co-workers' devotion. Soon, television shows would be interrupted with the *adhan*, the Islamic call to prayer.

The prayer lasted five minutes and we hated it, because it interrupted exciting soccer games. During these moments, it was common to turn on the radio and listen to the event, because radio broadcasts mercifully weren't interrupted.

As time passed, *imams* began to advocate that women wear the *hijab*, the Muslim head scarf. If you compare school class photographs from Nasser's time with those taken from the 1970s to the present, you will notice that in the earlier images the *hijab* was hardly worn, but after

Islamists gained influence, many women began wearing them. Likewise, husbands in the '50s usually wore a wedding ring made of gold. Later, silver became the metal of choice, because certain *hadiths* proclaimed the wearing of gold to be un-Islamic.

> *Gold and silk are allowed for the women of my nation (Muslims) but they are forbidden for men.*
> —Ahmad al-Nasai and Muhammad at-Tirmidhi

Hatred of non-Muslims, especially Jews, increased as well; this was true particularly in mosques not under government control. *Imams* began to preach more regularly that Jews were a race of pigs and monkeys that had poisoned Muhammad, and they should be fought until the End of Days. Under Nasser, such forms of religious preaching were uncommon. Popular songs in the years of Nasser and Sadat contained no anti-Semitism, but by 2000 a tune called "Ana Bakrah Israel" ("I Hate Israel") became a national hit. This is not to say Jew-hatred never existed, but in earlier periods it was considered a relatively muted political issue that coalesced around an Arab identity rather than an Islamic one. The former is much easier to treat than the latter.

Eventually, in mainstream mosques, too, *imams* began to speak of Sharia and even promote it in favor of secular government. Soon, they also began passively to justify violence. They might not have supplied the knives, so to speak, but the mainstream *imams* played a role in establishing and promulgating a theoretical foundation for brutality.

In the Revival's first phase, its effect on society was less one of incitement than a reinvigoration of strict Salafi practices and beliefs – a sense of pride in Islamic power. It was at this time, as the Islamic Revival got under way, that I entered high school.

Adolescence

I used to sit between two friends: Nagi Anton, who was a Christian, and Muhammad Amin, an atheist. Nagi and I would gang up on Amin in debates, seeking to prove to him the existence of God. I enjoyed these theological disputes and began to study religion in an effort to win more of them. Soon, Muslim and Christian students began to meet informally for theological sparring. It was, for the most part, friendly.

Occasionally a participant would insult an opponent, leading to animosity, but that was relatively rare. My Muslim classmates eventually chose me to lead the debates against the Christian students. I was a good debater and basked in the high esteem in which my classmates held me. I studied the Old and New Testaments in order to find ammunition with which I could best my Christian adversaries. The debates actually led to an ironic situation where I knew more of the Bible than I did the Quran. Such contests were innocent enough. My only goal was to win them and maintain the respect of my schoolmates.

At this time – between ages 15 and 16 – I began to think about God more spiritually. This happened while studying the structure and function of DNA as part of a homework assignment for biology class. I couldn't believe that the beautiful, extremely complex organization of life's six-foot-long central molecule was some evolutionary coincidence. It must have resulted from the unlimited power of a divine architect. I looked in the Quran for confirmations of my spiritual wonder at nature and found them.

> *Behold! In the creation of the heavens and the earth, and the alternation of night and day, there are indeed Signs for men of understanding … Men who celebrate the praises of Allah, standing, sitting and lying down on their sides, and contemplate the (wonders of) creation in the heavens and the earth, (with the thought): Our Lord! Not for naught hast Thou created (all) this! Glory to Thee! Give us salvation from the penalty of the Fire.* [3:190-191]

My father was often abroad by this time, and the influence of his atheism on me was receding. It is strange, looking back, that although I shared my father's attraction to science, it first led me in the opposite, religious direction.

My exposure to religion during the debates, the esteem of my peers, and my wonder at nature combined to fuel an earnest interest in Islam. The community as a whole seemed to give me more respect, as I sought to be a more dedicated Muslim.

I still did not go to the mosque very often, but I would pray at home. If we were watching a soccer game or eating supper, I would stop and pray in everyone's presence. I would go to wash my hands, feet, face and head, and then return to place the *sajjada*, or prayer mat, on the ground, adjusting it to face east toward Mecca. As I was praying, I would receive compliments from others in the room.

Some of my friends went further. They walked to mosque prayers – the more distant the mosque, the better. It was believed to be a sign of devotion to walk a long way to a mosque. Often, they would count their footsteps and relate the total as proof of their faith.

Time passed, and I recall the first time I looked at a Christian with disdain. We were in Arabic language class reading a passage from an obligatory textbook called *Al-Shaichan (The Two Wise Old Men).*[3] The book referenced what the *hadiths* supposed were Prophet Muhammad's words:

> *I have been instructed by Allah to declare war and fight all mankind until they say "No God except Allah and Muhammad is the Prophet of Allah."*

This passage can be found in *Sahih al-Bukhari* and *Sahih Muslim* – two of the most important Sunni *hadith* collections. Christian students went to their own religion class and Muslim students went to theirs. But this class wasn't religion – it was Arabic – so Nagi was present. The implications of the Prophet's supposed words dawned on me. I turned to him and said, "If we applied Islam correctly we should be doing this to you." To which he replied, "Your Muhammad is just a barbaric Bedouin!"

Medical School

After high school – and a summer attending prayers regularly at a local mosque – I entered the medical school at Cairo University. I was 17 at the time. Egypt didn't use the concept of undergraduate. Naturally, I continued to pursue my recently acquired fervor for Islam. Coincidentally, an Islamic organization called Jamaa Islamiya [4] had been gaining a foothold at the school. Although it was later classified as a terrorist group, Jamaa's activities were perfectly legal then. They began by receiving permission to build a small prayer room inside the medical school, which quickly developed into a small mosque. Shortly thereafter, a library was added to the area where Jamaa members promoted Salafist books.

Clearly, Egypt's Revival of Islam had made its way into academia. Jamaa members not only preached in the mosque but, as their influence spread, also started a tradition of meeting in the morning lecture hall 45 minutes before the teacher arrived. There, they would discuss Islamic topics. Most Muslim students thought it a good thing, but the more secular ones found it annoying, and the Christians were soon intimidated into silence.

It was the custom at the medical school to refer to professors by their title and first name. One day, "Dr. Edward," a Christian, was unable to begin his lecture because the Jamaa speaker had not finished. When Dr. Edward stepped up to the podium and asked the speaker to conclude, six members called the professor an infidel and started to berate him. They pushed Dr. Edward off of the podium, and he broke his arm. Secular students were disgusted, and Christian students were terrified. The reaction of Muslim students was mixed. Some approved of it; others thought it was excessive. Personally, I regretted the violence, but because I was a Muslim I thought Jamaa had the right to preach in class, and the professor should not have provoked them. I was not yet a member.

Behind one of our two main lecture halls was a cadaver room – the same one my father had shown me when I was a child. Sometimes, Jamaa lecturers would point in the direction of the cadaver room from the podium as evidence of the earthly world's expendable imperfection. For the nonbelievers and unobservant Muslims, they would utilize the same example to hector them about Hell. They read Quranic passages that would echo in the halls and in our minds:

> *For those who do not follow Allah, garments of fire shall be cut out*
> *for them (in the life to come); burning water will be poured over their*
> *heads causing all that is within their bodies, as well as the skins, to*
> *melt away. And they shall be held by iron grips; and every time they*
> *try in their anguish to come out of it, they shall be returned to there*
> *and (be told): "Taste suffering through fire (to the full)!"* [22:19-22]

They kept referring to the cadaver room to show us that only the afterlife was important – that earthly life was meaningless. And martyrdom guaranteed entrance to Paradise:

> *Those who desire the life of the present and its glitter, to them we*
> *shall pay [the price of] their deeds therein, without diminution ...*
> *(yet) it is they who, in the life to come, shall have nothing but the fire –*
> *for in vain shall be all good things that they have done in this [world],*
> *and worthless all that they ever did.* [11:15-16]

By a strange irony, Jamaa Islamiya employed the same example as my father had years earlier in order to teach me precisely the opposite lesson. As its influence grew, Jamaa began to intervene with the secular traditions of the medical school. They insisted on separate seating in the lecture halls for men and women, and they sometimes forcibly separated students who did not comply. Occasionally, they would use violence to stop students from playing music or singing – activities the members considered un-Islamic.

"Why medical students?" you might ask. Westerners are often astonished to observe highly accomplished Muslim doctors in the terrorist ranks. These include Dr. Ayman al-Zawahiri, a surgeon who currently heads al-Qaeda (more about him shortly); Dr. Abdul-Aziz al-Rantisi of Hamas, a pediatrician, now deceased; and more recently, a group of doctors including a neurosurgeon who planned attacks on Scottish and English transportation systems. [5]

How can this be? Doctors have taken the Hippocratic Oath and swear by another of Hippocrates's maxims: "First, do no harm." How, then, could a group like Jamaa Islamiya gain traction in a medical school? As I discovered when I became radicalized there, medical schools at the time had become vanguards of fundamentalism in most Egyptian universities.

Medical students are often more attracted to religion because they see the power of God in nature on a regular basis. After all, they study the miraculous structure and function of the human body. For me and many others, this wonder was a significant motivating element.

Once attracted to religion, Islamists inside the school fostered in students an abnormal fear of mortality. Because we witnessed death so closely in patients and regularly worked with cadavers, they were able to exploit our proximity to it. They encouraged us to think about the next world. They seized the opportunity to remind us continuously of the torture that would await us in the grave (Adhab al-Qabr) or in the afterlife (*jahannam*) if we did not obey their teachings. Some students were influenced by this approach; others less so.

Because we worked with the sick, Islamists would claim that we would be punished in the present for our lack of devotion by acquiring the diseases of our patients. Allah would curse us not only in the afterlife but also in this life. The tactic sometimes worked with students who feared disease more than usual.

Islamists also would manipulate our sense of guilt. Many students felt particularly relieved that they were spared the often-horrible illnesses of the patients they treated and would naturally thank Allah for it. Islamists insisted that strict devotion to their Islamic agenda was the only acceptable expression of gratitude; anything else was insulting to Allah.

Another reason why Islamists targeted medical schools: The students were bright and idealistic yet hard-working and practical. They were naturally concerned with life, death, pain and salvation.

A New Recruit

During my first med-school year, I was approached by a rising member of Jamaa named Muchtar. He was in his fourth year and known as an *amir*, or "prince." The title was short for "Prince of the Believers,"[6] a term taken from early writings about the Islamic Caliphate. Determination to serve Allah overcame my hesitancy that remained from witnessing the incident with Dr. Edward, and I agreed to join them in what I thought would be a commonplace gathering for prayer. En route to the mosque, Muchtar impressed upon me a concept that he called *al-fikr kufr* – that one becomes an infidel (*kufr*) by thinking critically (*fikr*). One's brain is similar to a donkey, he elaborated. You can ride it to the palace of Allah, but you must leave it outside when you enter.

It soon became clear why Muchtar had prepared me. Before the service, all new candidates were instructed to line up shoulder-to-shoulder and foot-to-foot. Muhammad Omar, the cleric, scrutinized us for 15 minutes to make sure there were no gaps and then proclaimed,

> *Truly Allah loves those who fight for His Cause in battle array, as if they were a solid cemented structure.* [Quran 61:4]

After prayers, I was advised to visit the library regularly and begin reading Salafi texts, which I did.

Jamaa Islamiya also counted women among its members. The women prayed in a separate room, however, though they were very dedicated. They wore the *hijab*, and the men related to them as comrades or "sisters-in-arms." There was no dating between members under any circumstances. Before I met my wife, she had been invited to join Jamaa. She declined. Perhaps her father's Sufi faith granted her a stronger immunity to the group than the atheist inclinations of my own father.

You might wonder what could possibly attract women to a group that advocates stoning women for adultery and limits their rights. Obviously, Jamaa women lived in a state of denial that overcame any natural aversion they might have felt toward the world their brothers-in-arms envisioned for them. But there was more to it.

As a new member, I was sometimes asked to speak to women students who might be prospective candidates for Jamaa. Sex in Paradise was less of an enticement for them, but fear of Hell played a significant role. They would sometimes cry when I laid out the eternal punishment that awaited weak Muslims. The prospect terrified many of the women, no less than it did the men. But also like the men, the women earned respect for joining Jamaa. Those from poorer backgrounds sometimes felt insecure around affluent young women, and they sought to claim a measure of superiority over them. Islamism gave them that superiority. They might not have wealth, but they did have religious devotion and found favor in the eyes of Allah. Poorer women allowed themselves to believe their well-to-do counterparts were spoiled, pampered and weak. Societal norms also played a role.

Young men wanted to date secular women, but when it came to marriage, they sought religious spouses. Observant women were more likely to be chaste – an important concern in Arab culture. Mothers would actually urge girls to wear the *hijab* because it encouraged men to seek them out as marriage partners and not for friendship and dating.

Phases of Indoctrination

After several months of attending Jamaa's sermons and reading their Salafi books, I began to change dramatically. I grew a beard, lost my sense of humor, and became aloof and judgmental. My father and mother tried to persuade me to relax my religious views and to leave Jamaa. Because Salafi Islam forbids many forms of art and music, my relationship with my uncle Kamal also suffered. I couldn't forgive him for his devotion to the un-Islamic diversions of theatre and film.

Still, an innocent person cannot convert to violent jihadist in one day. An individual changes incrementally and subtly – it is a gradual mental process that occurs broadly and in three stages: hatred, suppression of conscience and desensitization to – or acceptance of – violence.

LEARN HATRED

It's difficult to kill an innocent person if you don't hate that person. Hatred toward the infidels is not only promoted by jihadist groups such as Jamaa, but it also fits in the mainstream of Islamic teaching. The books, the jurisprudence and the commentaries assist in creating this hatred. Here are a few examples:

O ye who believe! Take not the Jews and the Christians for your friends and protectors: They are but friends and protectors to each other. And he amongst you that turns to them (for friendship) is of them. Verily Allah guideth not a people unjust. [Quran 5:51]

Shall I point out to you something much worse than this, (as judged) by the treatment it received from Allah? Those who incurred the curse of Allah and His wrath (the Jews), those of whom He transformed into apes and swine, those who worshipped evil – these are (many times) worse in rank, and far more astray from the even path! [5:60]

Those who say that God is Christ the son of Mary are Infidels. [5:17]

The following *hadith* has special significance for me. When I later lived in Saudi Arabia, I remember the Wahhabis had selected it for publication in one of their small booklets, which they would freely distribute in order to teach Muslims about Islam.

Prophet Muhammad has said: Do not initiate the Salam (peace greeting) to the Jews and Christians and whenever you meet any of them in a road, force them to its narrowest alley. —Sahih Muslim

This teaching is also promoted in the mainstream Islamic books used by young Muslims in the United States. [7]

SUPPRESS CONSCIENCE

Likewise, if instructed to kill someone, a person might at first consider the act unethical, even if he hated the potential victim. Murder is difficult to perform if the would-be murderer can't overcome his conscience.

Jihadism suppresses the conscience of its adherents by pressuring them to accept, promote and praise acts that are entirely at odds with normal senses of decency and justice, simply because such acts are recorded in the religious books. We used to praise Prophet Muhammad for marrying a girl of seven when he was 52 years old (as written in *Al-Bukari*). We openly advocated stoning women to death and killing apostates (converts from Islam or Muslims who have departed from the true faith. We even supported enslaving female war prisoners and having sex with them as concubines, following the practice of *ma malakat aymanukum*, or the treatment of slaves. All of these practices constitute an integral part of mainstream Islamic teaching. If we advocated them,

Paradise awaited us; if we even questioned these beliefs, we faced eternal damnation.

DESENSITIZE VIOLENCE

In the final stage, a jihadist might hesitate to commit a murder if he wasn't sufficiently desensitized to violence. Thus, radical Islam must remove from its followers any aversion to killing.

Again, Salafi religious interpretations lead the way. Current, mainstream Islamic teaching insists that good Muslims must declare war on infidels. Nonbelievers are offered three options: to convert to Islam; to pay the *jizya*, a humiliating poll tax; or be slain. Mainstream and so-called moderate Islamic books such as the *Fiqh us-Sunnah* insist that a Muslim who fails to pray five times per day must repent or be tortured and killed [8]. Ironic, but at the beginning of the third volume of this same book, the author maintains that Islam is all about peace. Islamists, Islamic scholars and many Muslims regard such concepts as applicable today as they were in the past.

Consider these examples:

> *After the raid on a Jewish tribe … the disciples of Muhammad brought Kinanah ibn Alrabbia in front of Muhammad, as he knew the place of the treasures of the Jewish tribe (Bani al-Nuder). The man denied that he knew the place of such treasures … The prophet (pbuh) said to one of his disciples (Alzubeer ibn Alawam) "torture him until you root out and extract all that he has" … So Zubayr kindled a fire on Kinanah's chest, twirling it with his firestick until Kinanah was near death, then prophet Muhammad pushed him forcibly toward Muhammad ibn Maslama to kill him … The latter beheaded him (to satisfy the prophet).*
> —Al-Sira al-Nabawiyya (The Life of the Prophet) by Ibn Kathir

> *There was a woman named Fatima Bint Rabiaa who was well-known as Um Kerfa. All her children were great leaders among the Arab tribes. She was one of the most respected women in the Arab society and was an example for dignity so that when two tribes had a fight they immediately stopped fighting if she intervened to make peace by sending her headcover on a post in between the fighting groups. This woman was a poet and she used to recite poems against Muhammad. In the 6th year after Muhammad left Mecca to Medina,*

he sent one of the best disciples, Zayd ibn Harithah in a raid to pun-
ish her. Zayd tied her legs with rope and then tied her between two
camels until they split her in two. And then after beheading the dead
body he carried the dead body to Medina and put her head on a post
to satisfy the Prophet.

—*Al-Tabaqut al-Kubra*
(The Raid of Zayd ibn Harithah to Um Kerfa) by Ibn Sa'd

Critics will contend that the Old and New Testaments also contain violent passages. But Judaism and Christianity teach these verses in historical context, as no longer practicable, to be understood metaphorically
or in the worldview of an earlier period of civilization. Islam today fails
to furnish a counterbalanced understanding. Violent exhortations are
still acceptable and applicable in countries or communities that implement Sharia law. They are found not only in the texts; Islamic scholars
agree almost unanimously about the validity and violent interpretation
of such injunctions.

As soon as a Muslim accepts cruelty at the psychological level, it is
a natural step to view it as a tool within a larger ideological program.
In my medical school, some of us stopped at the level of hatred; others
suppressed their conscience but went no further, while others reached
the last stage, ready to wage *jihad.* All of these phases are necessary to
manufacture the cruel mentalities that we see today, resulting in individuals who are prepared to target large numbers of innocent people. But if
these are phases that a normal person experiences on the path to terror,
it remains to identify the tactics used by Islamist groups to bring about
such a transformation.

Tactics of Indoctrination

It is very difficult to convey to non-Muslims the attraction to radical
Islam that believers can feel. It is a multi-faceted experience, greater than
the sum of its parts. Individuals can be drawn to militant Islam for different reasons – no single element of Islamism by itself can explain why
more young Muslims around the world fall victim to it each day. The
only requirement is a willingness to serve Allah and Islam. I remember
feeling exhilarated at Jamaa's unity and vision, the singularity of purpose and fearlessness the group displayed in the face of opposition from
government and moderates. It was a feeling of raw power – the power

to change the course of history and to sweep current society aside. It was, as some might say, not unlike a drug, an addiction, but it was more: Jamaa's program of religious study and their sermons spoke to my awakening interest in the divine.

For Jews and Christians, the Bible is a testament to God's covenant, to his deeds, to what he said to other people. God speaks to Moses, Moses paraphrases to his people, and the Old Testament tells us what Moses said. It is a history, a chronicle. Both the Old and New testaments have been translated into countless languages, and each translation is acceptable for prayer and study because the words themselves are less important than their meaning – it is the content that matters. For example, one of Judaism's greatest scholars – Philo of Alexandria – based his writings chiefly on the Septuagint (the Greek translation of the Old Testament). Likewise, Christians in America read the New Testament in English. They do not feel compelled to read it in Greek unless they are theologians, and they do not regard themselves to be less Christian as a result.

The Quran is different. It is the actual Word of God, transmitted to each believer directly and individually. It is as if each Muslim is Moses being personally addressed by the Lord. And because God spoke these words in Arabic, translations of the Quran are regarded as mere facsimiles.

This power of the Quran is augmented by the role that poetry plays in Arab culture. In the West, a quick examination of the sales ranking of books shows that poetry is not especially popular. Of course there are devoted readers, but their number is small. In the Arab world, poetry competitions are mainstream. Poems are read avidly; people still weep when they hear them, and children memorize collections as part of their education. Traditionally, Bedouin culture in Arabia didn't produce a musical tradition that spawned complex and endless variations of mathematical harmony. In the visual arts, a representation of Allah or the Prophet was and still is regarded as idolatrous and is forbidden. Human portraits only began to be permitted under the Ottomans. It was in epic and lyrical poetry that Arabic culture excelled. The language lent itself to a long and influential tradition.

Yet Islamists don't merely utilize the voice and language of the Quran. They deftly exploit a number of themes to bring young Muslims into their organizations.

SUPPRESS CRITICAL THINKING

The first tactic Jamaa Islamiya employed was to pressure me to suppress critical thought. I have already mentioned how Muchtar encouraged me to "leave my brain at the door" and his use of the phrase *al-fikr kufr* ("thinking critically makes one an infidel"). [9] Actually, the Quran encourages critical thinking in numerous verses; however, the leaders of Jamaa focused on a specific verse:

> He cannot be questioned for His acts, but they will be questioned (for theirs). [21:23]

In other words, nobody can question Allah about his instructions, decisions or actions. The suppression of my critical thinking was the most important factor that trapped me on the path to jihadism. All other techniques of indoctrination depend on it. Jihadists understand that it takes time for new recruits to lose their capacity to think critically, so its leaders prefer to keep members in situations where they can gradually erode it. But erode it they must. One cannot become a jihadist if reason and objectivity aren't thoroughly crushed.

PREACH SUPERIORITY

Another tactic Jamaa used was to persuade us that adherence to Islam and Sharia is the best way to regain the "superiority of Islam." They argued that the early Islamic Conquests succeeded in less than a century not only because Muslims practiced *jihad* against external enemies but also because they applied strict Islamic law at home. If modern Muslims did the same, Jamaa's leaders preached, we could subjugate the rest of the world again. Our inferior international status and our economic problems would become a thing of the past. Islamists in Jamaa supported these arguments with many citations from the Quran, the *hadiths* and other Islamic resources.

Islamists consider other Muslims who do not engage in *jihad* to be inferior. Recall how leaders of Jamaa like Muchtar were commonly addressed as *amir*, or prince, a term that refers to the leaders of the early Islamic Caliphate. The use of this expression cautioned members against integrating into wider society. That society included "lesser" Muslims, who did not practice Islam as strictly as we did.

ACCEPT A STATE OF WAR

Jamaa did not leave it up to recruits to decide if there was a war with the infidels. Our leaders insisted we were already at war with non-Muslims. Adherents and potential adherents faced the option of bravely joining the battle or cowardly avoiding it. The *imam* at the mosque had meticulously instructed us to stand "shoulder-to-shoulder and foot-to-foot." His command made us feel like soldiers, tasked with fighting for Allah against the enemies of Islam. We envisioned the victories of the Islamic Conquests. During prayer, I used to picture myself as a knight of Allah, standing with fellow warriors as "one cemented structure."

OFFER SEX AND PARADISE

Islamists brainwashed new recruits by exploiting sex in two ways: They simultaneously deprived young men of it and enticed them with it. Call it Sex Deprivation Syndrome, or SDS. Broadly speaking, students find it very difficult to marry because of financial limitations. Marriage carries with it great expense in the Middle East. It is not culturally acceptable for a young man to marry before he graduates and secures employment. Further, Jamaa cited the Quran to prohibit premarital sex:

> *And who never invoke any (imaginary) deity side by side with God,*
> *and do not take any human being's life – (the life) which God has*
> *willed to be sacred – otherwise than in (the pursuit of) justice, and do*
> *not commit adultery. And (know that) he who commits aught thereof*
> *shall (not only) meet with a full requital (but) shall have his suffering*
> *doubled on Resurrection Day: for on that (Day) he shall abide in*
> *ignominy.* [25:68-69]

Likewise, release of sexual desire in any other physiological manner is also forbidden by most Islamic scholars. In combination, these factors create a great deal of sexual suppression and frustration among young Muslim men. Sexual restrictions alone were not enough to sway us toward *jihad*, so jihadists directed our attention to the pornographic accounts in Salafi Islamic writings. Sexual release might be nearly impossible in this life, but it would be readily available in Paradise. Consider:

> *Narrated Anas: The Prophet used to go round (have sexual*
> *relations with) all his wives in one night, and he had nine wives.*
> > —*Sahih al-Bukhari*

Narrated Anas: That Prophet Muhammad used to have sex with all of his 11 wives in only one hour of a day or a night ... and he said that Muhammad has been given the power of 30 men in having sex.
—*Sahih al-Bukhari*

In Paradise: When the Muslim enters the room to have sex with the first lady of the 72 hur (beautiful ladies with wide eyes and white skin), he will find her waiting on the bed ... He will not become bored at having sex with her and she will not become bored of having sex with him ... and every time he has sex with her he will find her a virgin again ... and his penis will never relax (i.e. will be continuously erect) after the coitus ... Some disciples asked the prophet, "Are we going to have sex in the Paradise...?" Muhammad said "Yes, and I swear with the name of the one who controls my soul and body (Allah) that every time the man will finish his turn at sex with her ... she will return back a virgin."
—*Tafsir ibn Kathir*

A man was sleeping in the house of Aisha (the youngest wife of the prophet) and he ejaculated while sleeping. The concubine of Aisha saw him while he was cleaning it (the semen) with water ... She spoke to Aisha who explained to the man that she used to scrub the semen of the Prophet directly with her nails after it dried up.
—*Sahih Muslim*, Book of Tahara

The ladies of the Paradise awaiting the followers of Muhammad are so beautiful to the degree that light shines from their faces, their bodies are as soft as silk, they are white in color and they wear green clothes and golden jewelry ... These beautiful ladies say to the believers when they enter the Paradise ... "we are eternal for you (to enjoy us) ...We are very soft and will never get unhappy. We are continuously ready (for sex) and we are always satisfied and will never be discontent ... So blessed is this man who will have us and we will have him."
—*Tafsir ibn Kathir*

Jamaa maintained these texts in the library. We were encouraged to read them and believe them literally. Islamists constantly decry the West's export of lewdness and easy sex. Western scholars often concur and chastise their societies for it. Islamists, however, use the sexual lewdness in Islamic writings in place of the lewdness they fight against in the West. In combination, sexual prohibitions and enticements help drive some young Muslim men into a fever for *jihad*, which guarantees them sex in Paradise – as soon as they martyr themselves.

The striking difference in the percentage of suicide bombers between Shia and Sunni Muslims further elucidates this problem. In recent years, it has become obvious that young Sunni Muslims have contributed to suicide bombings significantly more than their Shia brethren. We can attribute this phenomenon, in part at least, to the fact that young Shia Muslims are permitted *nikah mutah*, a brief temporary marriage for premarital sexual relations. [10]

Young Sunni Muslims do not have this option; the Sunni branch does not recognize *mutah* at all. In other words, young Shias do not need to martyr themselves in suicide attacks in order to have non-marital sex, which is permitted to Sunnis only in Paradise. Unlike many young Sunnis, young Shias can easily find fulfillment on Earth. Note, however, that Shias can still conduct suicide bombings if their *maraji*, or highest religious authorities, order them to do so.

Sex Deprivation Syndrome is not the only factor that causes jihadism, but it is a significant contributing factor for many young Sunnis. I know; I experienced it personally. Leaders of Islamic terrorist organizations regularly promise their would-be martyrs that they will enjoy the *hur* – the white ladies of Paradise.

THREATEN HELL

Jamaa's leaders and other Islamic scholars manipulated our minds perhaps most effectively by using the graphic descriptions of Hell in religious writings. Torture in the Quran is not an abstract concept; the descriptions are vivid and gruesomely poetic.

> *But those of the left hand (did not obey Allah and Muhammad or follow them) – how unhappy those of the left hand. They will be in the scorching hot wind and boiling water, under the shadow of thick black smoke, neither cool nor agreeable ... They will be gathered together on a certain day which is predetermined. Then you, the erring and the deniers will eat Zaqum (a thorny tree), fill your bellies with it, and drink scalding water, lapping it up like female camels raging of thirst and disease. Such will be their entertainment, their welcome on the Day of Doom ... the welcome of boiling water and the entertainment of roasting in Hell. This is the ultimate truth.*
> [56:41-57]

*For we have truly made it as a trial to torment the disbelievers.
Zaqum is a horrible thorn tree that grows in Hell. The shoots of its
fruit-stalks are like the heads of devils. Truly they (the non-Muslims)
will eat it and fill their bellies with it. On top of that they will be
given a mixture made of boiling water to drink especially prepared.
Then they shall be returned to the Blazing Fire. [37:63-68]*

*Soon will I fling them into the burning hellfire! And what will explain
what hellfire is? It permits nothing to endure, and nothing does it
spare! It darkens and changes the color of man, burning the skin! It
shrivels and scorches men. [74:26-29]*

*We have prepared the doom of Hell and the penalty of torment in
the most intense Blazing Fire. For those who reject their Lord is the
punishment of Hell: Evil, it is such a wretched destination. When
they are flung therein, they will hear the terrible drawing in of their
breath and loud moaning even as the flame blazes forth, roaring with
rage as it boils up, bursting with fury. Every time a fresh crowd is cast
in, Hell's wardens will ask, "Did no warning come to you?" [67:6-8]*

*"This," it will be said, "is the Fire, which you used to deny!" Is this
magic fake? Burn therein, endure the heat; taste it. It's the same
whether you bear it patiently or not. This is my retaliation for what
you did. [52:14-16]*

*Those who shall dwell forever in the Fire are given to drink boiling
water that tears their bowels to pieces, and cutting their intestines to
shreds. [47:15]*

Repeated exposure to these passages terrified us of the dreadful consequences of disobeying religious teaching. To be saved from such a fate,
and to win the destiny of Paradise, was incentive enough to perform any
deed in the name of Allah.

MODEL PROPHET MUHAMMAD

Being a dedicated Muslim, I dreamed of emulating the Prophet in word
and deed. Young Muslim men everywhere typically think the same way
and are encouraged to do so, based on the following Quranic verse:

*Ye have indeed in the Messenger of Allah a beautiful pattern (of con-
duct) for any one whose hope is in Allah and the Final Day, and who
engages much in the Praise of Allah. [33:21]*

The Quran has many positive examples of Muhammad's conduct, and I will describe his role more thoroughly in the chapter on reformation. Jamaa Islamiya, however – and Islamists in general – employed purported instances of Muhammad's abusive conduct to encourage us to embrace *jihad*. It is essential to keep in mind that very few of these examples referenced by jihadists are found in the Quran – they come from *hadiths* and much later writings.

Here are three passages Jamaa leaders cited:

> *Allah granted Rayhanah of the (Jewish) Qurayza to His Messenger as booty, but only after she had been forced to watch him decapitate her father and brother, had seen her mother hauled off to be raped, and her sisters sold into slavery.*
>
> —Al-Tabari

> *After Muhammad attacked the Jews of Bani Khriza he killed all their men and divided the women for sexual pleasure among Muslims and enslaved their children and took their money and treasure.*
>
> —Sahih al-Bukhari (Kitab al-Maghazy)

> *One day a woman came to Prophet Muhammad (pbuh) and said to him "Do you have a desire in my body (for sex)? If so … I am offering myself to you … Muhammad's daughter said, "This lady does not have any dignity so she offers herself to a man!" … The Prophet said to his daughter "This lady is better than you … as she wanted to be with the Prophet of Allah so she offered herself to him."*
>
> —Sunan ibn Maga (Kitab al-Nikah)

These verses are widely propagated by Salafists; we were encouraged to read them in Jamaa's library at the medical school. They assist Islamists with the indoctrination tactics of superiority, state of war and sexual deprivation.

RESTRICT EMOTIONAL OUTLETS

Another key tactic of indoctrination was to suppress our ability to appreciate beauty. Islamists prohibited most forms of music, prevented female singing and dancing, and forbade drawing anything with a soul. This suppression had a rigorous theological base in Salafism. Women were also not allowed to wear perfume or makeup. We could not disobey because, again, we risked spending eternity in Hell.

What is the life of this world but play and amusement? But best is
the home in the hereafter, for those who are righteous. Will ye not
then understand? [6:32]

"Amusements" – such as music and dancing – were considered evil
activities. By inhibiting our capacity to enjoy beauty, Jamaa made us
more amenable to accept ugliness and barbarity.

In short, they managed these tactics to great effect, producing the
phases of transformation from devout young Muslims into jihadists.
When believers hear the Quran in Arabic, they experience these tactical
components as the literal Word of God expressed in poetry. It can have
a stirring effect when read or spoken alone, but in the hands of a gifted
cleric, Quranic verses can be mesmerizing.

'Doctor Ayman'

It happened one afternoon. A guest *imam* arrived to deliver a sermon.
His topic didn't concern itself with dry details of prayer and fasting. He
was fiery and charismatic; his passion was holy war. It was to be fought
on all fronts, against all nonbelievers, without compromise until all people converted, submitted to Sharia or were slain. He persuaded us that
Islamic victory was possible, that we could make the glorious days of
al-Futuhat al-Islamiya, the Islamic Conquests, return. After the sermon,
a fellow member, Tariq Abdul-Muhsin, asked me if I knew the *imam*.
When I answered that I didn't, he told me the speaker was Dr. Ayman
al-Zawahiri. Because I was a new member, Tariq offered to introduce
me to him.

In person, al-Zawahiri was polite and decent with the members of
Jamaa. It was hard to reconcile his fiery sermons with the quiet man
before me, but al-Zawahiri was only applying a Salafist understanding
of a holy verse:

Muhammad is the apostle of Allah, and those who are with him are
strong against Unbelievers, (but) compassionate amongst each other.
[Quran 48:29]

I remember feeling very proud when al-Zawahiri told me, "Young
Muslims like you are the hope for the future return of Khilafa (the
Caliphate or Islamic global dominance)." He made me want to fight for
him, to show him my courage and loyalty.

Al-Zawahiri came from a wealthy, well-known and well-educated family and was a top postgraduate student at the medical school. He was active in a number of Islamist groups, so he did not devote his time exclusively to Jamaa. We called him "Dr. Ayman."

The doctor's speeches employed *hadiths* and Quranic verses to great effect. He was a master at attracting new recruits and inciting them to *jihad*. It is worthwhile studying his use of Islamic texts in terms of the phases and tactics we have mentioned, particularly hatred, superiority and war:

> *Fight those who believe neither in Allah nor the Last Day, nor hold that forbidden which hath been forbidden by Allah and His Messenger (Muhammad), nor acknowledge the religion of Truth (Islam), (even if they are) of the People of the Book (Christians and Jews), until they pay the Jizya (Humiliating Poll Tax) with submission, and feel themselves subdued.* [Quran 9:29]

> *But when the forbidden months (a certain four months in the Arabic calendar) are past, then fight and slay the Infidels wherever you may come upon them, and seize them, beleaguer them, and lie in wait for them in every stratagem (to do harm to them); but if they repent (convert from their beliefs to Islam), and establish the regular (Islamic) prayers and practice the regular Zakat (Islamic charity), then open the way for them: for Allah is Oft-forgiving, Most Merciful.* [9:5]

> *Allah hath purchased of the believers their persons and their goods; for theirs (in return) is the garden (of Paradise): they fight in His cause, and slay and are slain: a promise binding on Him in truth, through the Law, the Gospel, and the Quran: and who is more faithful to his covenant than Allah? Then rejoice in the bargain which ye have concluded: that is the achievement supreme.* [9:111]

> *When ye meet the Unbelievers, strike off their heads.* [47:4]

> *So fight them (the Non-Muslims) until there is no more Fitnah (disbelief) and all submit to the religion of Allah alone.* [8:39]

*It is He who hath sent His Messenger (Muhammad) with guidance
and the Religion of Truth, to proclaim it over all religion, even
though the Pagans may detest (it).* [9:33]

No doubt al-Zawahiri was a potent speaker, but how did he propose
to create the world he wanted, and exactly what kind of world did he
want to create?

To answer this, we need to examine the differences among Islamist
organizations, particularly those in Egypt. The proliferation of such
groups is a frequent source of mystification to Westerners, but for all
intents and purposes the strategic goal of each organization is the same;
they differ primarily in tactical focus. At any moment, dozens of such
groups inhabit a given nation or geopolitical region. Most collaborate
on occasion and are typically on good terms with one another. In Egypt
during my indoctrination, several such groups were particularly noteworthy, although many others existed.

Islamic Jihad, for example, was extremely violent. [11] Its members
would concentrate on the assassination of important political leaders.
Their violence was not diffuse but highly targeted. Also brutal, and
broadly so, was Takfir Wa al-Hijra. *Takfir* means "consider others as
infidels," while *al-hijra* refers to the group's segregation from society.
They practiced murder and mass murder as a matter of policy. When
that wasn't possible they engaged in theft, physical assault and intimidation wherever and whenever they could. The group did not distinguish
among Christians, Jews and secular Muslims; they considered all three as
infidels and impediments to Islamic world domination. Takfir Wa al-Hijra provided recruits with weapons and didn't particularly care if their
targets were important on the national level.

On the opposite side of the Islamist spectrum was Jamaa al-Tabligh
Waal-Daawa; literally, "Party of Messengers." This group sought societal change toward Islamist rule through grassroots outreach. They did
not clearly condemn violence, nor did they deny the violent aspects of
Salafist teaching. Its members would travel door-to-door to preach a
return to strict Islamic orthodoxy while avoiding political discussion or
activity.

Another group from a similar mold was Ansar al-Sunnah, which
translates, awkwardly, as "Supporters of Following in Muhammad's
Footsteps." Their goal was to emulate Prophet Muhammad in every

aspect of life, including those abusive and sexual inclinations described by Salafist writings. They forbade a husband to see his wife completely naked, for example, while encouraging polygamy.

Ansar al-Sunnah members dressed like the Prophet, wearing white clothes, beards and short mustaches. Members also would apply a cologne called misk and utilize special toothpicks (*siwak*) made of sandalwood to promote healthy gums, because Prophet Muhammad was reputed to have used them. The group was obsessed with manners, such as eating only with the right hand, sitting on the floor, and finishing a glass in three gulps. The late Osama bin Laden exhibited this behavior.

Somewhere in the middle was the Muslim Brotherhood. Their flag illustrates their philosophy. The two swords, and beneath them the Arabic word *wu-aiidu* ("prepare"), are based on the Quranic verse:

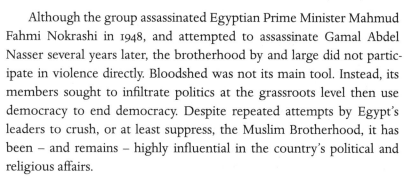

> *Prepare for them (the Infidels) whatever military power you have ... to insert fear into (the hearts of) the enemies of Allah.* [8:60]

Although the group assassinated Egyptian Prime Minister Mahmud Fahmi Nokrashi in 1948, and attempted to assassinate Gamal Abdel Nasser several years later, the brotherhood by and large did not participate in violence directly. Bloodshed was not its main tool. Instead, its members sought to infiltrate politics at the grassroots level then use democracy to end democracy. Despite repeated attempts by Egypt's leaders to crush, or at least suppress, the Muslim Brotherhood, it has been – and remains – highly influential in the country's political and religious affairs.

For years, we in the West have been debating whether the Muslim Brotherhood is a radical organization. It's been a difficult case to make for those of us who understand the group's true nature, because the brotherhood has managed to persuade key decision-makers in the United States and Europe that they are moderates. This, despite the fact that the brotherhood is the closest ally of, and shares the same ideology with, Hamas – a group the U.S. government has correctly classified as a terror organization.

It's a frustrating misconception, because even a cursory examination of the brotherhood's goals will reveal the group's dangerous nature. Basically, their modus operandi can be reduced to four stages:

1. *Al-daawa:* preaching

2. *Al-musharaka:* participation

3. *Al-tamkeen:* consolidating power while faking legitimacy

4. *Al-mughalab:* enforcing Sharia

Think about it. These sequential stages, taken in order, constitute an insidious strategy that inhibits outsiders from suspecting the brotherhood's creeping tyranny – until they accumulate enough power to impose Sharia to the exclusion of all civil authority.

This almost happened in Egypt just a few years ago. Following the removal of President Hosni Mubarak, in the so-called Arab Spring, the Muslim Brotherhood effectively took control of the government and installed one of their own, Mohamed Morsi, who quickly organized the brotherhood's campaign of replacing the country's legal system with Sharia. In fact, had the Egyptian people not turned against the brotherhood by the millions, only a year after Morsi's government took over, they could have faced a fate not unlike Sharia-ruled Afghanistan under the Taliban.

Yes, if the Muslim Brotherhood had succeeded in reaching its Stage 4 in Egypt, it would have become extremely difficult to remove them from power. Yet many Westerners, including the Obama administration, have continued to support the brotherhood, perhaps because they did not witness the consequences of the brotherhood achieving Stage 4. Egypt certainly understood the implications, because it declared the group a terrorist organization in late 2013. [12, 13]

It's also important to understand that the Muslim Brotherhood will accept circumstances that offend their beliefs – temporarily – if doing so will advance their goals. Examples are consuming alcohol or permitting Western dress for women. Such ideological sacrifices are based on the Sharia principle of *taqiyya*, or the deception of the infidel. You might recall that some of the 9/11 hijackers, in the days leading up to their attack, went to bars and strip clubs, and they drank alcohol, all to persuade any suspicious souls that they were not jihadists.

Other insidious aspects of the brotherhood:

+ Whenever possible, they avoid doing dirty work themselves. Instead, they support other radical groups and encourage them to perform certain tasks on the brotherhood's behalf. This is one reason why, after Morsi took power, he ordered the release of radical Islamists from Egypt's prisons. [14]

+   They pose as peacemakers to attempt to ease pressure on besieged radicals in other countries. That is what Morsi did when he objected to France fighting terrorists in Mali, and when he presented himself as a peace negotiator between Hamas and Israel. Many Western media hailed. [15, 16]

+   They employ Orwellian doublespeak to deceive their intended conquests. For example, Muslim Brotherhood members insist it is the right of any individual to choose his religion, suggesting support for freedom of religion. The attempted deception is easily detected, however, because it is not accompanied by a declaration that an individual has the right to leave his or her faith. Sharia demands that anyone who converts from Islam to another religion, or anyone who forsakes Islam, must be killed.

Tactics such as these have permitted members of the Muslim Brotherhood to portray themselves as moderates within Islam. And it often works, as I have described. But it belies the true nature of the group. Sayyid Qutb, one of the brotherhood's early leaders, who promoted the use of violence to enforce Islam, remains its spiritual model. He is the man whom some regard as exerting the principal influence on Osama bin Laden and Ayman al-Zawahiri. [17]

President Nasser, who executed Qutb for trying to assassinate him, once remarked that the first things Qutb asked him to do when they met in 1953 was force women to wear the *hijab*, close all theaters and ban movies. Radical Islamic groups, from Mali to Somalia to Afghanistan, typically make such demands when they attain power.

Last, Jamaa Islamiya (literally, "Islamic Group") concentrated on recruiting from society's best and brightest by entrenching themselves in universities and medical schools. Having done so, Jamaa prepared the theoretical foundations for *jihad* and propagated them to promising students who could best absorb them. Like the Muslim Brotherhood, Jamaa didn't participate directly in terror – it would have been counterproductive to provoke a crackdown from school administrations. Jamaa was more of a gateway group. It indoctrinated recruits and equipped them with jihadist knowledge, encouraging them to assume leadership positions in Islamic Jihad or the Muslim Brotherhood, or to practice *jihad* in other countries.

Intellectually, Ayman al-Zawahiri was much affected by the teachings of Sayyid Qutb. He used to praise Sayyid by saying "Rahimahu

Allah" whenever he mentioned his name. The expression means, "May Allah show him mercy and kindness." Qutb was an extremely persuasive writer; he was capable of painting pictures with his words that left the reader totally captivated. His deep knowledge of the Arabic language and his ability to use it were remarkable. Qutb's interpretation of the Quran, *Fi Zilal al-Quran (In the Shadows of the Quran)*, was an extraordinary work. Unfortunately, it also promoted hatred and violence.

As with all jihadists, al-Zawahiri's ultimate goal was to recreate the Islamic Caliphate. That is, he sought to unite the Muslim world under a single leadership headed by a prince. This caliph would not merely provide spiritual leadership but also would govern the totality of Islamic dominions.

It should be understood that Salafi Islam is political in its very essence, to the extent that it is fundamentally different in this regard from Judaism and Christianity. Judaism was forced to contend with the Diaspora at an early stage and learned to cooperate with host nations while preserving its religious identity. Likewise, when Christ was asked what deference should be given to temporal power, he responded with the well-known maxim:

> *Render therefore unto Caesar the things which are Caesar's, and unto God the things that are God's.* [Matthew 22:21]

In contrast, Salafi Islam teaches an aggressive military ideology designed to spread the religion, using murder, torture and enslavement if necessary to dominate the world. [18]

Al-Zawahiri wished to dispense with the idea of individual states. He wanted one state, Islam, bound by Sharia law and ruled by the caliph. For al-Zawahiri, it was the world of Islam against the world of war (i.e., against the infidels), or in Arabic, *dar al Islam* and *dar al harb*, respectively. In this sense, al-Zawahiri was no different from many traditional scholars who taught the theoretical underpinnings of violence. It was typical for an *imam* to rouse congregants in a prayer that cursed Jews and Christians. Al-Zawahiri differed from them by directly preaching actual violence against Islam's "enemies."

As we have witnessed time and again, this desire for a caliphate puts Islamists on a collision course with the governments of their host countries; in this case, Egypt. As it is written,

Those who do not judge with Allah's law are Infidels. [Quran 5:44]

In other words, al-Zawahiri did not view the leaders of Islamic nations as true Muslims because, as Jamaa Islamiya interpreted it, they did not rule by Islamic law. So it was that the Islamists not only objected to Anwar Sadat's peace with Israel in 1979 and his goal of better ties with America, they also objected fundamentally to Egypt as a secular state and Sadat as a leader with temporal power.

Al-Zawahiri equally decried the freedoms of the West as immoral weaknesses, as excesses, but also as threats. The West did not submit to Islamic law, yet it was both successful and powerful. He scorned the liberties of Western women, particularly their suggestive attire. Women, he believed, should be required by law to wear Islamic dress – at least the *hijab* and preferably the *niqab*, a covering for the woman's face as well as her hair. He envisioned a system similar to that implemented later by the Taliban in Afghanistan, one that compelled women to cover themselves completely with the *burqa*. [19]

If necessary, al-Zawahiri believed, it is sometimes acceptable to indulge the freedoms of the West but only as *taqiyya*, the vehicle for advancing the takeover by Islam.

Al-Zawahiri was faithful to his cause, but his spiritual identification became perverted. Islamist teachings twisted his religious fervor toward violence. Today, as head of al-Qaeda, he is certainly a leader of mass-murderers. But al-Zawahiri is also a pawn of a perverse doctrine that warped him into a terrorist. I often wonder how al-Zawahiri would have turned out if his childhood religious education had promoted love instead of hate and violence.

Second Thoughts

My entire relationship with Jamaa Islamiya lasted approximately from 1979-1982. It took about six months to become sufficiently indoctrinated. Over the next year, I became increasingly active in the movement. Eventually, my involvement reached the point where I thought myself prepared to train with jihadists in Afghanistan – to fight and kill the Russian invaders in the name of Allah.

It was at this time that my conscience began to awaken. I sensed I was on the wrong path. In the last eight months of membership I gradually withdrew.

One episode in particular gave me second thoughts. It transpired that I overheard a conversation between Ahmed Omar and other members of the group. A fourth-year medical student, Ahmed was an *amir* of Jamaa. He was planning to kidnap a police officer and bury him alive. His exact word was *netaweeh*, which actually meant, in Egyptian slang, "to dig a grave for someone and bury him alive."

The issue concerned a party planned for that day at the medical school and featuring music and women singers. The view of Jamaa, of course, was that such an event was un-Islamic. Members of Jamaa gathered that day by the thousands to protest the party and disrupt it by force. The police intervened and the medical school was placed under martial law.

It occurred to me then that the Quran doesn't actually forbid music. Jamaa and other Islamists base this prohibition not on Quranic verses but on non-Quranic sources such as the *hadiths*. It creates a contradiction between the Quran and other approved Islamic books. But in thinking this way, I was doing the opposite of what Jamaa had taught me: I began to analyze. The critical thinking with which my father had raised me helped me at the last moment. It ignited the essential spark.

I recalled the time I studied the Bible to debate the Christian students in high school. In particular, I remembered this passage:

For what shall it profit a man, if he shall gain the whole world, and lose his own soul? [Mark 8:36]

I pondered. What if Islam was to subjugate the world but lose its soul? That early exposure to the Bible was crucial in helping me question the violent aspects of Salafist teaching. Christ's statement played a pivotal role in giving me the moral fiber to swim against the stream of radical Islam – to resist it rather than appease it.

Then, I remembered another verse from the Quran:

O ye who believe! Stand out firmly for justice, as witnesses to God, even as against yourselves, or your parents, or your kin. [4:135]

This time, I beheld those words in a completely different light. I understood them to mean we should speak the truth even if it conflicted with the common beliefs of our culture. It meant we should say what we believe is good and useful to all of mankind even if it violated the dictates of traditional religious teachings.

I wondered, too, if the divine DNA molecule was violent. Did it attempt to conquer the rest of the cell? Did it try to force other cellular components to behave like itself? It did not. Rather, it worked harmoniously within an organism to create and sustain life.

Most of all, the existence of alternative forms of Islamic teaching helped me to desist from the path of *jihad*. Specifically, I was invited during this time to join a very small sect of Islam that followed only the Quran. They were known as Quranics, and they rejected the *hadiths* and other Islamic texts. Consequently, members of this sect stood against killing apostates, against stoning women for adultery, against killing gays. They viewed the Islamic Conquests as immoral and senseless.

The sect was not ideal – the respect many followers had for women's rights was not entirely satisfactory to me. Still, they were much less violent than the Salafists, and they allowed me to think critically, to approach the Quran in a non-traditional manner. I was able to develop different theologically based interpretations from those of other sect members without engendering animosity. Tolerating different views was an important creed of the Quranics. If this alternative sect had not been available, it would have been much more difficult for me to resist jihadism.

All of these influences combined to cultivate in me a new mentality that defied – and still defies – the violent injunctions promoted by prevailing Islamic instruction.

Jamaa, of course, was not pleased. They tried to persuade me to return. We became embroiled in intricate debates about stoning women and secular rule, which annoyed them greatly. They didn't threaten me with violence per se, but there were indirect threats: "Apostates such as you will be killed."

After I left Jamaa, I began to preach a peaceful understanding of Islam. Once, I gave a sermon at a local mosque, and after prayers a gang of radical Muslims confronted me and my dear friend Dr. Tarek Ragab. They punched him, and as we ran from the mob, they pelted us with stones. Fortunately, we weren't seriously injured.

Summing Up

It is vital that Islamic education systems teach young Muslims the value and skill of critical thinking. They must be exposed to other beliefs, cultures and religions, and learn to respect them. Most important, the Islamic world must foster an alternative, theologically rigorous doctrine that rejects violence. This approach is necessary to modernize Islamic societies and decrease the likelihood of young Muslims turning to *jihad*.

The consequences of not learning the lessons have been dire and will continue to be so. By the late 1970s, Islamists had penetrated into every aspect of Egyptian life. They established competing banks offering exceptionally high rates of return on deposits, sometimes 25 percent. As Egyptians gravitated to these banks, the result was a significant boost to the liquidity of Islamist coffers. In 1981, not long before I graduated, President Anwar Sadat was assassinated by a military lieutenant named Khaled Islambouli – a member of Islamic Jihad. The Iranians were delighted at the assassination and named a street after Islambouli. Al-Zawahiri was also a member of Islamic Jihad and was indicted for the assassination, but his connection to it was never proven. He was released from prison in 1984.

Takfir Wa al-Hijrra, among others, went on to slaughter many Egyptians and foreign tourists in Egypt. The so-called Blind Sheikh, Omar Abdel-Rahman, was a spiritual leader of Takfir. Americans will recognize his name – he resides now in a maximum-security federal penitentiary in North Carolina, in solitary confinement, for conspiring to blow up the United Nations building in New York City and for attempting to destroy the World Trade Center in 1993 – a job finished by al-Qaeda in 2001. Though estimates vary, about three-quarters of al-Qaeda's leadership is Egyptian. Of the 19 hijackers that perpetrated the 9/11 attacks, 15 were Saudis. The rest hailed from other Arab countries. Their leader, Mohamed Atta, who died crashing an airliner into the Trade Center's North Tower, was my countryman.

NOTES

2.   For example, in 1961, Nasser dismissed two grand *imams* at Al-Azhar University and relegated to himself the power to appoint future grand *imams*.

3.   The textbook was written by Taha Hussein, who was the Dean of the School of Arabic Language at Cairo University. A well-known scholar, Taha was blind since childhood, learning the Quran by verbal repetition at Al-Azhar school. Al-Azhar, better known as a university, actually consists of two parts – the university and a religious school for children. Taha didn't like the teaching at Al-Azhar and left because it was too fundamentalist. He was so critical of Al-Azhar that some called him an apostate. The *hadith* cited here refers to the first two Caliphs, Abu Bakr and Umar.

4.   Also transliterated as al-Gama'a al-Islamiyya, Gamaat Islamiya, Jamaat al Islamiya, al-Jam'ah al-Islamiyah, etc. The name should not be confused with a similarly named Islamist group based in Indonesia.

5.   Russel Goldman, "Can Terrorists Trained as Doctors Slip into the United States?" ABC News Online, July 4, 2007.

6.   It is short for Amir al-Muminin, a term employed during the Islamic Caliphate.

7.   See *Tafsir ibn Kathir* and *Minhaj al-Muslim* by Abu Bakr Jabir al-Jazairi.

8.   See *Fiqh us-Sunnah* by As-Sayyid Sabiq, Volume I: Purification and Prayer

9.   A saying made more effective by its use of the same three letters in its Arabic root, giving it a musical and therefore more memorable quality.

10.   I do not endorse *nikah mutah*.

11.   For our purposes, this group should not be confused with the Palestinian terrorist organization of the same name.

12.   Robert Spencer, "Obama White House," *Jihad Watch*, December 1, 2014.

13.   "Egypt Declares Muslim Brotherhood Terrorist Group," VOA News, December 25, 2013.

14.   Ahmad Ramin, "Morsi's Pardon of Islamists Stirs Controversy in Egypt," al-Monitor.com, August 1, 2012.

15.   "Egypt's Morsi opposes French intervention in Mali," France24.com, January 22, 2013.

16.   Bessma Momani, "With Gaza ceasefire, Egypt's Morsi becomes a serious player," *The Globe and Mail*, November 22, 2012.

17.   Robert Irwin, "Is this the man who inspired Bin Laden?" *The Guardian*, October 31, 2001.

18.   Although Moses was a powerful leader of the Hebrews, and well cared-for by them, God forbade him to enter the land of Canaan.

19.   It is an almost ubiquitous misconception in the West that the *burqa* is the garment covering a Muslim woman's entire body. Actually, the word, which originated in Turkey and then Egypt, describes the *burqa* as a portion of cloth that descends from the nose and covers the neck, leaving the eyes exposed. In Arab societies, the proper term for the full-body covering is the *niqab*. But given the current widespread understanding of the term, I have applied it accordingly in the text.

CHAPTER 2

Myths and Misconceptions about Islamism

Many myths surround the phenomenon that is radical Islam, and we need to address them if we are to understand fully what we're facing. Every medical doctor knows how difficult it is to treat a disease if it has been misdiagnosed or if the disease is confused with its symptoms. We need to diagnose jihadism correctly, lest we waste time, resources and lives attempting to fight it – we must identify the root causes before we can effect a cure.

Even then – even fully understanding its causes – jihadism is difficult to fight, because it defies persistent, commonly held political beliefs. Watch or read accounts of world leaders commenting on the latest terror attacks. You will quickly see most of them attributing the cause to every possibility but one: Islam as it is currently taught and practiced in the vast majority of Muslim communities.

For example:

\+ U.N. Secretary General Ban Ki-moon once said the genocide in the Darfur region of Sudan, which began in 2003 and rages on even today, had stemmed from global warming. He advanced the idea that the Janjaweed militias – the so-called devils on horseback – of Northern Sudan were exterminating the residents of Darfur because of drought brought on by climate change. [20, 21]

\+ Former President Jimmy Carter, in merely one in a long string of similar comments, blamed the January 2015 terror attack at the Paris offices of *Charlie Hebdo*, the French humor magazine, on the treatment of the Palestinians by Israel. [22]

+ President Barack Obama, reacting to the same event, condemned the violence without mentioning the words "radical Islam" or "Muslims," even though eyewitnesses reported that the attackers shouted "We have avenged the Prophet Muhammad" as they murdered the magazine's staff, calling out their names one by one. [23, 24]

+ Incredibly, President Obama characterized the murder of Jewish patrons of a Parisian kosher delicatessen, an attack related to the *Charlie Hebdo* incident, as an act by "a bunch of violent, vicious zealots" who "randomly" shot "a bunch of folks." He did the same when commenting on the mass-murder of Christians by al-Shabaab suicide terrorists at Garissa University in Nairobi. [25, 26]

+ Perhaps President Obama's most ill-informed utterance of all was his assertion that the terror group Islamic State in Iraq and Syria, aka ISIS – which the president persists in calling "ISIL," for Islamic State in the Levant – is "not Islamic." He has refused to call the members of ISIS jihadists or radical Islamists or Muslim extremists. He will deem them terrorists or extremists, but at this writing President Obama will not associate ISIS – or al-Qaeda, for that matter – with Islam. [27]

How Did We Get Here?

This reticence to call a spade a spade, so to speak, isn't difficult to understand. Islam has more than 1.5 billion adherents, making it the world's second-largest religion. Muslim communities reside in nearly every nation, and it is common for them to become vocal, aggressive minorities. Witness the political power Muslims have amassed in England, in France, in Germany and to a lesser extent in the United States. It's one thing to say that extremist groups such as the Muslim Brotherhood and ISIS and al-Qaeda and al-Shabaab and Boko Haram don't represent Islam, even though all claim fealty to the Quran and to Muhammad, and all claim they act in Allah's name. It's quite another to blame the emergence of jihadists on the theology of Salafism and its companion, Wahhabism, which currently pervade Islam. Doing so, and when criticism or particularly satire is directed at Prophet Muhammad, the backlash can be severe – witness the *Charlie Hebdo* massacre.

Western nations also maintain many economic and strategic ties with Islamic states, so criticism of Islam and the Muslim community for abetting or acquiescing to radical Islam does not come without risk. The common inclination, such as in the examples cited above, is to excuse the religion as it is practiced and find some other reason for a scapegoat.

No question, fear is a big contributing factor. Western academicians and politicians want to appear tolerant at all costs, even to the point of tolerating an illiberal, intolerant ideology. According to this conceit, to appear intolerant is to appear unenlightened, even unintelligent. Peer pressure and political correctness weigh heavily, as do opportunities for promotion or election. Intolerance, at least as deemed so by the multicultural establishment, is an intellectual mark of shame. On the so-called street level, citizens hesitate to ask pointed questions of their Muslim neighbors because of their fear of civil disorder and violence in retaliation.

Resentment, too, is a factor. Some consider terrorists as underdogs, that the position of terrorists reflects their own isolation, their sense of being outcast. They thus perceive jihadists to be individuals who are down on their luck and in their supreme frustration are attempting to punch back at an oppressive system.

Root Causes

Islamic terrorism indeed has root causes. But many supposed motivations are misleading or just plain wrong. Many view it as the outcome of external forces such as poverty, lack of education, Israel, U.S. policies in the Middle East and so on. Some of these arguments are easy to disprove; others play a catalytic role, feeding into and fostering jihadism. But none, by itself, is the true cause, though all remain stubbornly popular.

Let's examine them.

POVERTY

On February 15, 2015, State Department spokeswoman Marie Harf said on the MSNBC program Hardball, "There is no easy solution in the long term to preventing and combating violent extremism, but if we can help countries work at the root causes of this: What makes these 17-year-old kids pick up an AK-47, instead of try to start a business?" [28]

To put it kindly, statements such as this are naïve and unrealistic. There are lots of impoverished non-Muslims around the world, particularly in Africa and Asia, who don't become suicide bombers. Moreover, take a quick peek at the backgrounds of most Islamist leaders. You'll find that many if not most emerged from the upper socioeconomic classes of their home countries. Osama bin Laden was a Saudi billionaire. Ayman al-Zawahiri, the man who recruited me to join Jamaa Islamiya, is a medical doctor and the product of a wealthy family in Egypt. Khalid Sheikh Mohammed, the principal architect of the 9/11 attacks, received an engineering degree in the United States. Iran's Ayatollah Ruhollah Khomeini emerged from humble beginnings to become one of the leading clerics of Shiite Islam. Likewise, his successor, Ayatollah Ali Khamenei, arose from modest circumstances, but his background in no way could be said to have been abject poverty.

Many other Islamic terrorists, such as the homegrown variety in the United Kingdom, were born into middle- and upper-class families. Fifteen of the 9/11 hijackers were from Saudi Arabia, a country one can hardly consider poor. Most of the hijackers spent extensive time enjoying the affluence and privileges of American society; it didn't deter them from their mission at all.

If poverty is a root cause of Islamic terrorism, we would have seen the majority of jihadists hail from a low socioeconomic status and from the poorest Islamic countries, such as Somalia or Nigeria. True, terrorists do emerge from such circumstances – the brutal al-Shabaab arose in Somalia, and Boko Haram now runs rampant in Nigeria. But nations and communities that are desperately poor do not always spawn terrorists. There are no statistically significant numbers of terrorists from, for example, the ranks of Chinese rice farmers, Rio de Janiero's *favelas* or Mexico City's shantytowns.

Let's look at this another way. Elements of traditional Islamic ideology, such as the oppression of women, can contribute to poverty without engendering terrorism. Islamic countries lose a significant proportion of their potential gross domestic products when half of their populations are not sufficiently participating in the labor force. In Saudi Arabia, women are not allowed to drive. This creates excessive demand for taxi services and chauffeurs, so the country must employ relatively low-paid foreigners to address the shortage of drivers.

Not that terrorism doesn't depress economies. When Islamic terrorists perpetrated the Luxor Massacre in 1997, Egypt's tourism industry collapsed almost totally. Likewise, the Palestinians of the West Bank and Gaza can attribute much of their impoverished lives to the activities of Hamas.

Yes, terrorism is related to poverty, but its role is one of facilitation, not origination. Poverty creates a vicious cycle in which jihadists find it easier to recruit new members when candidates suffer from poverty, after which these new recruits perpetrate acts of terror, which in turn creates more poverty. This diagram captures the cycle.

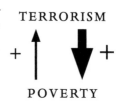

Terrorism and poverty work in a positive-feedback relationship. More important, terrorism is the primary factor in the cycle, while poverty is only secondary. It is vital to understand the mechanism precisely, because if we assess poverty to be the primary problem, our efforts at combating Islamic terror will fail.

What do I mean? Say, for example, that the West determines to authorize payments to poor Islamic communities in a global campaign to ease the root cause of terrorism. No doubt Western political leaders would hail the effort as an example of tolerance and charity. Unfortunately, in doing so, those leaders would only end up funding jihadists – men who would use the money to purchase weapons and intensify their recruiting efforts.

We must be sure to identify Islamism as the principal source of terrorism. When poor nations fail to produce terrorists, while Islamic societies spawn them in large numbers, the diagram above accurately describes what is going on. Therefore we must devote the bulk of our resources to fighting jihadist ideology.

DISCRIMINATION

This root cause would have it that Islamic terrorism is a backlash against discrimination: Muslims frustrated by inequality, injustice and prejudice in their respective societies and reacting to this perceived mistreatment by killing large numbers of infidels and apostates. The problem here is twofold. First, it fails to explain why Muslims who do not experience discrimination become terrorists. Second, it does not explain why non-Muslims who are discriminated against do not become terrorists.

Incidentally, not all Islamic terrorists are Middle Easterners. Some are Western converts to Islam. This leads to the subsidiary issue of whether such discrimination is directed against Arabs. Here again, there's a problem: Non-Arab Muslims have become terrorists while non-Muslim Arabs in general do not join the terrorist ranks.

Bottom line: Discrimination as a root cause of Islamic terrorism is questionable. According to recent FBI statistics, hate crimes against Muslims in the United States are not especially frequent compared to those against other religions or groups. [29]

FBI Hate Crime Statistics by Religion, 2013

BIAS MOTIVATION	INCIDENTS	OFFENSES	VICTIMS	KNOWN OFFENDERS
RELIGION	1,031	1,161	1,223	682
ANTI-JEWISH	625	689	737	393
ANTI-CATHOLIC	70	74	75	72
ANTI-PROTESTANT	35	42	47	17
ANTI-MUSLIM	135	165	167	127
ANTI-OTHER RELIGIONS OR MULTIPLE RELIGIONS	42	51	53	25
ANTI-ATHEISTS OR AGNOSTICS	7	7	7	7

Even if we grant the existence of discrimination against Muslims over and above what occurs against other groups, it doesn't explain why, for example, doctors in England – well-paid, respected professionals – were involved in attempts to destroy transportation targets. It also doesn't explain why Muslims commit acts of terror in Arab countries. The Muslims who perpetrated the 1997 Luxor massacre in Egypt, killing 60 tourists, were Egyptians. Do Egyptian Muslims face prejudice in Egypt? Jose Padilla, an American-born citizen and a non-Arab, was arrested in 2002 at Chicago's O'Hare Airport; at the time, he was attempting to leave the United States to participate in a plot to detonate a so-called dirty bomb. Adam Gadahn, aka Azzam the American, is another American-born convert to radical Islam who worked to attack his own country.

LACK OF EDUCATION

Another frequently cited cause of radicalism is the lack of education in Islamic societies. Anne Hidalgo, the mayor of Paris, typified this sentiment with her comment following the *Charlie Hebdo* killings. While in Washington, D.C., for the White House Summit on Countering Violent Extremism in February 2015, she said:

> *We must fight with security, but also through education and inclusion. It's important to deconstruct the myth the terrorists create around their activities. Their activities lead to death. [Real] heroes are people who succeed, go to school, engage with society and can talk to their neighbors even when they're different.* [30]

As mentioned, al-Qaeda's al-Zawahiri is a medical doctor, and his predecessor, Osama bin Laden, was likewise highly educated. Looking back over the past four decades of Islamic terror attacks worldwide, you can find many similar examples.

Education can play a positive role in combating terror, provided it teaches peace, critical thinking and real tolerance. But Salafist ideology, the most powerful force in mainstream Islamic education today, conveys virtually nothing along those lines. Moreover, highly educated people are better able to spread the religious texts that promote brutality, while illiterates usually cannot independently interpret Islamist writings much beyond the Five Pillars. An uneducated Muslim might well have a greater chance of maintaining his conscience unscathed, while the educated person would be more prone to rationalize violent religious indoctrination.

In the 1940s and 1950s, when Egypt had an illiteracy rate exceeding 90 percent, terrorism against tourists in the country was almost unheard of. Ironic, but when literacy improved and people became better able to assimilate Salafi Islamic theology, as indeed has happened over the past few decades, killing innocent tourists became commonplace.

Religious education can be beneficial if it teaches love, but if it teaches hatred and intolerance it can be catastrophic. Having knowledge or skills does not, by itself, make a person ethical or decent. We would do well to remember the quote often attributed to Theodore Roosevelt:

> *To educate a man in mind and not in morals is to educate a menace to society.*

ABSENCE OF DEMOCRACY

Back when I first wrote this book, there was a widespread belief that if we could only democratize the Middle East all would be well. Hillary Clinton, at the time the junior senator from New York, gave a speech at Princeton University in 2006 that exemplified the sentiment.

> *We must stand on the side of democracy wherever we can help it take hold, not just with speeches but with support that helps real people take charge of their own lives.* [31]

The previous year, Secretary of State Condoleezza Rice described President George W. Bush's "agenda for freedom" at a speech in Cairo.

> *There are those who say that democracy leads to chaos, or conflict, or terror. In fact, the opposite is true: Freedom and democracy are the only ideas powerful enough to overcome hatred, and division, and violence. For people of diverse races and religions, the inclusive nature of democracy can lift the fear of difference that some believe is a license to kill.* [32]

At the time I warned against attempting to impose democracy prematurely in the region; events then and since have borne me out. [33]

Many brave and noble individuals, such as Saad Eddin Ibrahim of the Ibn Khaldun Center for Democratic Studies, are championing democracy in the Middle East. It is an essential and critical battle. But in their zeal, many of these activists seem to be missing an important point: Insisting on elections before enlightenment can be dangerous. Egypt tried it and ended up with a legitimate, democratically elected Islamist government, which mercifully was removed after only a year in power by a massive popular revolution. In Libya and Yemen, the ballot brought non-Islamist governments, but as we have seen, those governments could not long withstand the relentless radical Islamic movements that currently dominate both countries.

Democracy advocates seem unable to perceive just how powerful and seductive Islamism can be, possibly because its barbarity is so alien to them. Many of them felt deep sorrow at Benazir Bhutto's assassination in 2007. But as my wife, Maha, noted at the time, why didn't the prime minister's death lead them to question whether lack of democracy is the source of Islamic terror? After all, the jihadists in Pakistan had just murdered their country's best chance for it.

Following the U.S. invasion of Iraq in 2003 and the ouster of Saddam Hussein, the Iraqi people ratified their own constitution and established a new democracy. Millions voted, proudly displaying their fingers coated with purple ink – signifying their participation at the voting booth – for a wide range of candidates. Seven years earlier in the Palestinian territories, Yasser Arafat was widely hailed as the democratically elected leader. His election, despite allegations of fraud, was certified by former U.S. President Jimmy Carter. In the time since, however, both of these societies have struggled constantly with Islamism and Islamic terror – the Palestinians with Hamas and Iraq with the Islamic State.

Consider also the outcome of the Arab Spring. Of all the revolutions that overthrew authoritarian regimes across the Middle East beginning in December 2010, only Tunisia emerged with a democracy. The others tried but failed miserably. In Libya, the ballot did not protect the nation from collapsing under the weight of Islamic barbarism.

Looking at these examples, we cannot escape concluding that democracy in the Middle East offers no magical solution to ending Islamic violence. In fact, these cases illustrate how countries jumping to democracy, perhaps without due preparation, gain no guarantee that violence will cease.

Without question, democracy should be the ultimate goal. Unfortunately, at the tactical level, defeating Islamism must take priority. Otherwise, Islamists will use democracy to end democracy. As Hamas did in Gaza, and the Muslim Brotherhood did in Egypt, they will participate in the democratic process, running candidates and taking office. But when they achieve a majority, or sufficient power, they will quickly shift to an authoritarian, Sharia-based government. That's what happened in Algeria in 1992, when the Islamic Salvation Front, a Salafi group led by Abbassi Madani, took power in an election and immediately declared the cessation of democratic government.

Islamists don't crave democracy; they are a parasite on democracy – they feed on a democratic host until the host perishes.

WESTERN COLONIALISM AND IMPERIALISM

Some Western academics and Leftist intellectuals, such as Edward Wadie Said, who died in 2003, blamed all trouble in the Middle East on Western and economic hegemony. The argument posits that European adventurism has left a legacy of enormous resentment and lingering hatred sufficient to fuel Islamic terror.

In a word: rubbish! If colonial injustice spawned radical Islam, then it should have inspired terrorism during or immediately after foreign occupations. The time gap belies the argument. It would be like a man with a chocolate allergy blaming a skin rash he just developed this morning on a bit of chocolate he ate 30 years ago.

The most common colonialist narrative is that Arab nations have been exploited since the 1930s by Western powers for their oil. More rubbish. Arab states required Western technology to extract their petroleum. They invited the multinational companies – Standard Oil, Royal Dutch Shell, British Petroleum and the others – as partners and granted them extensive drilling rights. Furthermore, after the establishment of the OPEC cartel in 1960, members began nationalizing their oil industries, retaining the multinationals only as outside contractors when necessary. And in any event, so-called economic imperialism has not left these nations destitute and humiliated. On the contrary, petroleum exporting has made several Middle Eastern nations fabulously wealthy.

One nation in particular thoroughly discredits the link between colonialism and *jihad*. Saudi Arabia, up to now the largest exporter of Wahhabism, the radical Islamic ideology that ultimately breeds terrorism, has never been colonized by a Western power. The Arabian Hejaz has been under continuous Muslim rule since the beginning of Islam. Yes, the Saudi coastal strip along the Red Sea encompassing the holy cities of Mecca and Medina was conquered and controlled by the Ottomans – but they were Muslims.

The brutal slaughter we see today of Muslims by Muslims has no relation whatsoever to Western occupation, the last of which ended decades ago. Sunnis massacre Shias in Iraq for reasons other than British colonialism. Algerian Muslims slaughtered each other not because of French colonialism but because of Islamist ideology. Women in Islamic societies who fail to wear the *hijab* have their faces burned with acid not because of colonial edicts but because of Sharia. Women are stoned for adultery not by colonial police but by Islamists. Gays are executed because their sexuality is considered immoral by Islamists.

Looking outside the sphere of Islam, why didn't Hindus in India, who were subject to the British Raj for more than a century, become international terrorists? Indeed, Gandhi went quite the opposite route by pursuing nonviolence. Why didn't the Swahili culture of Kenya and

Tanzania, likewise ruled by the Brits, take to violence during colonization? Yes, the Americans violently threw off British rule and formed the United States; the Catholics in the Irish Republican Army often brutally resisted their Protestant government in Northern Ireland; and Zionists in Palestine – not the Palestinians – battled British overseers prior to the establishment of Israel. But none of these instances resulted in a global campaign of terror.

No, colonialism did not spark *jihad*. On the contrary, when Islamic nations were colonized, Sharia- and Islamist-based crimes tended to drop significantly. In fact, Islamic nations in many respects were more civilized under occupation than they are now; we virtually never heard of suicide bombings or attacks against or kidnapping of tourists during that period.

Last, this argument seems suspiciously inconsistent. Anyone who blames *jihad* on the colonization of the Middle East by the West must also condemn Islamic subjugation of the region. Western colonization – where it can be said to have occurred – changed no language or religion of the Middle East's inhabitants. The Islamic Conquests can lay no such claim. They wiped out numerous native religions and forced the Arabic language on everyone they subjugated.

THE ARAB-ISRAELI CONFLICT

This argument runs that the recurring wars between Arabs and Israelis have created resentment among the world's Muslims, who express their anger at Israel via terrorism. We can dismiss this potential root cause entirely. The problem is that the argument fails to explain the global reach of *jihad* and the vast number of targets that have no relation to Israel.

Take, for example, the estimated 200,000 Algerians who perished in their civil war. Thousands of innocents were massacred, particularly by the Algerian Islamic Group, which was Salafist. Or, consider the Buddhists in Thailand who, for years now, have been enduring a protracted campaign of Islamist terror.

Here are four more-recent examples:

+   In 2004, 1200 students were taken hostage by jihadists in Beslan, Russia. Of these, 385 civilians perished, including 168 schoolchildren murdered at point-blank range. [34]

+   In 2014, in Peshawar, Pakistan, seven gunmen affiliated with the Taliban mowed down 141 people, including 132 schoolchildren. [35]

+   Also in 2014 and into 2015, in Nigeria, Boko Haram terrorists have been massacring innocent civilians by the thousands, including an incident, reported in the news as these words were being typed, where the terrorists disguised themselves as preachers and shot and killed at least 24 non-Muslims. [36]

+   In 2015, in Mosul, Iraq, ISIS members executed a group of teen-age boys, apparently for the crime of watching Iraq's national soccer team on television. [37]

As revolting as these incidents are, they represent nothing new. Shia and Sunni Muslims have been killing one another for over a millennium, ever since the early caliphates, and the hostility often spills across Middle Eastern borders.

Back in 1991, for example, more than 280,000 Palestinians were expelled from their homes. They had sided with Saddam Hussein during operation Desert Storm and suffered that consequence when allied forces defeated his army. Yet, the country that expelled the Palestinians experienced no world condemnation for its actions and has experienced, essentially, no retributions involving terror. The expulsion has not been mentioned in jihadist manifestos and has never been cited as a motivation. The reason for the indifference is the country that expelled them wasn't Israel; it was Kuwait.

If the predicament of the Palestinians were the source of global *jihad*, shouldn't we expect that Kuwait would experience a protracted campaign of terror, and that Muslims everywhere would attribute 9/11 to Kuwaiti expulsion of the Palestinians?

It's obvious there is no factual basis for blaming *jihad* on the Israeli-Palestinian conflict. Why, then, does this fallacy remain so persistent? The argument is prevalent throughout the global media, and it saturates the halls of academia. Blaming Israel is attractive to proponents of many competing, often conflicting, ideological positions. But most of all, blaming Israel is attractive because it is easier than leveling criticism at those 1.5-billion Muslims worldwide.

Likewise, using Israel as an excuse for *jihad* garners fewer consequences than, say, blaming the petrodollars collected by the Arab OPEC members that have been used to finance terror groups such as al-Qaeda. Despite plunging oil prices, members of the cartel remain tremendously powerful economically. They own or control a large chunk of the world's oil. Countries remaining dependent on this oil are therefore reluctant to provoke diplomatic and economic crises by accurately placing the blame for Islamic terror where it belongs, on current Islamic teaching, instead of the Palestinian problem.

Many Muslims seem to have this tendency to point fingers at anyone but themselves. Take my native land, Egypt. In January 2011, the country experienced a popular uprising that resulted in the removal of President Hosni Mubarak and the rise of the Muslim Brotherhood, capped by the election of Mohamed Morsi. Then, a little more than two years later, Egyptians rose up again, this time deposing Morsi and installing Abdel Fattah el-Sisi.

The reasons for the turmoil, which for the time being seems to have ended well, were clear. The brotherhood was in the process of imposing Sharia law on one of the most cosmopolitan societies in the Middle East, and certain members of the group even began calling for the destruction of Egypt's priceless landmarks such as the Sphinx and the Pyramids. [38] Yet instead of blaming themselves for choosing Islamists after the January 25 Revolution, many Egyptians persist in blaming America for their own missteps.

No surprise; American and European neo-Nazis view the destruction of Israel as a positive development, so they find it convenient to blame Israel for terrorism and apologize for the jihadists. Some neo-Nazi websites bitterly lament Islamophobia. They oppose the phenomenon not because they care about Muslims but because they are anti-Semitic. They tend to follow that old maxim: The enemy of my enemy is my friend [39]

Even casual observers will note that many Middle Easterners automatically blame Israel for everything. They seem incapable of accepting responsibility for mistakes in handling their own affairs.

Last, the international Left has its own motivations to blame Israel for the rise of Islamic terror. The Arab-Israeli conflict seems to find favor in Leftist thought, because it fixes the source of the evil in external, material conditions. War, exemplified by the Arab-Israeli conflict, creates Islamic terror, as their story goes, and not vice-versa. But there is more. A common Leftist template is that most of the world's problems stem from capitalist exploitation by imperialist nations. They claim that problems in the developing world – civil war, poverty, starvation, genocide – are the vestiges of this exploitation.

The problem is that Israel does not fit this template. Israel has allied itself with the West, particularly with the "Great Satan," the United States. It has utilized free markets and global trade and its close alliance with America to become a developed nation in less than 50 years.

Instead of hailing Israel as an example of liberal democracy in a geopolitical region where liberal democracy is conspicuously absent, instead of defending a small nation bullied and attacked by its larger, oil-rich Islamic neighbors, the Left has chosen to demonize Israel as an oppressor of the Palestinians, with global Islamic terror the result. The international Left is overwhelmingly, almost entirely, anti-American, and for this reason its members harbor deep animus toward Israel.

Yes, Osama bin Laden once named the Arab-Israeli conflict as a reason for his actions. But bin Laden also listed a variety of other motives – and frankly, much of his accusations were rambling and vague.[40] His first video after 9/11 did not name Israel. Rather, it cited the presence of American military bases on Saudi soil as the impetus for the attack on the World Trade Center. Both reasons, however, were tactical obfuscations borrowed, it seems, from Leftist talking points. His real motivation was to subjugate the world to Islam – a goal supported by statements of jihadists everywhere and on every level.

ISIS and Boko Haram never mention Israel as the reason for what they are doing. To pretend that Israel is their primary concern would be patently absurd. How does ISIS throwing gays from the tops of buildings or burning people alive, destroying ancient monuments and kidnapping Christian and Yazidi women and selling them as sex slaves connect with Israel's conflict with the Palestinians? How does Boko Haram's kidnapping schoolgirls and forcing them into marriage? Make no mistake; both groups intend to conquer the world for Islam, no matter the outcome in Gaza and the West Bank.

U.S. FOREIGN POLICY

I hear or read frequently that U.S. foreign policy in the Middle East lies at the root of Islamic terror; for example, that aforementioned video by Osama bin Laden after 9/11, in which he cited the presence of American troops on Saudi soil during the first Gulf War as the reason he ordered the attack.

U.S. architects of foreign policy have made plenty of serious errors and miscalculations – as have diplomats from every nation on Earth – but this is not the cause of Islamism. On the contrary, the United States has often come to the aid of Muslims and Muslim nations. Look at the liberation of Kuwait from Saddam Hussein's invasion in the first Gulf War in 1991. Look at how the United States fought back the attempted genocide of Bosnian Muslims by the Serbians later in the 1990s. Look at how American forces chased the Taliban out of Afghanistan and removed Saddam Hussein from Iraq, thereby freeing innocent Muslims from murderous rulers. Can anyone not admit that despite the flaws in all of those efforts, millions of Muslim lives have been saved by actions of the U.S. military?

Going back a bit farther, America financed the Mujahideen resistance to the Soviet invasion of Afghanistan in the 1980s. Why, didn't Osama bin Laden thank the United States for its support in that war, and why did he not harbor animus toward Russia? Incidentally, why hasn't the Left admonished Soviet imperialism?

No. The reason for the jihadists' animosity toward America is because they seek domination by Islam through Sharia. America, because of its freedoms, its military power, and its secular society and government, stands as the greatest obstacle to this obsession. Radical Islamists base their quest on an interpretation of the following Quranic verse:

It is He who hath sent His Messenger with guidance and the Religion of Truth, to proclaim it over all religion, even though the Pagans may detest (it). [9:33]

Jihadists would not be able to exult as much in Islamic superiority if they defeated countries like Russia or China, because those countries are not the strongest. But defeating the United States, the most powerful nation the world has ever seen, will provide that feeling of elation. Jihadists also know if they attacked China, that government would most likely respond too severely and without regard for collateral damage. They have witnessed similar responses by Russian forces to terror attacks in the Chechen Republic. In contrast, jihadists know that American concern for human rights constrains its retaliation and blunts its wrath toward the Muslim community.

More important, American involvement in the Middle East has been, on the whole, positive – though we almost never hear about America's contributions, never find them cited in balance to criticisms or see it pointed out that other nations haven't made the same extensive efforts. The United States has assisted the economic and infrastructural development of many Islamic nations. Prior to its nationalization, Standard Oil explored and drilled Saudi oil fields and built Arabia's refineries. Americans have consumed and still consume a great deal of that oil. Petrodollars from America and the West have afforded the Saudis and other OPEC nations a luxurious lifestyle. Dubai has become a beautiful and desirable destination in which to live and work, and U.S. investments played a key role in that development.

Let's talk plainly. If America truly were an imperial or ruthless power, it would have long ago conquered and obliterated the OPEC nations and taken over their oil. America easily holds the military capability to do so, and it has for decades. Instead, America has spent billions of dollars to establish democracy in Iraq – to win the hearts and minds of the Iraqi people. Yet to date America has reaped no financial rewards and, the wisdom of such an action aside, has withdrawn its entire military force from Iraq. U.S. troops are gone, and in their absence the dark shadow of ISIS is rampaging across the landscape, murdering, torturing or enslaving anyone who will not submit to them – and many if not most of their victims are Muslims.

Given this context, attempting to place blame for Islamic terror on American foreign policy is ludicrous.

The Meaning of *Jihad*

Apologists for jihadism frequently claim that the true meaning of the word *jihad* is unconnected with violence. Typically, one hears it means "peaceful struggle" or "defensive struggle." The non-violent interpretation is often advanced by Muslims to avoid criticism of Islam. This was particularly common after 9/11.

The truth is the violent meaning of *jihad* is the prevailing one in mainstream Islamic writing. If *jihad* were commonly understood to be peaceful, we would find Islamic charities and advocacy groups with the word in their titles. But one never hears of a truly peaceful Islamic organization using *jihad* in its name, while *jihad* is often found in the titles of Islamic terror groups. I have already mentioned Egypt's Islamic Jihad and the Palestinian group of the same name. There are many more: Jama'at al-Jihad al-Islami, an al-Qaeda affiliate active in central Asia; Jihad Rite in Australia; Laskar Jihad in Indonesia, and even a Turkish Islamic Jihad. Most people do not know that a less-common name for al-Qaeda is Qa'idat al-Jihad, and that the group commonly called Al-Qaeda in Iraq goes by the formal name Tanzim Qaidat al-Jihad fi Bilad al-Rafidayn.

Technically, *jihad* has at least five different meanings and some of them are indeed peaceful. Others are quite violent. In the strict, literal sense, *jihad* means to struggle or resist something that pressures or oppresses. According to the Salafist interpretation, however, *jihad* means either to defend the Muslim community from an enemy or convert non-Muslims via holy war. Early Muslims justified making such war on neighboring nations using the more aggressive interpretation of *jihad*, and that interpretation prevails to this day. It is unanimously endorsed by the *madhhab*, the four main Islamic jurisprudence schools: Maliki, Hanbali, Shafi'i and Hanafi. It also flourishes unchallenged in mainstream Islamic texts such as *Fiqh us-Sunnah* and *Minhaj al-Muslim*.

In contrast, the Sufi branch of Islam usually understands *jihad* as "internal struggle," that is, to resist the evil ideas and desires within oneself. This view derives from a *hadith* about Prophet Muhammad. After one of his raids, Muhammad said to his disciples:

> *"We have returned from the smaller jihad to the bigger jihad" ... The*
> *disciples of Muhammad said to him: What is the greater jihad? Then*
> *he said "Jihad al-Nafs," which means internal struggle against evil*
> *thoughts and human fleshly desires.* —Al-Baihaqi and Al-Khateeb

This excellent understanding of the word *jihad* is not the dominant one in our mosques and the Islamic education system. If you ask a Muslim child in the Arab world to define *jihad*, in most cases the answer will be "war against the infidels."

The small Quranic sect to which I belonged viewed *jihad* as preaching the Quran only by the word rather than the sword. Their view is grounded in the following verse:

> *Fight them (do your jihad) by preaching the Quran. [25:52]*

There is also a meaning of *jihad* that's been used in the Quran but is uncommon in traditional Islamic instruction: to struggle in search of God by studying his miracles in nature. This rare understanding is based on the following verse:

> *And those who strive in our (cause) – We will certainly guide them to*
> *our Paths: For verily Allah is with those who do right. [29:69]* [41]

In the preceding passage, a derivative of the word *jihad* – *jahadu* – is employed to mean "strive in our cause." In short, *jihad* definitely can be understood in a nonviolent manner, but the dominant sense in Islamic books is violent. It is misleading and dishonest to claim that the nonviolent understanding is in any way typical today. We need a new interpretation of Islamic texts that promotes the peaceful meanings of *jihad*. This certainly would benefit Islamic instruction and improve our security.

Jihadists 'just want to be heroes'

Some have suggested that the motivation for Muslims to commit acts of terror lies in their desire to be heroic. For example, in a 2007 interview on the Australian radio program The World Today, Dr. Marc Sageman stated that new jihadists "don't know much about Islam, but they just want to be heroes." [42] Ultimately, the hero-worship analysis dangerously minimizes the role of Islamist ideology. There are two problems with this analysis: its overemphasis of secondary factors and its methodology.

The desire of a person to be a hero and admired by his community is not unique to Muslims. Individuals all over the world, from every culture, every geographic location, every economic background and every religion have sought to be heroes.

In itself, the desire to be a hero is not a bad thing – it is in many respects a virtue. A person might wish to save lives and decide to become a doctor or wish to defend his country by serving in the military. A man or woman might strive to be a star tennis player or campaign heroically to stop toxic pollution. But when large numbers of Muslims commit acts of terror to be heroes – and the community lauds them for it or does nothing – the problem is not the desire to be a hero but a cultural and ideological disease in the community as a whole. If the Muslim community cultivates these jihadists, praises them, and sanctions or dismisses the problem, we must focus chiefly on the community and less on a member's desire to please it.

Take the case of two brothers; as often happens, both Muslim and both exposed to the same Islamist indoctrination. One harbors a greater desire to be a hero, the other less so. Normally, neither would become a terrorist, but when we introduce Islamism, one becomes a suicide bomber while the other does not take the final step. The solution in this case is to remove the Islamism, not the desire for heroism. It is impossible, and not even necessarily commendable, to smother a young Muslim's desire to be praised and recognized by his community. But the community must praise the right behavior.

It is likewise difficult, if not impossible, to evaluate a person's psychological proclivity toward heroism. It is possible, on the other hand, to defeat the Islamist ideology.

Salafism, in other words, can be called the activating agent. To understand this better, permit a medical metaphor. Imagine two cells in the human body. One cell has a predisposition to become cancerous; the other is normal. Neither cell, however, will develop cancer unless a carcinogenic chemical is introduced.

If that happens, the cell with the predisposition becomes cancerous, and the protocol is to eliminate the carcinogenic chemical, not to destroy all cells, even those predisposed to cancer. So it is with jihadism. We must eliminate the cancerous ideology – Salafism – not crush the predisposition of young men to be heroes. Dr. Sageman's assertion that providing Muslim men with alternative models of heroism is noble but perhaps naive, because the powerful ideology currently driving jihadism would remain.

The heroism argument also fails to explain the division of labor present in all jihadist organizations. Take Ayman al-Zawahiri. Despite his lengthy history as an Islamic radical, Dr. Ayman has yet to detonate himself on a bus or in a pizza parlor, and he is unlikely ever to do so.

We might ask, does the person who funds the terror, arranges fake passports, drives bombers to the target – who never becomes famous or is even heard of – does he participate because he wants to be a hero? If terrorism derives from a quest for personal glory, what explains the motives of those in a terrorist group who devotedly but anonymously perform the drudgery?

In the same interview about terrorism, Dr. Sageman also stated, "Right now what's fueling it is a sense of moral outrage that young Muslims see in terms of Iraq." [43]

Unfortunately, the hero theory – in the absence of an ideological component – fails to explain why Arab Christians, suffering from identical pressures of the current civil wars in Iraq and Syria, are not interested in becoming heroes, while their Muslim neighbors are. Suicide bombings inside and outside Iraq are always conducted by Muslims rather than Christians.

'Al-Qaeda resembles the IRA'

I have had many discussions with bona fide counterterrorism experts, most of whom earned their spurs fighting the Irish Republican Army or, in a few cases, the Baader-Meinhof gang. I have also sparred intellectually with a number of pundits who were advertised as "experts" on terrorism. Unfortunately, I think because we tend to be comfortable only within our own frames of reference, it has become fashionable to treat all forms of terrorism broadly as being the same. Pundits in particular never fail to draw comparisons between Islamic terrorist organizations and other terrorist groups, usually the IRA. In a 2005 editorial in *The Guardian*, religion writer Karen Armstrong opined that "Islamic terror" was an inadequate and unfair phrase for Islamic terror.

> *We rarely, if ever, called the IRA bombings "Catholic" terrorism*
> *because we knew enough to realise that this was not essentially*
> *a religious campaign. Indeed, like the Irish republican movement,*
> *many fundamentalist movements worldwide are simply new forms of*
> *nationalism in a highly unorthodox religious guise. This is obviously*
> *the case with Zionist fundamentalism in Israel and the fervently*
> *patriotic Christian right in the [United States].* [44]

As to her poor comparison of Islamism with Zionist fundamentalism and the American Christian right, I will address the topic in a later chapter. And regarding the IRA, I agree that Catholic terror is an incorrect description of that group's bombings. But I would argue that Armstrong is grossly mistaken to say Islamic terror inaccurately describes terror perpetrated by jihadists.

Why? If it were correct to use the phrase Catholic terror, it would imply that Catholics across the globe – from the Middle East to Europe to America to Indonesia – were committing terrorist acts. It would imply that Catholic communities everywhere have large contingencies of terror supporters. It would mean Catholics murder Buddhists in Thailand, or blow up nightclubs in Bali, or detonate themselves on Israeli school buses or fly planes into skyscrapers. If Catholics were to engage in these types of attacks around the globe, with wide community support, we would indeed be justified in calling it Catholic terrorism.

But Catholics have not done so, except for limited instances in Ireland and the United Kingdom. So, we correctly refrain from using the phrase "Catholic terror." Yes, members of the IRA happened to be Catholic, but the goal of their terror had limited, not universal – and certainly not religious – focus. Their complaints were irredentist and national. Had the English settlers in Northern Ireland been Catholic instead of Protestant, it's hard to believe the conflict in Ireland would not have existed.

Where Armstrong and others err is to assume Islamic terrorism is similar to terrorism by non-Islamic groups. In reality, Islamic terror is being perpetrated on a daily basis, worldwide, and it is doctrinally driven.

If you think I'm exaggerating, please see Appendix 1.

Large numbers of Muslims in places as disparate as America and Thailand are supporting, financing and taking pride in acts of terror by their fellow Muslims. Millions more are silent, even in the face of the carnage perpetrated by their own people.

Equally important, Islamic terror organizations refer to themselves in Islamic terms. The IRA never referred to itself as the Catholic Republican Army. In contrast, Islamic Jihad and Jamaa Islamiya are bona fide terrorist groups that use "Islam" in their names. They do not call themselves "Egyptian Jihad" or the "Egyptian Brotherhood."

Most crucial, Islamic terrorist groups indoctrinate young Muslims with Islamic writings and Islamist ideology. It is entirely accurate to refer to Islamic terror as "Islamic terror." Moreover, it is inaccurate and dangerous to draw simplistic and ignorant comparisons between Islamic terror and other forms of terror. The goals of the IRA were narrowly focused, and the conflict in Ireland has died down considerably because of political concessions and police actions.

If we tried to apply the same strategies to Islamic terror, we would utterly fail to stop it. Worse, we would jeopardize all modern, democratic societies. Islamists care nothing for national boundaries; al-Qaeda will not be satisfied with turning one country into a Taliban-style nation of misery. Islamic terror seeks to subjugate the entire non-Muslim world to Islam, by force. It sees the world as its battleground and the stakes as universal.

NOTES

20.   Ban Ki-moon, "A Climate Culprit in Darfur," *The Washington Post*, June 15, 2007.

21.   See also http://worldwithoutgenocide.org/genocides-and-conflicts/darfur-genocide

22.   "Jimmy Carter Blames Terror Attacks on 'Palestinian Problem,'" DailyCaller.com, January 13, 2015.

23.   White House statement issued January 7, 2015.

24.   "Charlie Hebdo attack: Three days of terror," BBC News, January 14, 2015.

25.   Tom McCarthy, "White House backs Obama claim that victims of Paris deli attack not 'targeted,'" *The Guardian*, February 10, 2015.

26.   President Obama's statement on the Garissa University College attack, April 3, 2015.

27.   "Transcript: President Obama's Speech on Combating ISIS and Terrorism," CNN, September 10, 2014.

28.   Ian Hanchett, "Harf: 'We can't kill our way out of war' against ISIS," Breitbart. com, February 16, 2015.

29.   U.S. Department of Justice, Federal Bureau of Investigation, Criminal Justice Information Services Division, Hate Crime Statistics, 2013, Table 1.

30.   Oren Dorell, "Mayor: 'Without Jews Paris would not be city that it is,'" *USA Today*, February 20, 2015.

31.   Senator Hillary Clinton speech at Princeton University, January 18, 2006.

32.   Secretary of State Condoleezza Rice remarks at the American University in Cairo, June 20, 2005.

33.   Tawfik Hamid, "Democracy Will Not End Radical Islam," Newsmax.com, August 19, 2009.

34.   "Beslan school hostage crisis," Wikipedia.org.

35.   "Peshawar attack: 132 children among 141 killed, all 7 Taliban gunmen dead," Associated Press, December 17, 2014.

36.   "Boko Haram disguised as preachers killed at least 24 in Nigeria," Reuters, April 6, 2015.

37.   Yaron Steinbuch and Jamie Schram, "ISIS executes 13 teens for watching soccer," *New York Post*, January 19, 2015.

38.   "'Destroy the idols,' Egyptian jihadist calls for removal of Sphinx, Pyramids," al-Arabiya News, November 12, 2012.

39.   "French Nazis ban a march against Islamization by French patriots but allow one against 'Islamophobia' by Muslims and the fascist left wing," BareNakedIslam. com, January 18, 2015.

40.   "Full text: bin Laden's 'letter to America,'" *The Guardian*, November 24, 2002.

41.   In both verses (25:52 and 29:69) the word *jihad* is used in the Arabic text of the Quran but in different derivatives, respectively, *jahidhum* and *jahadu*.

42.   Transcript of Marc Sageman interview with Eleanor Hall on The World Today, October 3, 2007.

43.   Ibid.

44.   Karen Armstrong, "The label of Catholic terror was never used about the IRA," *The Guardian*, July 11, 2005.

CHAPTER 3

The Failure of Islamic Societies

Background: Sufi and Salafi

The attacks of September 11, 2001, surprised and shocked America. Prior to that awful day, people went weeks or even months without thinking about Islamic terror. It seemed worrisome, to be sure, but a minor worry, something that occurred in distant, hopeless lands, motivated by obscure passions and unfathomable complaints. Compared to 9/11, Sheikh Omar Abdel-Rahman's attempt to bring down the twin World Trade Center towers in 1993 seemed an amateurish side note.

The day forever known as 9/11 seemed to spawn the same question in the minds of millions: What kind of creatures could have executed such savagery? Unlike the bombing of Pearl Harbor, the perpetrators were not the military forces of a country. Nor were they an anomalous collection of isolated, deranged individuals in the mold of Timothy McVeigh, the man who had parked an explosives-laden truck outside a federal building in Oklahoma City, Oklahoma, in 1995 and killed 168 people, including 15 children at a daycare center. [45]

Instead, the assaults on the World Trade Center in New York City, the attack on the Pentagon in Washington, and the associated but unsuccessful fourth airline hijacking all were conducted by a group of fanatics called al-Qaeda and headed by a tall, slim, bearded individual named Osama bin Laden, scion of a wealthy Saudi family. In describing him, words such as "Islamism," "*jihad*" and "Wahhabi" suddenly emerged in media reports. Experts scrambled to explain the background of the attacks; some insightfully, others less so. They published countless analyses; some illuminating, many profoundly misguided.

Frankly, few of those early attempts to make sense of Islamic terror helped much. Most were compiled by non-Muslims trying to digest categories of Islamic belief into a bird's-eye view that would be accurate and practical. They failed, their analyses largely reaching dubious conclusions colored by ideological agendas and clouded by irrelevant or exaggerated details.

One of the biggest and most consistent missteps: attempting to dissect Islam by focusing on the differences between Sunni and Shia, which constitute approximately 90 percent and 10 percent of the world's Muslims, respectively. The problem is that Sunni and Shia do not differ doctrinally in significant ways – though clashes between the two sects can be and often have been murderous.

The truth is the Sunni-Shia conflict is largely sectarian, with roots going all the way back to the early caliphates. The Sunnis asserted, at least superficially, that Islam has no favorites among believers, and therefore any Muslim is technically entitled to become caliph. The Shia insisted the caliphate must be headed only by a descendent of Muhammad. The first battle over this dispute was joined at Karbala, in present-day Iraq, in the year 680, or 1335 years ago! The Shia side was massacred. Since then, many Sunni regard Shia as false Muslims, and the Shia have enshrined their loss at Karbala into a victimized ethos of the disinherited.

In some ways, the behavior of the two sects toward each other resembles the divisions between Protestants and Catholics during the Middle Ages, where theological differences resulted in frequent bloodshed – except that the Sunni-Shia rift is more superficial. This isn't to say the conflict is unimportant. On the contrary, in terms of human rights as well as geopolitical decision-making, the Islamic divide is of utmost importance. But for our purposes it plays a negligible role in global Islamic terrorism. As we see and hear and read in the news almost every day, there are Sunni and Shia terrorist groups scattered around the planet – though despite al-Qaeda and ISIS, which are Sunni, Shia-dominated Iran is the world's largest sponsor of terror.

All jihadists are motivated by the same objectives and utilize largely identical tactics. Most important, they are sworn enemies of Western values. When we speak of Islamic terror, we should focus on the differences between Salafi Islam, or Salafism, and Sufi Islam. Salafism corresponds closely to what is called Islamic fundamentalism. Salafism, during the early days of the faith, was most prevalent in the Arabian Hejaz, the holy peninsula of Islam.

Sufi Islam, or Sufism, encompassed in the past the rest of the Islamic dominions. Now, we can consider Sufism the equivalent of secular Islam or liberal Islam.

Sufism

Sufi Islam emphasizes mysticism and a personal relationship with the creator. It might be characterized as a mixed form of Islam. Some suggest that its early influences included Hindu and Buddhist currents, as well as shamanic elements from Central Asia. Members sometimes engage in trancelike meditation – accomplished by repetition of Quranic verses – to bring about communion with the creator. The sect features a number of mainstream and non-mainstream orders, plus a variety of past and present luminaries, or masters, who have contributed many spiritual innovations.

Sufism permits art and music to flourish. Perhaps the most famous examples of Sufis, though not nearly the most prevalent, were the Whirling Dervishes, who would dance – or whirl – to music to achieve ecstatic, transcendent states. Sufi Muslims often visit shrines where virtuous individuals are buried. These are known as Awliya Allah al-Saliheen, or the Righteous People of Allah, from whom Sufis seek blessings.

There are no reliable statistics that I know of on the total number of Sufis, but they certainly number in the millions. Moreover, many Muslims share elements of Sufism and Salafism simultaneously, which makes it difficult to estimate the world's Sufi population.

Sufism is relatively – but not entirely – peaceful. Sufis typically consider *jihad* as internal struggle against the individual's evil inclinations. Hence, Jews and Christians were able to survive under Sufi governance. In fact, as the venerable historian Bernard Lewis has pointed out, Christian dissenters and Jews sometimes found existence to be more tolerable under Sufi-influenced Islamic societies than during Medieval Christendom. We should note, however, that "survive" can be a relative term.

Technically, traditional Islamic teaching permits non-Muslims to reside in Islamic communities, but only as *dhimmis*, or second-class citizens. Some Muslim rulers forced *dhimmis* to pay the *jizya*, a humiliating poll tax, but otherwise did not molest them. In a few Islamic areas, Jews and Christians even thrived at various times. Under the Egyptian Mamluks and the Turkish Ottomans, for example, some Jews even became *viziers*, or consuls, to the caliph or sultan.

Tolerance within Sufism is exemplified by the following poem:

O Marvel! A garden amidst the flames.
My heart has become capable of every form:
It is a pasture for gazelles and a convent for Christian monks,
and a temple for idols and the pilgrim's Kaa'ba,
and the tables of the Torah and the book of the Quran.
I follow the religion of Love: whatever way Love's camels take,
that is my religion and my faith.
>—"The Mystics of Islam," from the *Tarjuman al-Ashwaq*
>(*Interpreter of Desires*) by Ibn al-Arabi,
>translated by Reynold A. Nicholson

The poem was written by Muhammad ibn Ali ibn Arabi (1165-1240 AD) also known as Muhyiddin (Reviver of Religion) and Shaykh al-Akbar (Greatest Master). He was born into the Moorish culture of Andalusian Spain and traveled widely in the Islamic world.

Salafism

Sufism is a true branch of Islam, while Salafism, in contrast, is not precisely a discrete sect or formal organization. It is more of a force, a powerful reactionary energy that can impose itself on any Islamic society or group. Very few Muslims would identify themselves or think of themselves as Salafist. Many Muslims who are in every respect Salafist would not even know the term. An adequate English approximation for Salafist would be "fundamentalist."

Salafism seeks a return to the envisioned purity and perfection of early Islamic times. It strives for a strict and literal interpretation of the Quran, and it holds up the early leaders of Islam as examples for believers; the Arabic word *salaf* means "ancestors." Salafists base their doctrine on one of Muhammad's *hadiths*:

>*The people of my generation are the best, then those who follow them,*
>*and then those who follow the latter. —Sahih Muslim*

Prophet Muhammad, naturally, is their best role model, and Salafists seek to emulate his behavior as closely as possible, most notably in dress and table manners but also in warlike zeal, as described in traditional Islamic writings. Bin Laden, for example, sat on the ground to dine, he ate with his right hand – even though he was left-handed – and dressed in a style that fit Sunnah models as taught by Salafists.

Salafists insist that Islam has gradually been diluted with sensuality and worldly indulgence, a sinful departure from the religion's austere roots. Exploiting Quranic verses, and particularly the *hadiths*, Salafism places strict limitations on the rights and behavior of women. It restricts art, especially the visual arts and music. And these restrictions are enforced by violence and barbaric punishments spelled out in doctrine.

Salafists desire a return to the Islamic Caliphate. They do not respect secular states or weak Islamic regimes. They believe Sharia law should constitute, ideally, the only legal system in any society, because it is divine law. Here is an archetypical passage employed by Salafists:

> *Ibn Abbas reported that the Prophet, on whom be peace, said, "The ties of Islam and the principles of the religion are three, and whoever leaves one of them becomes an unbeliever, and his blood becomes lawful (it is acceptable to kill him): testifying that there is no God except Allah; the obligatory prayers, and the fast of Ramadan."*
>
> —Abu Ya'la with a *hassan* chain

As we see, Salafism can create hardhearted individuals who accept ruthless conduct. It suppresses a Muslim's conscience while making him think he is devout.

Since 9/11, we have heard that the Wahhabi sect in Saudi Arabia has been exporting terror, and we have similarly heard the word "Wahhabism." What is the relation of Wahhabism to Salafism? The answer is simple: Wahhabism is a concrete manifestation of Salafism. In other words, the Wahhabists apply existing Salafist doctrine; they never invented new theology.

The sect was founded in Saudi Arabia by Muhammad ibn Abd al-Wahhab (1703-1792). Wahhabists reject visiting shrines, except for the grave of Muhammad, and consider such behavior to be idolatrous. For this reason, al-Wahhab destroyed all of the shrines in Saudi Arabia but left Muhammad's intact. Muhammad's grave is customarily visited by pilgrims during the *hajj*.

Wahhabism, then, is the prevailing Islamic force in Saudi Arabia, and it furnishes us with an important example of Salafism. Women there are forced to cover their faces completely with a black mask known as the *niqab*. Muslims are required by law to attend prayer five times per day. It is strictly forbidden to build a Christian church in Saudi Arabia. It is, indeed, a nation of religious apartheid. In Mecca, there are separate freeways for Muslims and non-Muslims. People are beheaded for so-called crimes such as adultery, homosexuality and converting from Islam. Lesser crimes such as theft meet with amputation of limbs. The national flag of Saudi Arabia features the scimitar and the words, "No God except Allah and Muhammad is the Prophet of Allah." This utterance is required for every person converting to Islam. The words are regularly cited as justification to subjugate and subdue non-Muslims, who are given the option to convert, pay the humiliating *jizya* or be killed.

One of the most prominent Salafi scholars in Saudi Arabia, Sheikh Saleh al-Fawzan, authored the religious textbook *Al-Tawhid* (Monotheism), which is used to teach not only Saudi high school students but also their Western and non-Western counterparts abroad. In recent years, al-Fawzan has declared that "slavery is a part of Islam" and "slavery is part of *jihad*, and *jihad* will remain as long as there is Islam." Al-Fawzan insists those who promote the view that Islam can exist without slavery are "ignorant." Indeed, he calls them "infidels" and adds that they are not scholars but merely writers. [46]

By declaring that Muslims who reject slavery are infidels, al-Fawzan is declaring them to be apostates. The portion of Sharia concerned with apostates is known as Redda law, and according to the literal implementation of Redda in Saudi Arabia, the punishment for apostasy is death. In other words, al-Fawzan has declared that Muslims who reject slavery in Islam should be killed.

Sheikh al-Fawzan is hardly a fringe radical. He is a member of Saudi Arabia's Senior Council of Clerics, their highest religious body. He serves on their Council of Religious Edicts and Research. He is also the Imam of the Prince Mitaeb Mosque in Riyadh and a professor at Imam Muhammad ibn Saud Islamic University, also in Riyadh, the main Wahhabi center of learning.[47] For Salafists, the perfect world is one in which apostates are slain, adulterous women are stoned to death, enslavement of war captives is permitted, polygamy is admired and wives can be beaten when the husband deems it appropriate.

Salafism is intimately connected with violence. In some cases, Salafists actually perpetrate terror and brutality, as do jihadists. These groups adhere to the concept of *al-takfir wa al-istihlal*, which allows them to consider non-members of their organization as infidels. It explains why they show little compunction in killing fellow Muslims.

Examples of Salafist groups that follow *takfir* were those in Algeria who exterminated 200,000 Muslim innocents and burned the faces of many Muslim women for refusing to wear the *hijab*. Many Salafists believe violent *jihad* is the solution for most of the problems in the Muslim world. They look to the early successes of the Islamic Conquests, when Muslims declared wars on the infidel, won those wars and established an empire.

As mentioned, Jews and Christians could often survive and sometimes flourish under Sufi-influenced rule. The same cannot be said for Salafi Islam in the Arabian Peninsula, from whence Jews and Christians were evicted. We see the outcome today. One would be hard-pressed to find a single Saudi Jew or Saudi Christian. True enough, Jews were also expelled from Egypt under the Nasser regime, but that expulsion was political rather than religious, and in any event Egypt still harbors communities of Jews along with its ancient Coptic Christians. In contrast, the whole Saudi nation has been ethnically and spiritually cleansed by the Salafi Islamic sword.

Secular Islam

For completeness sake, I must mention one other force in the Islamic demographic: Secular Islam, an expression predominantly used in the West to describe what is perceived as liberalism among Muslims.

Broadly speaking, secular Muslims apply various elements of their culture rather than follow a text-based belief system. They tend to follow culturally transmitted Islamic moral codes but do not study the texts. Like Sufis, secular Muslims can be influenced by surrounding non-Islamic cultures, e.g., Judeo-Christian traditions in the Middle East or Hindu and Buddhist philosophies in parts of Asia. These infusions have resulted in the passive rejection of some Salafist tenets. Polygamy, for example, is relatively unacceptable in Egypt but much more tolerated in Wahhabi-dominated Saudi Arabia. Polygamy is less common in Egypt because Egyptian Muslims have long lived alongside Jews and Christians, who do not practice it.

There are also Muslims who do not fit easily into any of these categories because they represent a variable mix of all combined groups. Some, however, might display a moderate façade, while their minds have been primarily influenced by Salafism.

Salafism Explodes (Wahhabis Become Wealthy)

Wahhabism has been active in the Saudi peninsula since the 18th century. Only within the last 50 years, however, has it emerged as a global force. This happened because the sect acquired access to the petrodollars flowing into Saudi coffers.

The effect of Wahhabi wealth has operated on three levels. First, when the Saudis became wealthy, they were widely admired in the Islamic world. Muslims elsewhere wondered why the Saudis should be so blessed, and attention turned to their Salafist religious practice. Muslims in less wealthy states reasoned that they, too, would be blessed if they adopted Salafist beliefs. They began pushing aside relatively moderate implementations of Islam to make way for Salafism.

Second, the booming Saudi economy required skilled labor and outside expertise. To fill the void, numerous non-Saudi Muslim immigrants sought the work. They were exposed to overpowering Wahhabi influence in their daily lives. Many of the foreign workers returned home potentially radicalized – or, at least, sympathetic to Wahhabism. Most of the workers became wealthy by the standards of their societies, which helped fortify the perception that adherence to Salafism would bring blessings and wealth to its followers. The workers often supported Salafism in their home communities by financing Salafi institutes and charities.

Third, and most important, the Wahhabis used their new wealth to fund the propagation abroad of their Salafist version of Islam. To this day, they continue to finance Salafi mosques in countless locations overseas and have made their literature available, at little cost, to Muslims around the world.

Relatively moderate Islam lost ground in societies everywhere – "moderate" in the sense that Jews and Christians were not eradicated from non-Saudi states, and "relatively" because the Islam taught outside of Saudi Arabia still considers non-Muslims to be second-class citizens, or *ahl al-dhimma*.

Jihad: from *Umma* to **Individual**

Salafi ideology presented weak Islamic or secular Arabist regimes with a dilemma. A growing percentage of their home populations subscribed to a doctrine that categorically rejected the nation-state itself. They did not respect temporal power and sought to replace it with Sharia. On the other hand, if the regimes moved to crush Salafi adherents and their

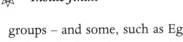

groups – and some, such as Egypt and Syria, did – they would appear barbaric both to their own citizens and those in the West who defend freedom of religion. Faced with this predicament, most regimes compromised. They granted Salafists some freedom to organize and espouse their beliefs – as long as they did not threaten the government.

In addition, some regimes found Salafists useful despite the danger they posed. Salafists could, for example, be given room to destroy political opponents; in the case of Egypt, some claim that Anwar Sadat used them against the Nasserists.

Yet, although Arab regimes were granting Salafists some freedom, they still limited Salafi activities. Salafists therefore sought a strategy to defeat the regimes – a strategy that would also be essential to mounting another global Islamic conquest – and they found it. The solution was to transfer, via reinterpretation of doctrine, the responsibility of violent *jihad* from the Islamic collective, or *umma*, to the individual Muslim.

Traditionally, the responsibility to declare war on the infidel rested with the *umma*. This was the mainstream interpretation of Islamic law, and all Islamic schools of jurisprudence in the past supported this understanding. During the last 50 years, this interpretation has changed. By shifting *jihad* to the individual, every Muslim became obliged to share in it and help reestablish the Islamic Caliphate. A Muslim should not – indeed must not – wait for collective bodies to give the green light.

This individualization of *jihad* was based on the following verse:

Then fight in Allah's cause – You are held responsible only for yourself – and rouse the believers (to fight). [Quran 4:84]

The transfer of responsibility could not have been achieved without the backing of theological rigor. It became a topic of debate. Should Muslims wait for the reestablishment of the caliphate to declare war on the infidels, or should they personally undertake the battle at once? I witnessed these doctrinal disputes between various members and leaders of Jamaa Islamiya, as well as in numerous mosques.

It might seem that a narrow doctrinal shift of this type would not be significant, but in fact it became critically important. It provided the theological justification that enabled the small-group and so-called lone-wolf Islamic terrorism we have seen in recent years. An already barbaric concept was energized by a new and aggressive focus. Among many others, Ayman al-Zawahiri was its champion.

Passive Terrorism

The seeds of Islamic terror could not have sprouted into voracious weeds if they had not found fertile soil in which to germinate. Such soil is the world's Muslim community. A large percentage of Muslims today passively approve of Islamic terror. They minimize it, shift the blame or do nothing about it. Some of these behaviors are deliberate strategies by Islamists to support terrorists by misleading their pursuers. In other cases, there is simply an unwillingness to face the problem. Therefore, the term "passive terrorism" refers to a broad category of enabling behaviors and beliefs, both conscious and unconscious, which serve to exacerbate jihadism.

Passive Support

For every jihadist in the world there is a much larger number of individuals who quietly approve of his conduct. Islamic terror often makes passive terrorists secretly proud. The relationship of passive terrorism to active terrorism constitutes a vicious cycle. The "success" of active terrorists boosts the self-esteem of passive terrorists, giving them a sense of victory and power. In turn, the pride felt by passive terrorists prepares the ground for active terrorists and gives them tacit approval to continue.

Within the Muslim community, passive terrorists often behave actively by suppressing moderate voices. This suppression typically takes the form of ostracizing the moderate Muslim and his family or by using harsh language, physical threats and even violence. [48] Outside the community, support for terror often takes the form of *taqiyya*: misleading the infidel with the aim of weakening him. One example of *taqiyya* is when Islamists give Westerners interpretations of Quranic verses that are different from the ones they follow themselves.

For example, many Islamic organizations and scholars attempt to prove to Westerners that Islam promotes freedom of religion by citing this Quranic verse:

> *Let there be no compulsion in religion.* [2:256]

This sounds commendable, until we realize that many of the same scholars also support Redda law, which enjoins Muslims to kill apostates or kill any Muslim who denies a fundamental component of Islam. Note that it is inadequate to proclaim the "freedom to leave Islam," as some fake moderates do, because such moderates still permit Muslims to kill those individuals who have freely left the faith. Such ostensible expressions of moderation are deceiving to Westerners. There is no substitute for rejecting Redda law in its entirety.

Likewise, many of these scholars proclaim to Westerners that Islam does not force a non-Muslim to convert. But there's an unspoken qualification: Salafist teaching grants a non-Muslim the right to practice his faith, but only as a *dhimmi* who agrees to pay the *jizya*. In the view of these Islamic bodies, this is tolerance and mercy. Non-Muslims are perfectly free not to convert – as long as they agree to live as second-class citizens and pay the demeaning tax. These justifications for Islam as a religion of peace can be meaningful only if the same Islamic scholars denounce the barbaric Redda law and insist that non-Muslims be treated as equals, not as *dhimmis*.

Alarm at the widespread, passive support for Islamic terror is not unwarranted – there are hard data. In the Arab world, a poll taken by Al-Jazeera in 2006 showed 57.9 percent of respondents supported the views of Ayman al-Zawahiri as he expressed them in a videotape.

Al-Jazeera had conducted a similar poll in 2004. The television network asked viewers whether they supported Al-Qaeda in Iraq kidnapping and killing civilians. Nearly 75 percent approved.

Then, in 2007, Al-Jazeera asked its Arab viewers whether they supported al-Qaeda attacks in Algeria against civilians. Over 50 percent of respondents approved.

Al-Jazeera conducted another 2004 poll to see how many of their Arab viewers would support al-Qaeda attacks in Algeria against innocent civilians. Over 50 percent agreed.

The situation is little better in the United Kingdom. According to polls there, nearly 60 percent of British Muslims would prefer to live under Sharia. Nearly 35 percent between ages 16 and 24 believe leaving Islam should be punished by death – compared with only 19 percent of those over age 55. And 13 percent of young people ages 16 to 24 reported admiring al-Qaeda. [49]

The news isn't all bad, however. In a Pew Global Attitudes Survey, taken in 2013, which polled Muslims in 11 countries, 67 percent of respondents said they were concerned about Islamic extremism in their country – though 27 percent remain unconcerned. Also, 57 percent expressed an unfavorable opinion of al-Qaeda, and 51 percent opposed the Taliban. Also, 89 percent of Pakistanis opposed violence in the name of Islam, as did 81 percent of Indonesians, 78 percent of Nigerians and 77 percent of Tunisians. On the other hand, 62 percent of Palestinians supported such violence. [50]

In an earlier Pew poll, conducted in America, the results were much more discouraging. Of American Muslims, 8 percent said suicide bombings are sometimes justified and the results are worse for Muslims between ages 19 and 35. Among the younger crowd, 15 percent approved. [51]

Conservatively estimated, there are perhaps 3 million Muslims in the United States today, meaning about 240,000 American Muslims consider suicide bombings sometimes justified. Furthermore, the numbers did not show the percentage of Muslims who accept terrorist acts by techniques other than suicide bombings. Also, a significant percentage of respondents were likely to have answered dishonestly because of *taqiyya*. As we can see, the numbers are far from heartening when we examine them carefully. Yet, if Muslims seem at all moderate in poll results, their host nations can be lulled into complacency. For many more such polls, please see Appendix 2.

Passive Denial

The Pew survey also showed that 60 percent of American Muslims do not believe Arabs perpetrated the 9/11 attacks. [52] A bizarre result indeed, because Osama bin Laden himself stated in one of his authentic videotapes that he was responsible. This denial, a form of passive terrorism, occurs for a number of reasons. For one, it presents Islamists with a conundrum. If they admit that bin Laden was behind 9/11, they would either have to support him or denounce him. If they supported him, it would reveal their hand to Western host countries prematurely. If they denounced him, they would have betrayed their Muslim brother. To avoid this Catch 22, many Muslims have skirted the issue by claiming that bin Laden, and Arabs in general, were not behind the attacks.

Of course, someone or some organization must have been responsible, so the common practice has been to suggest other perpetrators. Some Muslims have claimed that a conspiratorial cabal of Jews was behind it or that somehow it was an inside job by U.S. intelligence agencies. This redirection of blame serves a secondary purpose of refocusing anger toward Americans and Jews.

I also suspect that a portion of the respondents denied bin Laden's involvement out of shame, although it is not clear how sizable this number is. Arab culture places a high priority on honor, though it has been characterized, in fact, as a shame-based culture. Muslims worry about their image, not realizing that denial only harms it further.

Redemption from shame is not and can never be the product of denial. It comes, rather, from honestly admitting fault and then confronting it – openly, specifically and vigorously.

It is true, therefore, that fear plays a role in passivity; it prevents peaceful Muslims from taking charge of their communities. Nevertheless, the number of moderate Muslims should not be overstated; you can see why by examining the poll results. If Muslims truly denied or passively supported Islamic terror out of fear, it would follow that an anonymous poll would provide the best opportunity to express disagreement and dissatisfaction. There would be no risk in doing so; the community would not know who answered and would not be able to target dissenters. Yet the polls show disappointing amounts of support and denial; hardly the numbers we would hope to see.

False Uproar, Deafening Silence

In recent years, we have seen the Muslim community across the globe often protesting in large numbers, loudly and angrily. It is by no means a disorganized, apathetic community. But what have they protested?

+   In 2006, they demonstrated, violently, against the late Pope Benedict XVI because he cited a historical text critical of Islam. [53]

+   Also in 2006, many cities erupted in mayhem because a Danish newspaper published a cartoon of Muhammad that depicted him with a bomb on his head. [54]

+   Two years earlier, furor over a film produced by Theo van Gogh in the Netherlands sparked protests and probably led to his murder on the streets of Amsterdam. [55]

+   In 2010, France banned the wearing of the *hijab* in public, and again Muslims took to the streets. [56]

Equally meaningful is what the Muslim community has selectively not protested. We never saw even one protest against Osama bin Laden or other, specific, terrorists and terrorist organizations and their atrocities. Nor have we yet seen any appreciable protests about the incessant and massive violence among Muslims.

Take the case of the Bangladesh Liberation War back in the 1970s. In its attempt to gain independence from Pakistan, Bangladesh lost an

estimated 3 million people in what could accurately be called genocide. Mass graves are still being uncovered today. Although outside estimates of the death toll are lower (Pakistan estimates 26,000; the United
Nations between 200,000 and 3 million), there is no question the toll was
profoundly large. But beyond the mass murder, it is noteworthy that
both sides were Sunni Muslim. At the time, Pakistani Muslim scholars
had issued a *fatwa* enjoining the forces to rape any Bangladeshi women
captured, citing a passage in the Quran called *ma malakat aymanukum*,
and claiming any incident of rape to be permitted by the holy book. As
a result, possibly more than 20,000 women were raped. [57]

Where was – and is – the outrage of the global Muslim community in these cases? So silent it was amid the Bangladesh war that today
even educated Westerners might not be familiar with the event and its
atrocities.

Protest by the world's Muslims typically takes two forms: public
demonstration and statements, and the *fatwa*. Simply put, a *fatwa* is a
judicial decree by an Islamic religious body. The plural form, in Arabic,
is *fatawa*, and there are *fatawa* for nearly everything: marital relations,
table manners, rules of war, how to properly have sex and so on. The
fatwa is also used for purposes relevant to our topic: to declare a person
an apostate, which is similar to excommunication but with potentially
dire physical consequences. A *fatwa* can declare an act to be un-Islamic,
and it may define who is a Muslim and who is not.

Since 9/11, we have seen a few Muslim demonstrations or *fatawa*
against "terrorism." But this terrorism could be any violent act. I have
heard an Israeli reprisal against Palestinian attacks characterized as terrorism; likewise, American military involvement in the Middle East. The
word is deliberately left vague; it has no agent. Who is the perpetrator?
Whom should we bring to justice? The word is easily manipulated by
those who wish to deceive Westerners.

In Arab culture, denouncing a crime is not taken seriously unless
one denounces the criminal by name. This is important, so permit me to
repeat it: *Among Arabs, denouncing a crime is essentially meaningless unless
the criminal is also denounced.* Failure to ascribe responsibility for a criminal act is understood by the perpetrator to be a tacit approval of his deed
and also a cover for it. This applies to passive terrorism – denouncing the
word "terrorism" without explicitly denouncing the terrorist is both an
endorsement and a cover.

So, we have seen a few demonstrations and *fatawa* against "terrorism," but we have seen no condemnations by Muslims of specific Islamic terrorists and groups. Only when we observe masses of Muslims demonstrating against ISIS and al-Qaeda can we assume that the majority of Muslims are against them. Without this explicit rejection, claiming that most Muslims oppose Islamic terrorists is dubious speculation.

This specificity should embrace another requirement: that Muslims denounce terrorists for the right reason. One example of a bad and dangerous motivation is to denounce terrorism because it "damages the image of Islam," or that it sometimes kills Muslims. Would it be fine if it killed only non-Muslims? You can be sure that terrorists read these admonishments as they are intended: Violence is acceptable as long as it doesn't damage Islam's image, and it is acceptable as long as targets are restricted to non-Muslims.

This ambiguous condemnation of Islamic terror is a recurring and significant problem. Such denouncements, when they happen, do not cover the general war against non-Islamic civilization, and they do not condemn terrorism simply because it is immoral and barbaric. Nearly all statements issued by Islamic organizations have avoided denouncing ISIS by name; at best they denounce "those who perpetrated the attack," which is deliberately vague. On the rare occasion when a group like ISIS is mentioned, it is to express regret that they also murdered Muslims in Iraq.

Another common dodge, which we have heard even from the President of the United States, is to ascribe a different name to the terror organization, such as "ISIL" instead of ISIS – a name ISIS does not use.

Whenever Saudi religious authorities denounce terrorists, they typically use the phrase, *al-fidaa al-dala*, or "those who are on the wrong path," or perhaps also "the misguided." This condemnation has become ubiquitous and is understood in Arabic to be extremely mild, as one might expect from the translation. It is taken for granted that *al-fidaa al-dala* are not apostates but mistaken believers. The phrase is popular because it seems to satisfy Westerners while dulling the blade of rebuke at home.

Another phrase used for "terrorist" is *irhabi*, or the plural, *irhabeen*. Sheikh Omar Abdel-Rahman took this label as a badge of honor after he masterminded the 1993 World Trade Center attack by citing this Quranic verse:

Prepare for them (the Infidels) whatever military power you have to the utmost, including steeds of war, to insert fear into (the hearts of) the enemies of Allah and your enemies, and others besides, whom ye may not know, but whom Allah doth know. Whatever ye shall spend in the cause of Allah shall be repaid unto you, and ye shall not be treated unjustly. [8:60]

Islamic jargon does have powerful words to denounce terrorists. The strongest possible condemnation can be expressed by calling terrorists *al-murtadeen*, literally, "the apostates." This is not a tactical invention; there is precedent for it. It was originally used by the first caliph, Abu Bakr, to designate those who failed to pay the Islamic charity tithe, or *zakah*. A war was fought against this group, known as the Redda War, from which we get Redda law, or the law concerning apostates.

The phrase *al-murtadeen* is extremely strong, but unfortunately it is rarely if ever used to refer to terrorists. It isn't perfect, of course; it suggests that anyone who commits terror isn't Muslim, an assertion that yields different but preferable complications. It also implies that the named terrorist should be killed – a good thing – because he is an apostate – a bad reason. Still, it is the strongest condemnation available in Islamic jurisprudence and will help make jihadism less savory to young Muslims.

Certainly, *al-murtadeen* is preferable to the phrase used the day after 9/11 by Salman al-Oudah, a Saudi sheikh who in a letter to Osama bin Laden described him as "my brother." [58] The sheikh helpfully added that bin Laden's actions had a negative impact on Islam, from which we could infer that bin Laden's actions would have been fine if they hadn't negatively impacted Islam's reputation.

Public statements and *fatawa* sometimes masquerade as peaceful and moderate, but under careful scrutiny they also exhibit ambiguity and deliberate leeway for interpretation as approval. These *fatawa* placate Westerners who take the peaceful tone at face value, but such weak condemnations do not deter young Muslims from *jihad*.

Over the years, I have assembled a substantial collection of terrorism-related statements and *fatawa*. For the sake of brevity, here is a small sampling of them. Compare them, for example, to the *fatwa* issued against Salman Rushdie in 1989 for his publication of his bestseller, *The Satanic Verses*. The contrast is remarkable and highlights the insidious nature of the dual-purpose *fatwa*.

First, here was the *fatwa* against Rushdie, delivered by none other than Ruhollah Musavi Khomeini, the Grand Ayatollah and Supreme Leader of Iran:

> *In the name of God Almighty. There is only one God, to whom we shall all return. I would like to inform all intrepid Muslims in the world that the author of the book entitled* The Satanic Verses, *which has been compiled, printed, and published in opposition to Islam, the Prophet, and the Qur'an, as well as those publishers who were aware of its contents, have been sentenced to death. I call on all zealous Muslims to execute them quickly, wherever they find them, so that no one will dare insult the Islamic sanctities. Whoever is killed on this path will be regarded as a martyr, God willing. In addition, anyone who has access to the author of the book, but does not possess the power to execute him, should refer him to the people so that he may be punished for his actions. May God's blessing be on you all.* [59]

Now compare that language with this *fatwa* against the 9/11 attacks, enunciated by Mohammad Khatami, President of Iran at the time:

> *[The] terrorist blasts in America can only be the job of a group that have voluntarily severed their own ears and tongues, so that the only language with which they could communicate would be destroying and spreading death.* [60]

Khatami's words might seem impressive, but notice he never declared that the attacks were actually wrong. He simply stated that the terrorists – whoever they were – had no better means of expressing themselves. In other words, they were creatively challenged.

In the aftermath of 9/11 in America, condemnations of the attacks by Muslim leaders seemed better but were likewise highly flawed.

> *The American-Arab Anti-Discrimination Committee (ADC) today condemned the horrifying series of attacks on the World Trade Center towers in New York and government buildings including the Pentagon in Washington DC. Arab Americans, like all Americans, are shocked and angered by such brutality, and we share all the emotions of our fellow citizens. Arab Americans view these attacks as targeting all Americans without exception. No information is available as to what individuals or organizations might be responsible for these*

attacks. No matter who is responsible, ADC condemns these actions
in the strongest possible terms. ADC urges the public and the media to
proceed with caution and to resist rushes to judgment. [61]

Here was the *fatwa* issued by CAIR, the Council on American Islamic
Relations, immediately following 9/11:

We at the Council on American Islamic Relations (CAIR), along with
the entire American Muslim community are deeply saddened by the
massive loss of life resulting from the tragic events of September 11.
American Muslims utterly condemn the vicious and cowardly acts of
terrorism against innocent civilians. We join with all Americans in
calling for the swift apprehension and punishment of the perpetrators.
No political cause could ever be assisted by such immoral acts. [62]

What are we to make of the phrase "political cause?" What about
religious causes? And are Israelis or Thai Buddhists "innocent?" Is it
acceptable to use terrorism against those considered "guilty" by the
Islamic establishment? Rest assured; jihadists knew how to interpret
this *fatwa*.

Also weighing in about 9/11, Sheikh Rached Ghannouchi, chairman
of Tunisia's en-Nahda movement, member of the European Council for
Fatwa and Research, an assistant secretary-general of the International
Union of Muslim Scholars, and one of the founders of the World
Assembly of Muslim Youth:

Such destruction can only be condemned by any Muslim, however
resentful one may be of America's biased policies supporting occupa-
tion in Palestine, as an unacceptable attack on thousands of innocent
people having no relation to American policies. Anyone familiar with
Islam has no doubt about its rejection of collective punishment, based
on the well-known Quranic principle that 'no bearer of burdens can
bear the burden of another. [63]

We have already shown that the Israeli-Palestinian conflict is not
the reason for global terror, that it is used by Islamists as a diversion.
Jihadists would have taken this *fatwa* to mean their rage was understandable, and the lack of direct attribution to bin Laden was also read as a
go-ahead. Critical here is the phrase, "innocent people having no relation
to American policies." Did it mean terrorism was justified against those

connected with U.S. policy? As one might expect, the answer is "Yes." In fact, jihadists view every American as being responsible for American policies, because Americans elect their government.

The calculated dissembling of the *fatwa* by Yusuf al-Qaradawi provides another instructive example. Al-Qaradawi is a famous and, in some circles, still highly regarded Islamic scholar who was born in Egypt and is now believed to be residing in Qatar. Before his travails, al-Qaradawi was widely regarded as a moderate by many in the West; for example, by Ken Livingston, the former mayor of London; or historian and Arab scholar Raymond William Baker, who has hailed al-Qaradawi as a democratic reformer. Here are al-Qaradawi's thoughts about 9/11:

> *We Arab Muslims are the most affected by the grave consequences of hostile attack on man and life. We share the suffering experienced by innocent Palestinians at the hands of the tyrannical Jewish entity who raze the Palestinian homes to the ground, set fire to their tilth, kill them cold-bloodedly, and leave innocent orphans wailing behind ... With this in mind, the daily life in Palestine has become a permanent memorial gathering. When Palestinians face such unjust aggression, they tend to stem bloodletting and destruction and not to claim the lives of innocent civilians ... I categorically go against a committed Muslim's embarking on such attacks. Islam never allows a Muslim to kill the innocent and the helpless ... If such attacks were carried out by a Muslim – as some biased groups claim – then we, in the name of our religion, deny the act and incriminate the perpetrator. We do confirm that the aggressor deserves the deterrent punishment irrespective of his religion, race or gender ... What we warn against, even if it becomes a reality, is to hold a whole nation accountable for a crime carried out by a limited number of people or to characterize a certain religion as a faith giving support to violence and terrorism.* [64] [65]

Al-Qaradawi didn't seem to know who perpetrated 9/11, but whoever did, they certainly were frustrated by the plight of the Palestinians at the hands of Israelis. Looking at al-Qaradawi's other public statements he declared, for example, that all Israelis are guilty and are therefore legitimate targets. In other words, blowing up an Israeli school bus is fine, because no Israeli is innocent. He could not seem to muster very strong criticism for bin Laden at the time, either. In a 2004 interview with French Scholar Gilles Kepel, al-Qaradawi opined about bin Laden this way:

> [He] has never published anything that would allow one to judge his learning on actual evidence; he could not possibly call himself a doctor in law, and therefore can pass no juridical opinion, or fatwa: he is a 'preacher' – the lowest rank in the current hierarchical classification.

The problem with bin Laden, according to al-Qaradawi, was not that he was a brutal mass murderer but that he was a lousy scholar.

There are countless examples of such statements and *fatawa*, but let's examine one more – a *fatwa* that shows how incredibly subtle the dual nature can be. This *fatwa* to condemn terrorism was issued by the Amman Conference, a collaboration of the most renowned international Islamic bodies, representing all the major *madhhab*, or schools of jurisprudence. Please see Appendix 3 for the full text.

> [I]t is not possible to declare whoever subscribes to the Ash'ari creed or whoever practices true Sufism an apostate. Likewise, it is not possible to declare whoever subscribes to true Salafi thought an apostate. Equally, it is not possible to declare as apostates any group of Muslims who believes in Allah the Mighty and Sublime and His Messenger (may Peace and Blessings be upon him) and the pillars of faith, and respects the pillars of Islam and does not deny any Maloom Mina Al-Din Bil-Darura (necessary article of religion). [66]

Here, "true Sufism" or "true Salafi" means that jihadists know they can always claim their targets aren't true Sufis or Salafists; therefore, killing could be justified. But how do you empirically determine if a professed Muslim actually "believes in Allah the Mighty" or is merely putting on a show? Likewise, what is meant by "necessary article of religion?" Here, too, jihadists can claim their targets didn't follow necessary articles.

Such flaws, however, pale in comparison with two overarching defects: The *fatwa* does not condemn the killing of apostates, and it does not condemn the killing of non-Muslims. It merely attempts (and fails) to narrow the criteria for apostasy.

As I hope you can see, passive terrorism is a widespread, pernicious problem. Large swaths of the Muslim community quietly ignore jihadism or secretly approve of it. Though Muslims protest every perceived insult to Islam by the West with loud, widespread demonstrations that often turn violent and are always intimidating, they do not similarly demonstrate against the hijacking of their religion.

Islamic terror is not likely to decrease until Muslims cease being passive terrorists and become active defenders of hard truth, true peace and real tolerance.

Theological Deception

One of the tactics Islamists use to deceive the West is to present the same religious information to non-Muslims in one way and to Muslims in another. For example, it was common after 9/11 to find Islamic scholars using the following *hadith* to persuade Westerners that *jihad* means peaceful struggle:

> *You have come from the minor jihad to the major jihad."...then he said "it is the striving of the servant against his desires."*
>
> [Hadith 29]

Certainly this could yield a peaceful understanding of *jihad*, but distinguished Islamic books teach that it is a weak *hadith*.

> *Abu Bakr Al-Jazairi, a lecturer at the Nobel Prophetic Mosque in Saudi Arabia, wrote in his well-known, widely distributed book, Minhaj Al-Muslim, that this hadith is based upon a weak hadith that was reported by Al-Baihaqi and Al-Khateeb in the Tarikh. They reported it from Jabir. [Vol. 2, p. 167]*

This demonstrates how on the one hand Islamists show non-Muslims a peaceful *hadith* to improve Islam's image and on the other teach Muslims that it is weak and, by implication, Muslims should not follow it. In contrast, Islamists teach Muslims that the following *hadith* from *Minhaj al-Muslim* is *sahih*, or strong, accurate and authentic, and thus cannot be ignored:

> *I have been commanded to fight all mankind until they testify that none has the right to be worshiped except Allah and Muhammad is the messenger of Allah, they perform the salah and pay the zakah. If they do this, they have protected their blood and their wealth from me except by the right of Islam and their reckoning will be with Allah the almighty. (Agreed upon) [Vol. 1, page 402]*

The phrase "agreed upon" at the end means it is narrated as *sahih* by both *Al-Bukhari* and *Muslim*, which communicates to Muslims that it is extremely powerful.

Using such *hadiths* as justification, some disciples of Prophet Muhammad declared wars on non-Muslims to subjugate them to Islam. In this case, Muslims are taught that the violent *hadith* is strong and the peaceful one is weak. This theological tactic deceives countless non-Muslims.

Another example of this theological deception is the *hadith* used by many Muslims to make Islamic teaching look peaceful:

> *Whoever harms a non-Muslim citizen (of the Islamic state), then I will be his opponent on the day of resurrection.*

This seems like a benign *hadith*, but *Minhaj al-Muslim* declares:

> *Recorded by Al-Khateeb and it is weak.* [Vol. 1, p. 226]

Here again, the peaceful *hadith* is considered the weak one, and the same world-renowned Islamic book teaches that the following *hadith* is strong:

> *Do not initiate the greetings of peace with the Jews and the Christians. If you meet any one of them on the road, force him to go to the narrowest part of it. (Muslim)*

As before, the appended word "Muslim" refers to the fact that it is written in *Sahih Muslim*, which is considered one of the two most authentic Islamic books of *hadiths*. It bears repeating that the author of *Minhaj* is merely referencing mainstream Islamic teaching. He did not classify the *hadiths*.

In short, Westerners are not being told what is being taught to young Muslims. Many Westerners incorrectly conclude that Islam is a religion of peace based on these peaceful *hadiths*. Islamists teach that these *hadiths* are weak and should be ignored; only the violent *hadiths* are authentic.

Shifting the Blame

When some Muslims react to criticism directed at their community, perceptive observers often note that this reaction is almost always defensive and sometimes hostile. Likewise, when Muslims are confronted with questions about terror, they usually point fingers at America or Israel or a conspiracy – anything but themselves. This refusal to take personal responsibility for their actions is a gigantic stumbling block to preventing terror and treating the Islamist disease in the community at large. It is also a problem one sees to a much lesser extent among other groups. In America, thousands protested the Vietnam War; they marched for civil rights, free speech, abortion and more. In Israel, thousands of Jews protested their country's involvement in Lebanon during the 1980s. Yet we rarely see Muslims take members of their own community to the woodshed.

By now, it should not be surprising to learn that this lack of personal responsibility has roots in Salafi Islam. In Arab societies, it is common to hear the phrase, *al-Shaitan wa zenne* ("Satan has inspired me"), or as it is said in English, "The Devil made me do it." Every year during the *hajj*, pilgrims circle a symbol of Satan and throw rocks at it with great vehemence. The purpose is to express anger at Satan for making them sin and to deter him from doing so in the future. They are not responsible for their sinning; the devil is. Muslim children are taught and often forced to memorize the following *sura*:

> I ask refuge with the God of all humans ... the king of all humans ...
> From the mischief of the Whisperer (of Evil), who withdraws (after
> his whisper) [Quran: 114:1-4]

In this verse, it is widely understood that the "Whisperer" is Satan, or Shaitan. The verse rhymes in Arabic, making it particularly easy to remember.

The consistent attribution of mistakes to the Devil creates a mentality within which the individual does not consider himself responsible. When a Muslim learns to blame the Devil, it becomes easy to characterize any external force as the Devil or his work. Thus, Muslims call America the "Great Satan," responsible for most problems in the Muslim world. This culture of deflection makes it very difficult for Islam to correct itself because Muslims will not acknowledge responsibility for the crisis.

Who is a 'Moderate Muslim?'

Many Westerners will tell you that the majority of Muslims are moderates. It is a persistent theme in public discourse and has become an obligatory preface to discussing jihadism. In itself, this fact should be disconcerting – it doesn't seem to be necessary to speak of moderate Buddhists, and we rarely hear exhortations to moderate Christianity.

The problem with "moderate Islam" is why the phrase is even necessary. How can we assume any Muslim is moderate if we lack a clear understanding of what the word signifies? Many people suspect something is wrong with the way the term is used, but they fear articulating what that might be or admitting their suspicions. Furthermore, it is rare when someone offers a precise definition of "moderate" as it pertains to Muslims; we almost never hear a clear delineation. Where does that leave us? We're forced to accept what is basically a fallacy just to make ourselves comfortable. Or, if we deign to suggest the truth of what the evidence is telling us, we risk ridicule.

When we press those who use the word "moderate" about what they mean, they usually say it's someone who does not commit a terrorist act. Unfortunately, this makes most suicide bombers moderates until the very moment of the explosion. In fact, many of the Islamic terrorists who have attacked European cities were considered moderate prior to their involvement. Before 9/11, the hijackers looked in every way assimilated. Many were were clean-shaven, wore jeans and T-shirts, and would even visit strip clubs. Neighbors of the 9/11 hijackers were shocked when they discovered their superficially irreligious acquaintances were violent agents of fundamentalist Islam.

How is this possible? One tactic of jihadists is to deceive the infidel until he is weakened and thereby ripe for conquest. As mentioned previously, jihadists use the word *taqiyya* to describe the practice. Those who assimilate into infidel societies in order to wage *jihad* are not considered un-Islamic. Al-Zawahiri advocated this approach years ago.

Superficial indications of secularism, modernity, hospitality and westernization cannot be used as a guide to determine who is moderate and who is not. Indeed, Muslims who in every respect are kind and gracious can harbor Salafist religious beliefs and hatred for non-Islamic societies. In cases where it is unconscious, it can be termed Double Mind Theory, or DMT, a psychological condition similar to George Orwell's notion of Doublethink. We have seen the phenomenon most notably among citizens in the former Soviet Union, who described their own society in their criticisms of the West.

DMT is part of a larger psychological paradigm known as cognitive dissonance – the capacity to believe in mutually contradictory notions without being aware of it. In the case of passive terrorists, the schism is one between the cultural mind and the religious mind.

It is an integral part of Arab culture to show great hospitality to guests, and Muslim Middle Easterners in Western societies often show such hospitality to their neighbors. Depressingly often, however, their religious sense could simultaneously support declaring war on infidels to subjugate them to Islam. This contradiction has led to confusion among many Westerners. An instructive example is that of Jill Carroll, a peace activist and freelance journalist with the *Christian Science Monitor,* who was taken hostage in Iraq in 2006. She was released after three months of captivity and promptly spoke to the media, where she enthused about her kidnappers' hospitality. These same kidnappers were planning terrorist attacks and indicated so to her. [67]

Whichever mind is dominant at a given time determines hospitality or aggression. The presence of a mind that accepts violent religious teachings is the primary reason most Muslims did not demonstrate with any real zeal against the likes of bin Laden, or ISIS now, or why the highest Islamic organizations cannot bring themselves to issue *fatawa* of apostasy against such individuals.

A natural definition of moderate might be "non-Salafist," but using the term no doubt would raise objections that some are "mild" Salafists. It might be possible to distinguish between hardcore Salafists and so-called mild Salafists, but whenever a Muslim promotes the view that Sharia should be the single binding law, with all of its violent edicts and oppressive rules, or seeks to emulate ancient codes of dress and behavior, that Muslim, deny it or not, is a Salafist.

I met Salafi Muslims after 9/11 who claimed to Westerners that they were Sufi with the goal of appearing moderate. Many wonder why there has been so little outcry or protest by the Islamic mainstream against promotion of Sharia. The answer is that much of the Islamic mainstream is Salafist and actually supports Sharia.

It is difficult to find mainstream clerics and mainstream Islamic books that stand unambiguously against Salafist tenets, while it is easy to find examples of militancy and obfuscation. Omar M. Ahmad, the founder and former chairman of the board of the Council on American Islamic Relations, CAIR, declared the following in 1998:

Islam isn't in America to be equal to any other faith but to become dominant. The [Quran], the Muslim book of scripture, should be the highest authority in America, and Islam the only accepted religion on Earth. [68]

Omar denied having said this despite witnesses to the contrary, and he worked up a good dose of outrage when his words were exposed in the media. CAIR, under Omar and today as well, is considered to be the preeminent Islamic organization in the United States. The organization's own statement proclaims that CAIR's mission is to enhance understanding of Islam, encourage dialogue, protect civil liberties, empower American Muslims, and build coalitions that promote justice and mutual understanding. [69]

According to columnist Joseph Farah, however, "You should see the hate mail I get from CAIR's members. It would make your hair stand on end." [70]

When asked about the overwhelming numbers of Muslims in the terrorist ranks, CAIR's current executive director, Nihad Awad, obfuscated, saying, "They are Muslim, but they're not Islamic. Their actions are not inspired by Islam. It's like Islam philosophy." [71]

In other words, terrorism isn't fueled by Salafism, and terrorists aren't Salafists – it is the product of un-Islamic Muslim philosophers. Ahmed Bedier, who is CAIR's Florida communications director, is no better. He once informed Florida Representative Ginny Browne-Waite that "Catholic priests pose more of a terrorism threat by having sex with young altar boys than those who flew planes into the World Trade Center." [72]

In 2006, I attended the Secular Islam Summit, a conference to which CAIR objected strenuously. Radio host Glenn Beck, who at the time was working for CNN, was onsite to cover it, and he wanted to get perspectives from both sides. So he interviewed Bedier and me on his show. Bedier objected that I wasn't American, I didn't understand Islam in America, and I couldn't genuinely represent American Muslims. He added, "In order to have legitimate reform, you need to have the right messengers." [73]

Bedier was speaking as if Islam is taught in America differently than in other parts of the world. A single visit to any Islamic bookstore in the country would have revealed that violence and intolerance are taught here just as much as they are in Islamic countries. The same Salafist references are used and recommended in both places.

Looking at the threat of Islamism only within the borders of the United States – as Mr. Bedier did – presents a primitive and shallow approach to the problem. Salafism permeates a wide variety of Islamic organizations that rarely call themselves Salafist. But by accepting, or not clearly opposing, the violent tenets of Sharia, organizations reveal themselves to be in the Salafist camp. Although Salafists fear, hate and fight against modern values of freedom and civil rights, Salafists nevertheless complain bitterly about violations of their own civil rights when they reside in modern societies.

Such complaints are tactical, however; the goal is to establish a Sharia-based society with no civil rights by achieving strength in non-Sharia societies. Just as Salafists seek to use democracy to end democracy, as they have done in Algeria and they did temporarily in Egypt, so do they use the civil protections of modern nations with the goal of ending civil protections. In the Salafist mind, civil protections are weaknesses that can be exploited and even championed for the sake of ultimate Islamic subjugation.

Indeed, Salafists also might temporarily support a government that implements most aspects of Sharia. Such is the case with Saudi Arabia, where the ruling system was and still is supported by Wahhabi clerics. Other Salafists, such as Osama bin Laden, considered Saudi Arabia insufficiently Islamic; the country grants entry to non-Muslims, permits women to be educated and to work in some fields, permits secular TV channels, and justifies the existence of a Western (non-Sharia) banking system.

More common than incitement to violence are the continuous, low-level promulgation and reinforcement of doctrinal justifications for violence and the incitement to commit such acts. A Salafist will normally assert, among fellow adherents, that when members gain sufficient strength war should be declared on the infidels. Traditional Islamic teaching permits numerous violent or inhumane concepts. Therefore, Muslims and Islamic scholars must stand clearly and unambiguously against them in order to be considered truly peaceful.

One way to expose the positions of Islamic leaders about Salafism is to ask them pointed questions. Along those lines, I have developed a quiz that I call the Radical Islam Support Test (RIST):

+ Apostates: Do you support killing them? Should leaving the faith of Islam be punishable by death?

+ Beating women: Is this ever acceptable? If not, do you reject those decrees of Islamic law that sanction the beating of women? Do you also reject stoning women to death for adultery?

+ Calling Jews "pigs and monkeys": Do you believe that Jews are in any way subhuman? If not, do you reject Quranic interpretations that claim they are?

+ Holy War: Do you support war against non-Muslims to subjugate them to Islam? Do you believe it is fair and reasonable to offer non-Muslims conversion, paying the *jizya* or death?

+ Enslavement: Do you support the enslavement of female war prisoners and having sex with them as concubines? If not, do you reject those interpretations in Islamic law, such as *ma malakat aymanukum*, which justifies such actions?

+ Fighting Jews: Do you support perpetual war against Jews to exterminate them? If not, should those Muslims who incite such war be punished? [74]

+ Killing gays: Do you believe it is acceptable to kill homosexuals? If not, do you reject those edicts in Sharia law that claim it is?

A number of years ago, I was speaking in a public gathering in Michigan. During the speech, an *imam* in the audience stood up and proclaimed that he was a moderate. I responded by asking him if he was prepared to invite Jewish representatives to attend Friday prayers at his mosque, and also if he would state clearly before his congregation that Jews are not pigs and monkeys. The *imam* looked down, stepped back and said nothing.

I assure you, if a Muslim or Islamic organization fails this quiz, then regardless of how they describe themselves, they are Salafi. We can speak endlessly of peaceful Muslims when we focus on the cultural mind. But when we evaluate the religious mind, the outcome can be something else entirely. The question is simple and clear: Can a Muslim who does not reject the violent concepts challenged by RIST be a moderate? If a Muslim is truly moderate, he or she should not hesitate to reject, clearly and unambiguously, the hateful aspects of Sharia.

The central problem we face in confronting radical Islam is that the violent injunctions of Sharia are not bizarre, extremist or anachronistic

Islamic interpretations; they are mainstream. They are promoted in Islamic books. A careful analysis of all currently approved Islamic interpretations and schools of jurisprudence reveals this serious, pervasive, deeply disturbing problem.

New interpretations of Islamic texts are essential to our security. Accepting the injunctions of Sharia without extensive reinterpretation prepares the ground for jihadists to take the next logical step. Without providing theologically based alternatives that clearly reject the injustice and brutality of mainstream Sharia, a war between civilizations is inevitable.

Muslims who unquestioningly adhere to a violent value system will eventually force it upon their host nation when their numbers reach critical mass. Our experience in Iraq – particularly since the rise of ISIS – has shown that so-called insurgents can put the future of a whole nation at risk. We should not allow the same to happen in the Western world; we cannot allow passive terrorism to fester. Political correctness should not be allowed to stand in the way.

Developing techniques – such as RIST – to expose radical or dangerous views, will help keep us safe from Islamism and permit truly moderate Muslims to exist without fear of persecution.

Oppression of Women

The plight of women in Islamic societies is appalling in its barbarity and massive in scope. It is well documented. Although the women's movement in the West has been almost entirely silent on the matter, a small number of human rights activists, such as Phyllis Chesler, Nonie Darwish, Ayaan Hirsi Ali and others have worked extensively to raise awareness of the problem. [75]

Based on research these women have conducted, it is estimated that over 90 percent of Pakistani wives have been struck, beaten or abused sexually. In Iran, a girl is legally marriageable when she reaches the age of nine. To divorce a wife, a Muslim man needs only to say "I divorce you" three times, which leaves the woman with no income and the status of outcast.

I recall a case in Saudi Arabia where a woman was gang-raped by four men while a fifth recorded the event on his smartphone. The woman received a sentence of 90 lashes for being alone in a car with a man who was not her husband. When she appealed, her sentence was more than doubled to 200 lashes. The late King Abdullah pardoned her but only after much Western pressure. [76]

In addition, gender apartheid governs the nation. Women are forbidden to drive cars, to vote, to walk in public without wearing the *niqab*. In many parts of the Islamic world, girls undergo clitorectomies – also known as female genital mutilation. It is believed that doing so makes a woman chaste and docile.

Slavery is still legal in parts of Sudan and Mauritania, which gives rise to sexual slavery. Honor killings are more prevalent in Muslim communities – both in Islamic countries and in Western nations.

Indeed, the oppression of women in the Islamic world is so involved a topic that it is beyond the scope of a general book about Islamism. It is a human-rights concern by itself.

Meanwhile, the abuse of women in Islamic societies has another consequence that is less talked about, yet it contributes extensively to Islamic terror and violence.

To Westerners, the most noticeable aspect of many Muslim women is their dress. After a period of relative liberation in the 1950s and 1960s, women in many Islamic societies began to suffer from proliferating Islamism in the 1970s. They began wearing the *hijab* in greater numbers – in some cases by choice; in others by force.

Unfortunately, some Western women have chosen to wear the *hijab* when they conduct diplomatic missions to Islamic states. For example, former House Speaker Nancy Pelosi wore the *hijab* when she visited Bashar al-Assad of Syria in 2007; first lady Laura Bush donned one when she visited Gulf nations that same year.

These gestures might appear respectful, but they are in fact harmful. The women seem to be operating under the false belief that the *hijab* is a neutral – or merely traditional – fashion statement, not unlike the sari worn by women in India. But the *hijab* is not simply a clothing accessory. It harbors deep Islamic doctrinal connections to slavery and discrimination. Western women who cover themselves are unwittingly endorsing an inhumane system.

When I was a member of Jamaa Islamiya, we used to despise women who did not wear the *hijab*. We considered them vain and concerned with earthly pleasures and trivialities, and we believed they would burn in Hell. Our belief was based on the following *hadith*:

> *[It was] narrated by Abu Huraira that Prophet Muhammad (peace and blessings of Allah be upon him) said: "There are ... the people of Hell whom I have not seen ... women who are clothed but naked, walking with an enticing gait, with something like the humps of camels on their heads They will not enter Paradise nor even smell its fragrance* —Sahih Muslim

Within Salafi Islam, the *hijab* serves to differentiate between slave girls and women who are considered free. In this sense, it creates a feeling of superiority among the women who wear it (and their men) toward women who do not.

> *O Prophet! Tell thy wives and daughters (Not the concubines), and the believing (Free) women, that they should cast their outer garments over their bodies, that they should be known (as free women) and thus not molested. And Allah is Oft-Forgiving, Most Merciful.*
> [Quran 33:59]

Tafsir ibn Kathir, one of the most reputable authorities in explaining the Quran, discusses the context, or *asbab al-nuzul*, of this verse. According to it, some people from Medina would look at a Muslim woman, and if they saw a complete veil or cover they recognized she was free and would not sexually harass her. On the other hand, if a woman was seen without a veil, they marked her as a slave girl and could rape her without guilt. The verse exists to differentiate between free women and the concubines, so free Muslim women would not be molested. Most Islamic authorities and scholars affirm this purpose of the *hijab.* [77] The role the *hijab* plays in promoting or recognizing slavery is further supported by various *hadiths*:

> *Narrated Anas: The Prophet stayed for three days between Khaibar and Medina, and there he consummated his marriage to Safiyya bint Huyai (after taking her as a prisoner of war). I invited the Muslims to the wedding banquet in which neither meat nor bread was offered. He ordered for leather dining-sheets to be spread, and dates, dried yoghurt and butter were laid on it, and that was the Prophet's wedding banquet. The Muslims wondered, "Is she (Saffiyya) considered as his wife or his slave girl?" Then they said, "If he orders her to veil herself, she will be one of the mothers of the Believers (the wives of Prophet Muhammad); but if he does not order her to veil herself, she*

*will be a slave girl. So when the Prophet proceeded from there, he
spared her a space behind him (on his she-camel) and put a screening
veil between her and the people (accordingly they understood she
became his wife not just his slave girl).—Sahih al-Bukhari*

Umar ibn al-Khattab was one of the foremost disciples of Muhammad.
The Prophet personally promised al-Khattab a place in Paradise, so the
disciple is a role model for many Muslim men. The behavior of Umar
is narrated in many Salafist books, such as those written by Ibn Tameia:

*Umar ibn al-Khattab used to beat any slave girl if she dared to cover
her body as the free Muslim women did; so that free Muslim women
became distinctive from the slave girls.*

Also:

*When Umar ibn al-Khattab traveled in Medina ... If he saw "Ama"
or a slave girl, he would beat her with his Durra (a special type of
stick) until the hijab fell off and he would say: "How come the slave
girls are trying to emulate the free women by wearing the hijab!"*
　　　　　　　　　　　　　　　　　　—Tabakat ibn Saad

Obviously, the *hijab* plays a role in the discrimination against women.
Its purpose is not modesty or to encourage observers to focus on a
Muslim woman's personality. Its purpose, according to the most authen-
tic *hadiths* and interpretations, is to create a society where superior free
Muslim women are distinguished from inferior slave women.

In Australia, the foremost Islamic cleric is Sheikh Taj el-Din al-Hilali.
Back in 2006, he gave a sermon in which he analyzed the notorious
Sydney gang rapes – four women brutally raped by a group of Muslim
men. When those men received long jail sentences, the sheikh complained that their offense had been provoked, because the women had
swayed suggestively, worn cosmetics and dressed immodestly. Al-Hilali
called the women "weapons" used by Satan to manipulate men. He
offered this analogy:

*If you take out uncovered meat and place it outside on the street, or
in the garden or in the park, or in the backyard without a cover, and
the cats come and eat it ... whose fault is it, the cats or the uncovered
meat? ... The uncovered meat is the problem ... If she was in her
room, in her home, in her hijab, no problem would have occurred ...*

It is said in the state of zina (adultery), the responsibility falls 90
per cent of the time on the woman. Why? Because she possesses the
weapon of enticement (igraa). [78]

When young Muslims hear sermons like that it breeds hatred. I previously noted that hatred is the first phase in constructing the jihadist
mentality. It also breeds hatred by women who wear the *hijab* for those
who do not. Before she discarded the *hijab* and began wearing ordinary
modern dress, my wife – who had worn it for years – thought uncovered
women were cheap.

The *hijab* not only fosters gender discrimination in Islamic societies
but also encourages hatred for non-Muslim women who wear modern
clothing. Many terrorist attacks have taken place in areas where Western
women wear bathing suits or dance with men. Discotheques in Israel
were a favorite target, as were the Bali nightclubs, in which 202 people
were killed and 209 injured in the 2002 bombings perpetrated by Jemaah
Islamiah, an Asian cousin of my old group Jamaa Islamiya. [79]

Beaches in Egypt and Indonesia have been victimized by jihadist
attacks, and there have been plots to bomb the discos in London. In
such cases, hatred of women who do not wear the *hijab* can be a pivotal
factor. Furthermore, the proliferation of the *hijab* is strongly correlated
with increased terrorism. The *hijab* is both a sign of Salafism and a factor
that perpetuates it. Growth in terrorism to this extent has almost never
stemmed from Muslim communities where the *hijab* is uncommon.

Terrorism became much more frequent in Indonesia, Egypt, Algeria
and England after the *hijab* became prevalent among Muslim women
in those countries. Also, wearing the *hijab* preceded an increase in fundamentalism within Muslim communities in Kosovo. There, Islamic
fundamentalism was a factor in fueling conflict between Muslims and
Christians. It is true as well in Iraq; terrorism has been much more prevalent in the Sunni areas where the *hijab* is common (such as al-Anbar
Province – which at this writing has fallen almost completely into the
hands of ISIS) than in Sunni communities where the headscarf is seen
less frequently, such as among Sunni Kurds.

As the *hijab* becomes ubiquitous, young women are wearing it at pro-
gressively earlier ages. According to the *hadiths*, girls are only supposed
to wear the *hijab* after puberty (to hide sexual attractiveness). The current trend of some Muslims to make young girls wear it could indicate a

perverse way of thinking: When Muslim fathers require their daughters to wear the *hijab*, it can imply these girls are sexually desirable enough to merit covering. Young Muslims – male and female – who grow up in this twisted atmosphere of Salafist gender oppression become fodder for future *jihad*.

Another form of mistreatment, polygamy, leads to suppressing conscience, something I mentioned in Chapter 1. This polygamy is not consensual; it does not matter what the wife thinks about the additional woman, because under Salafism it is accepted that Allah has permitted it, and the Prophet practiced it.

As with much else that is wrong with many Islamic societies, oppression of women has deep roots in Muslim and especially Salafist writings. Salafism fuels the reactionary interpretations of scripture that justify it. In turn, the abuse of women plays a central role in desensitizing young Muslim men to violence. As I also mentioned earlier, desensitizing violence is one of the tactics jihadists use to indoctrinate and train recruits. When a Muslim man becomes indifferent to a woman being beaten, maimed or stoned to death, it becomes a much smaller step for him to commit acts of terrorism.

You might have seen videos of Saudi *imams* explaining the "humane" technique for beating a wife. [80] Doing so is sanctioned by a frequently cited passage in the Quran:

> *Men have authority over women because God has made the one superior to the other, and because they spend their wealth to maintain them. Good women are obedient. They guard their unseen parts because God has guarded them. As for those from whom you fear disobedience, admonish them and send them to beds apart and beat them. Then if they obey you, take no further action against them. Surely God is high, supreme.* [4:34]

Wife beating leads to the third phase of jihadist indoctrination: the acceptance of violence. The failure of many Islamic societies to embrace modernity and teach values of true tolerance and respect for others has contributed to the development of Islamic terrorism. This failure stems partly from promoting a violent understanding of Islamic texts. Proper educational reforms are vital for the future success of the Islamic world and for security worldwide.

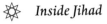

NOTES

45.   "Oklahoma City bombing," Wikipedia.org.

46.   Daniel Pipes, "Saudi Religious Leader Calls for Slavery's Legalization." Daniel Pipes Weblog, comment posted November 7, 2003.

47.   Ibid.

48.   See, for example, "Inside Islam: Faith vs. Fanatics," from the documentary series Islam versus Islamists, aired on Fox News, October 20, 2007. The episode was scheduled to be aired on PBS but apparently was considered too politically incorrect. After negotiations with the producers and PBS, it was aired on Fox. The series DVD can be purchased online.

49.   Munira Miraz, Abi Senthilkumaran and Zein Jaifar, "Living apart together: British Muslims and the paradox of multiculturalism," *Policy Exchange*, London, 2006/2007.

50.   "Muslim Publics Share Concerns about Extremist Groups," Pew Global Attitudes Surveys, September 10, 2013.

51.   "Muslim Americans: Middle Class and Mostly Mainstream," Pew Research Center, May 22, 2007.

52.   Ibid.

53.   Anthony Shadid, "Remarks by Pope Prompt Muslim Outrage, Protests," *The Washington Post*, September 16, 2006.

54.   "*Jyllands-Posten* Muhammad cartoons controversy," Wikipedia.org.

55.   "Gunman kills Dutch film director," BBC News, November 2, 2004.

56.   "Islamic scarf controversy in France," Wikipedia.org.

57.   "1971 Bangladesh Pakistan War Criminals" http://gatok-dalal.tripod.com. (The Wikipedia entry, "Bangladesh Liberation War," fails to mention the *fatwa* and shamefully understates the Islamic component in the war).

58.   Amad S., "Shaykh Salman al-Oudah's Ramadan letter to Osama bin Laden," MuslimMatters.org, September 18, 2007.

59.   Reference page: "Blasphemy Salman Rushdie," Constitutional Rights Foundation website.

60.   Charles Kurzman, "Islamic Statements Against Terrorism," University of North Carolina.

61.   "ADC Condemns Attack on Trade Center, Government Buildings," American-Arab Anti-Discrimination Committee, September 11, 2001.

62.   "Anti-Terrorism statements" reference page, CAIR Florida.

63.   Charles Kurzman, op. cit.

64.   "Sheikh Yusuf Al-Qaradawi Condemns Attacks Against Civilians: Forbidden in Islam," IslamOnline, September 13, 2001.

65.   See the excellent piece by Lee Smith, "The Myth of Islamist Democracy," *Slate*, July 16, 2004.

66.   "The Three Points of the Amman Message V.1," The Official Website of the Amman Message.

67.   "The Jill Carroll Story – Introduction," *Christian Science Monitor*, August 14, 2006.

68.   "CAIR tries to squash criticism of agenda through intimidation and lawfare, critics say," *The Daily Caller*, September 22, 2010.

69. "Our Vision, Mission, and Core Principles," Council on American Islamic Relations.

70. Art Moore, "Should Muslim Quran be USA's top authority?" *World Net Daily,* May 1, 2003.

71. "CAIR Outraged over President's Use of Term 'Islamic Fascists,'" Fox News Online, August 15, 2006.

72. Daniel Pipes, "CAIR Criticized," Daniel Pipes Blog, July 16, 2003.

73. Robert Spencer, "CAIR vs. Human Rights," FrontPageMagazine.com, March 12, 2007.

74. Policymakers should note: This clerical promulgation and widespread belief remain a major obstacles to solving the Arab-Israeli conflict.

75. See, for example, the excellent booklet *The Violent Oppression of Women in Islam* by Robert Spencer and Phyllis Chesler.

76. "Saudi king pardons gang rape victim," *The Guardian*, December 17, 2007.

77. See *Tafsir al-Tabari* for Sura Ahzab 45/22 and *Tafsir al-Baidhawi* 386/4. There are many other examples.

78. Richard Kerbaj, "Muslim leader blames women for sex attacks," *The Australian*, October 26, 2006.

79. "The 12 October 2002 Bombing Plot," BBC News Asia, October 11, 2012.

80. Middle East Media Research Institute, TV Monitor Project, "Saudi Cleric Muhammad Al-'Arifi Explains Wife Beating in Islam to Young Muslims in a Ramadan Show."

CHAPTER 4

The Failure of the West

It pains me to write this, but at this point in history the West is losing the struggle against radical Islam. The reasons are many, but some are clear – even obvious. Unless the situation is reversed, and the threat of *jihad* is eliminated, millions more peaceful and peace-loving people in the world will soon find themselves at risk because their governments have failed to protect them. That failure can be seen in the following manifestations.

Lack of Reciprocity

Back in 2007 in the United Kingdom, in the wake of the London Subway bombings two years earlier, an expensive and widespread advertising campaign began. The effort, called Islam Is Peace, placed ads on TV, in print, on billboards and on city buses. The supporting entity also launched a website to invite certain visitors to engage in dialogue – to create permanent channels of communication and debate between the Muslim community and the rest of Britain. [81]

As Ifhat Shaheen-Smith, one of IIP's organizers, told the BBC at the time, "In the current atmosphere of suspicion and fear about Islam and British Muslims, truth is often confused with fabrications and stereotypes." [82]

I studied the campaign while it was ongoing, and I observed a curious trait that is common to many such efforts. As it turned out, Islam Is Peace did not truly want dialogue or debate. Instead, the group wanted the criticism and introspection to run in one direction only: toward non-Muslims and the British government. Worse, virtually no one in England demanded reciprocity. It was a case of Western delicacy, if not outright cowardice, failing to counter an Islamic effort at intimidation.

Westerners commonly criticize their own societies with great gusto, but rarely do they display the same attitude toward Muslim communities. In contrast, Muslims frequently and openly criticize Westerners, but rarely themselves. And when some individuals have dared to satirize or criticize the Muslim faith, they have done so at their peril. Remember Salman Rushdie, who was targeted with an execution *fatwa* for his book *The Satanic Verses*? Or Theo van Gogh, who was stabbed to death on an Amsterdam street for his film *Submission*? Or more recently, the French journalists at *Charlie Hebdo* magazine who were massacred for satirizing Muhammad?

This isn't dialogue or debate; it's intellectual and moral absurdity that often manifests itself as hatred and violence.

Here are several small but telling examples of what I mean.

+   When Western women leaders visit Islamic countries, they often don the *hijab*, just as they cover their heads when entering Catholic churches. But where do you see traditional Muslim women doff their *hijabs* and display uncovered heads, and wear dresses and pantsuits, when they visit Western countries? Yes, Western cultures tolerate a broad range of clothing, so Muslim women are free to appear in public in traditional garb – though most non-Muslim countries have banned the *burqa*. But this has been an enduring case of lack of reciprocity, and it should be considered unacceptable even if the *hijab* did not represent a division between free and slave women and did not play a key role in gender apartheid.

+   In the 1985 film *A Passage to India*, there is a scene where Mrs. Moore, a British woman, has entered what she thinks is an empty mosque. There, she encounters Dr. Aziz, a Muslim, who at first scolds her presence. But she replies that she had removed her shoes and left them outside – and she is wearing a light scarf. Dr. Aziz comments that he would not have expected a British woman to obey the rules when no one was there to see. Mrs. Moore says, "God is here," to which Dr. Aziz replies, "That is very fine." At that point, the two begin a friendship based on an act of respect and tolerance. Why don't we see or hear of such acts by Muslims toward their fellow citizens of other faiths?

+   In 2004 in the United Kingdom, the town of Derby planned to replace a statue of a wild boar it had proudly displayed from 1840 until 1942, when the sculpture was decapitated by a German bomb. Controversy erupted, however, when the local Muslim community claimed the statue was offensive. [83]

  +   In another incident, the UK town of Dudley passed a law forbidding workers to place figurines of pigs on their desks. Apparently, a Muslim employee had complained that such desk ornaments offended his faith. According to Mahbubur Rahman, who was then Councilor of Dudley, the law represented "tolerance and acceptance" of Muslim beliefs. [84]

  +   Many Muslims took offense in 2006 when Pope Benedict XVI, speaking at the University of Regensburg, Germany, cited a passage from a 1391 tract criticizing Islam. Even though the citation was made in the context of a larger lecture, Muslim riots erupted around the world. In order to quell the unrest, the pope visited Turkey and prayed in a mosque, facing Mecca. Yet if dialogue was the goal, why didn't Muslims show Pope Benedict reciprocal gestures of respect? Why didn't Muslim scholars visit the Vatican and make the sign of the cross upon entering St. Peter's? [85]

  +   In 2007, the management of the Empire State Building in New York City decided to illuminate the skyscraper in green to honor the end of Ramadan and the Islamic holiday of Eid. But why didn't New York Muslims reciprocate the honor by, for example, wishing fellow city residents a Merry Christmas or a Happy Chanukah?

  +   Elsewhere, the lack of tolerance by Muslims has been more severe. In Egypt in 2006, veiled women stormed an art museum crying "Infidels, Infidels!" and attempted to destroy three works of art. The reason: A sculptor had violated a *fatwa* issued by the Grand Mufti of Cairo, which banned images of living beings. [86]

If Westerners yield to Muslim objections to trivial pig figurines and the statue of a boar, what will be the breaking point? If Muslims deem Christmas trees offensive, should communities remove or ban them? If Muslims declared that women's rights are offensive or that prohibiting slavery insults their faith or that banning marriages to underage females interferes with Sharia, should Western governments surrender as a matter of religious tolerance?

When Salafism has its way, the results are always depressing and irreparable. It should have come as no surprise when the Taliban destroyed the historically priceless Buddhist statues of Bamiyan by dynamiting them in 2001; [87] likewise when ISIS in 2014 and 2015 blew up or bulldozed Christian churches in Iraq as part of its conquests [88, 89, 90] or when the jihadists burned the Mosul Public Library and destroyed priceless ancient artifacts at the Mosul Museum. [91, 92]

Not that Christianity is under assault only by radical Islam. Indeed, it is strange how Christianity is constantly assailed by Western progressives, both in word and in the actions of organizations such as the American Civil Liberties Union. The ACLU worked diligently to remove a monument of the Ten Commandments from an Alabama courthouse in 2002, a "victory" disapproved of by 77 percent of Americans. [93] In contrast, the ACLU has hardly worked at all to stop Islamic infiltrations into secular institutions. The ACLU said nothing about installing Islamic footbaths in restrooms at the Minnesota Community and Technical College – a taxpayer-funded public institution – in 2007. School president Phil Davies claimed that the footbaths were a sign of tolerance and "hospitality," but at the same time he insisted that departmental Christmas cards not exhibit "any sign of favoring one religion." He added, "As we head into the holiday season ... all public offices and areas should refrain from displays that may represent to our students, employees or the public that the college is promoting any particular religion." [94]

Apparently, Dr. Davies saw no contradiction; the footbaths did not accommodate or promote a particular religion, but Christmas cards did.

Why must religious tolerance extend only in one direction? If Christians complained that the Islamic scarf was offensive to them, would the same decision-makers require Muslim women to stop wearing the *hijab*?

I cannot help but recall the way Jamaa Islamiya gradually dominated our medical school, using tactics similar to those I have described above – though not nearly to the extent exhibited by the Taliban or ISIS. First, they asked for permission to build a prayer room. Then, they demanded and received a library. Next came Salafist sermons before lectures and angry demonstrations to prevent music. Their gradual but relentless incursions wore down the school administration's resistance.

We in the West are experiencing an escalating series of incursions, and make no mistake, it is a vicious cycle. The more we surrender, the more Islamists will demand. If we continue to accommodate them, democracy itself will eventually be considered offensive, and the push will be on to impose Sharia – the ultimate goal of every Islamist. It is a certainty.

The West must insist on reciprocity in honoring religious freedom within the bounds of our respective national secular laws – something, for example, the ACLU selectively and pedantically enforces in America, but only against Christianity. This one-directional, self-destructive desire to appease Islamists – and to intimidate Christians – has led to such absurdities as the public outcry and threats against a humble pizza restaurant in Indiana having to close, albeit temporarily, because one of their employees told a local TV reporter that they probably would not cater a same-sex wedding – if asked. [95] Meanwhile, a similar report about several Muslim bakeries refusing to cater gay weddings elicited not even a whisper of indignation or protest by the public. [96]

The merits or demerits of the issue aside, there is no doubt Christians and Muslims in the West are now treated differently. There is no hesitation in protesting or challenging Christians who attempt to follow the tenets of their faith, while similar actions against Muslims are, if the news media are a reliable indicator, virtually nonexistent.

One of the strengths of the West is its tolerance and freedom, but Islamists view such traits as signs of capitulation and weakness. If there is to be any solution to this conflict, if Muslims and non-Muslims can go forth peacefully, there must be mutual respect for one another's cultures. Meanwhile, appeasement is generating the opposite outcome and must stop. It would behoove us to remember a little bit of history. Upon returning from the Munich Conference in 1938, British Prime Minister Neville Chamberlain smugly announced:

> *My good friends, for the second time in our history, a British Prime Minister has returned from Germany bringing peace with honour. I believe it is peace for our time. Go home and get a nice quiet sleep.* [97]

Winston Churchill's response was prescient indeed:

> *You were given the choice between war and dishonour. You chose dishonour, and you will have war.* [98]

Must history repeat itself?

Political Concessions

Nowhere is there a greater need for courage and determination in combating the jihadists than in our political leaders. Time after time, Western heads of state, and most especially President Barack Obama, have bent over backwards to avoid admitting any association between Islam or the Islamic ideology and jihadist terrorism. Mr. Obama continually refuses to call ISIS what it is, an Islamic state, as its name unequivocally conveys. In fact, the change from ISIS (Islamic State in Iraq and Syria) to IS (Islamic State) is extremely significant. When they regarded themselves merely as ISIS, the scope of their ambitions was limited to the two nations in which they operated. When they changed their name to IS in 2014, it was because they felt strong enough to announce their ambitions of a global caliphate. The change should have signaled to the West a dramatic expansion of the scope and scale of their operations. The IS attacks in France and Denmark [99] would have come as no surprise if we had not willfully chosen to ignore the importance of the name. Our continued official unwillingness to call radical Islam "radical Islam" will only exacerbate the problem. As I have described above, such actions are not helping and they are emboldening radical Islam.

Likewise, the following:

+   *Apologies.* Normally, issuing an apology for making a mistake is a respected act among civilized people. But when your self-sworn enemy considers an apology a sign of weakness and actually becomes more vicious in response, you must think twice before apologizing.

Take the rioting in 2006 over Danish cartoons lampooning Prophet Muhammad. The cartoons had been published the previous September in Denmark by *Jyllands-Posten* magazine. Until the end of January there was virtually no response on the Muslim street – four months of relative peace. Then, on January 31, the magazine issued an apology for publishing the cartoons. Within a few days, violent demonstrations erupted throughout the Islamic world. Perhaps it was only a coincidence, but in my view if the magazine had not apologized, the violent demonstrations probably would not have occurred. This mentality seems totally alien to Westerners, but it is real. Islamists react violently only if they perceive that their opponents are weak. Worse, the more concessions they receive, the more aggressive they become.

Another example that illustrates this bizarre attribute of the Islamist mind is the reaction of jihadists to antiwar demonstrations in the United States during the Iraq War. Jihadists perceived those demonstrations as a sign of disunity among the infidels and therefore an opportune time to step up their terrorism. One of the worst weeks in Iraq, in terms of civilian casualties, occurred immediately after actress and antiwar activist

Jane Fonda spoke at a rally in Washington in early 2007. Coincidence or not, I noticed the correlation, as it was widely reported that more than a thousand innocents were killed that week. [100]

I don't doubt that Jane Fonda and her ilk had no intention of facilitating the deaths of civilians. But their demonstrations almost certainly contributed to the loss of more innocent lives than would have occurred otherwise, and their misguided efforts served only to impede and delay victory in Iraq.

Please don't forget that I am a former Islamist. I know how such actions can boost morale and determination within the terror groups.

My belief is that if ISIS and al-Qaeda saw millions of Americans demanding vengeance by the U.S. government instead of demonstrating against their own country – particularly if many Muslims stood with them – the terror groups would feel weakened, and their ability to recruit future jihadists would likely decline.

I find it ironic that Leftist demonstrators on the one hand impeded victory in Iraq and at the same time blamed any failures in Iraq on the administration of President George W. Bush. I am not suggesting that the United States government made no mistakes or wrong decisions regarding the war in Iraq. But during the years of the Obama administration, things in Iraq have gotten steadily worse. President Obama, in announcing the complete withdrawal of U.S. troops in 2011, assured the American military and the American people that the troops were leaving behind "a sovereign, stable and self-reliant Iraq." [101] Perhaps Iraq technically remains a sovereign state, but given the terrible violence perpetrated by ISIS, and Iraq's steady and now-inevitable domination by Iran, the country is by no means "stable" and "self-reliant."

Anyone who understands the mentality of radical Islam could have predicted what happened in Iraq, beginning as soon as the last American soldier departed. President Obama, by refusing to allow American troops to remain as a stabilizing force – and a deterrent to any attempted invasion by ISIS from Syria – created a vacuum that the jihadists filled with impunity.

+   *Acquiescence.* In 2003, Muslims were permitted to build a controversial mosque in Grenada, Spain. The Spanish, as you might imagine, have a particularly sensitive history regarding the Islamic Conquests, because the nation was dominated by the Moors for centuries. At the time, a BBC report gushed that the mosque "heralds a new dawn for the faith in Europe," and mosque spokesman Abdel Haqq Salaberria agreed, stating "It will act as a focal point for the Islamic revival in Europe." [102]

Earlier in these pages, I described what the words "Islamic Revival" meant in my Cairo medical school. Construction of this historic mosque under these circumstances, especially after 9/11, was perceived by Islamists as Western acquiescence, a concession – even a retreat – and the act prompted more violence. Almost a year later, on March 11, 2004, al-Qaeda bombed the Madrid transit system, killing 191 and wounding more than 2,000. [103]

At first, authorities and the public suspected that the Basque separatist group ETA was responsible. The Spanish demonstrated by the millions against the Basque group, but when the truth emerged that al-Qaeda was responsible (i.e., Muslims), the demonstrations stopped at once. Shortly thereafter, Spanish Prime Minister Jose Aznar and his Partido Popular, or People's Party, lost the general elections. Aznar had supported President George W. Bush and the Iraq War. The new Prime Minister Jose Zapatero, of the left-wing Spanish Socialist Workers' Party, withdrew his country's forces from the war effort.

The Islamists considered Spain's retrenchment a significant victory. They built a massive new mosque and then intimidated Spanish voters into installing a weaker government willing to engage in appeasement. Yet Spain's withdrawal from Iraq failed to protect the country from again becoming the target of an Islamist plot. Later in 2004, 32 jihadists were arrested for planning to bomb the National Court in Madrid. [104]

The message here could not be clearer: When Westerners make concessions, such as installing weaker governments or withdrawing from combat zones, the actions only embolden the jihadists.

Something else should be evident from the Spanish actions: Western behavior is not the primary reason for jihadist atrocities and has little bearing on their recruitment efforts. This has been evident for some time. Back in 2004, French Muslims rioted in large numbers in 274 French cities. The riots lasted 20 days, during which 8,973 cars were firebombed, 126 police and firefighters were injured and one person was killed. Damage was estimated at 200 million euros. [105]

A smaller repeat of the riots occurred in 2007. In both cases the French media, government, academics and Islamic groups made every effort to blame factors other than Islamism. Rioters were called "youths," underprivileged immigrants or victims of segregation – anything but

Muslims. The apologists apparently did not recall that farther back, in the 1990s, Islamists in the Algerian Civil War engaged in acts of terrorism that ended the lives of tens of thousands of their fellow countrymen.[106]

Even earlier, in the 1980s, the Iran-Iraq War cost hundreds of thousands of lives, Sunni versus Shia, but all inflicted by Muslims on Muslims. [107]

In view of these facts, how can anything Western governments or societies do be blamed for expansion of the rolls of jihadists?

Nor can we blame economic hardship imposed on Muslims in Western countries. The French rioters received government benefits and enjoyed a standard of living typically higher than could be found in their ancestral homelands. The rioters, who were often chanting "Allahu Akbar," were the beneficiaries of extensive French efforts at appeasement. The French government had never supported the invasion of Iraq by the United States and never sent troops. French political leaders criticized the "cowboy" foreign policy of President George W. Bush at every opportunity. It scored them no points.

What's more, as Bat Ye'or describes in her seminal work, *Eurabia: The Euro Arab Axis*:

> *The existence of unassimilated Muslim enclaves – called banlieue*
> *in France – originated in large part from explicit non-assimilation*
> *agreements between the European Union and Islamic countries.* [108]

We can expose the real cause of the riots in France using straightforward logic. If non-Muslims living in France under the same socioeconomic circumstances had participated in the riots to the same degree as Muslims, then it could be concluded that the problem was likely related to socioeconomic circumstances. Non-Muslim participation in the riots was virtually nonexistent; therefore Islamism underpinned the protests.

+ *Denial.* Why don't we hear about violence occurring to the same degree among other immigrant minorities living in the West, particularly religious minorities? Why is there a tendency to riot and commit other violence only among the people who follow the dictates of mainstream Islamic teachings?

These are critical questions for all Western governments to ask and answer. Indeed, they are questions the governments should have been investigating for the past two decades, as the stream of Muslim immigrants has steadily proceeded. Most haven't, however, and as a result

serious problems have arisen in many democratic nations. Call it mis-
placed tolerance or even fearful denial; whatever, it has enabled jihadists
to enter secular democratic states and propagate violent Salafist beliefs.

Take Canada, which since the 1970s has allowed steady immigration from Islamic states. The immigrants are treated well. They receive
healthcare and welfare benefits. Like the French, the Canadians did not
support the Iraq War and did not send troops. Nevertheless, in June 2006
authorities broke-up a 17-person Islamic terror cell. The conspiracy had
plotted to assassinate the prime minister and blow up a variety of government targets. [109] The jihadists had accumulated three metric tons
of ammonium nitrate, nearly a ton more than was used by Timothy
McVeigh in the horrendous Oklahoma City bombing of 1995. [110]

When the London subway attacks occurred in July 2005, the terrorists who had conducted the barbaric acts had not sneaked into the country like the 9/11 hijackers. This bunch was homegrown; they were born,
reared and educated in the United Kingdom. Yet authorities and the
media pushed the idea that the young Muslims had turned into jihadists
because they had each visited Pakistan, where they ostensibly had been
trained in al-Qaeda camps. The Brits simply could not believe that children of Pakistani descent educated in England could be inculcated with
Islamist ideology and become suicide bombers. [111]

What the British did not seem to comprehend was that from the
standpoint of creating and developing jihadists, physical training camps
are not as important as ideological breeding grounds. The budding
young terrorists did not need to travel to Pakistan, because mosques
in England were already inspiring hatred from the likes of Abu-Hamza
al-Masry, who preached for years before being convicted of inciting
hatred and then was extradited to the United States for his part in several
terror-related plots. [112]

In 2007, an undercover investigation conducted by British television
exposed disturbing evidence of Islamic extremism at several important
mosques and Islamic institutions in the country, including an organization that had been praised by Prime Minister Tony Blair. Secret video
footage revealed, among other things, Muslim preachers exhorting their
followers to prepare for *jihad*, to beat women who did not wear the *hijab*
and to create a "state within a state." Many of the preachers, the investigation found, were linked to Saudi Wahhabis funding a number of
England's leading Islamic institutions. Their mosques sold books calling

for the beheading of lapsed Muslims, for constraining women indoors and for prohibiting interfaith marriage. And the preachers spewed similarly inflammatory injunctions to their charges. [113, 114]

England's knee-jerk reaction in the wake of the bombings was to blame another country. But the conclusion was ridiculous on its face. If years of British education could not dissuade young Muslims from becoming jihadists against a few months spent in an Islamic country, then perhaps England needs to question the effectiveness of its education system.

+ *Unwise immigration policies.* If we allow this form of teaching to infiltrate the minds of young Muslims under the guise of religious or ethnic tolerance, we shouldn't be shocked when the fruits of Islamist teaching emerge, full-blown, in Western society. I'm speaking not only of terrorism but of other forms of brutality such as rape, which commentator Andrew C. McCarthy calls "the unspoken epidemic of Western Europe." [115]

Because of the rape epidemic, quiet Scandinavia is quiet no longer. In Denmark, three-quarters of all rapes are committed by immigrants, almost entirely Muslim. Likewise, in Norway, where Muslims constitute only 2 percent of the population and (as in Denmark) almost the entire immigrant community, more than half of all rapes in Norway were committed by immigrants. [116]

Among Norwegian immigrants there is a severe problem with arranged, usually forced, marriages. In an article for the *Christian Science Monitor*, Bruce Bawer noted:

> *There are, naturally, no statistics on forced marriages in Norway. But HRS's [Oslo-based Human Rights Service] figures for henteekteskap, or "fetching marriages" – in which one spouse is "fetched" from the other's ancestral country – are startling. Between 1996 and 2001, 82 percent of Norwegian daughters of Moroccan immigrants who got married, married Moroccan citizens. For Norwegian daughters of Pakistani immigrants, the corresponding rate was 76 percent.* [117]

In the Netherlands, the government has introduced measures to curb importation of spouses. When artist Theo Van Gogh was murdered for his film *Submission*, it was because Muslims had become enraged at the Dutchman's stand against Islamist practices such as forced marriage. Author and activist Ayaan Hirsi Ali received constant death threats in response to her criticisms of Islam's treatment of women and was forced into hiding even while serving as a member of the Dutch Parliament. She eventually emigrated to the United States. [118]

Back in 2004, Dutch intelligence published a report, "From Dawa to Jihad," which estimated there were 50,000 potential jihadists in the Netherlands at the time, that the number of jihadists was growing, that the country was ill-prepared to manage the problem and that the Dutch Islamic community showed low resistance to Islamist infiltration. [119]

A decade later, things had not improved and in some ways had gotten worse. In late 2014, Dutch intelligence estimated that 130 of the country's citizens – including some former members of the military and even a few teenagers – had gone to Syria to fight with ISIS, and thousands more Dutch Muslims were seen as sympathetic to the jihadist cause. "It's a time bomb in our society," said Geert Wilders, a member of the Dutch Parliament who is known for his outspoken opposition to the Sharia movement in the Netherlands. [120]

It would be exhausting to itemize every single example of unwise (and sometimes absurd) Western immigration policies, but suffice it to say that similar difficulties and potential crises have arisen in Sweden, Belgium and Germany, as well as Australia, Thailand and elsewhere. When properly implemented, immigration is a good thing. Immigrants contribute monumentally to the success of a nation – indeed, they are essential. It is only when nations fail to be judicious about whom they let in and how they administer immigration that the problems begin. And once the problems develop, particularly with Muslim communities prone to Sharia and constantly indoctrinated by Salafism, they can be astonishingly difficult to resolve.

Weak Military Responses

The failure of the Western nations to address the growing threat of radical Islam lies not only in their words and domestic policies but also in their geopolitical decisions and, particularly, military responses. Western foreign policies have at times been disastrously wrongheaded. Worse, military responses have typically been absent, half-hearted, superficial, ineffective or excessively delayed.

It's important to distinguish the weak responses of U.S. foreign policy regarding terrorism in recent years from the Leftist contention that American foreign policy is an understandable motivation for Islamism.

Islamism and terrorism are never – under any circumstances – natural, logical or justified. The question is not whether U.S. military involvement in the Middle East is the source of Islamic terror but whether the U.S. military has attacked the problem with sufficient force and determination.

Let me declare here that my analysis of U.S. policies and attempts to confront Islamism are not partisan. Every U.S. administration that has faced the problem of Islamic radicalism (with the notable exception of Thomas Jefferson's, but that's another story) has made errors in dealing with this threat – some of them grievous. But if we are ever to learn from our mistakes, we must be objective.

What we know now, in hindsight, is that Islamism and terror have been permitted to grow and fester throughout the world while Western nations have juggled political and economic priorities they deemed more pressing. Only since 9/11 has the West realized how much of an existential threat radical Islam has become.

Modern Islamism is not a recent development; it has intensified steadily since the 1970s during various shifts in Western leadership. But the single event that perhaps ignited the current Islamist wildfire was President Jimmy Carter's mismanagement of the Iranian Revolution and the resulting hostage crisis in 1979. It began when Islamic radicals, headed by the Ayatollah Ruhollah Khomeini, deposed the Shah of Iran.

It sounds inconceivable now, given Iran's sponsorship of terrorism, its hegemony in the Middle East and its relentless pursuit of nuclear weapons, but for many years the relationship between the United States and Iran remained exemplary. In 1964, President Lyndon Johnson said, "What is going on in Iran is about the best thing going on anywhere in the world." [121]

True at the time, but just as Egyptian presidents Nasser, Sadat and Mubarak discovered to their dismay, the Shah of Iran found it impossible to wipe out Islamic jihadists – in his case the Shia variety. Eventually, opposition to the Shah grew so fierce that he was forced to leave the country – a moment when the United States, even if it couldn't prevent the Shah from being deposed, should have embraced him as a steadfast and longstanding ally.

But Jimmy Carter reacted badly. Even though Carter invited the Shah to the White House in 1977 and called Iran "an island of stability," his support for the Shah faded quickly. Carter spoke out frequently about the Shah's human-rights behavior, he began conditioning U.S. aid on changes in Iranian policies and, in an ill-fated move, he withheld covert payments to selected *mullahs* – who immediately switched sides and began calling for the Shah's removal. [122]

When Islamists drove the Shah from the country, Carter then refused to grant him a visa to receive medical treatment in the United States. Then, when radicals overwhelmed the U.S. Embassy in Tehran and took 52 of the staff as hostages, Carter condemned the act but otherwise did nothing. Five months later, when he finally authorized a rescue of the embassy personnel, the attempt failed. Carter rightly accepted responsibility, but he doubled the failure by refusing to order additional rescue attempts. Khomeini allowed the hostages to return to America, but only in January 1981, or 444 days after the embassy siege, and only because of fear of retaliation by incoming President Ronald Reagan. [123]

That might have been the end of the story. But the ordeal of the American hostages in Tehran did not go unnoticed among those involved in radical Islam. The episode sent two unmistakable messages: 1) that the United States would, under sufficient pressure, abandon its friends and allies, and 2) the United States that had defeated Nazi Germany and crushed Imperial Japan had somehow lost its willingness to engage enemies with sufficient force to defeat them utterly. America perhaps had become a fair-weather friend, an untrustworthy partner in any endeavor.

Who would not be wary of depending on America when agreements and governments had been jettisoned so easily, such as President Carter had done with the Shah? Moreover, who among radical Islamists would not be encouraged to think that the American government and its military would hesitate in the face of aggression?

Carter's indecisiveness spawned those questions.

In the wake of the U.S. embassy takeover, according to columnist and security analyst Amir Taheri, Iran's Ayatollah Khomeini had expected a swift and forceful response from the White House. But Carter surprisingly equivocated. His representative at the United Nations, Andrew Young, even referred to Khomeini as "a 20th-century saint" and begged the ayatollah to show "magnanimity and compassion." [124]

Also, the botched rescue operation could not be kept from world audiences, as footage of crashed helicopters appeared on newspaper front pages and TV screens. As a result, America's humiliation deepened, and Islamist exhilaration exploded – temporarily at least, until the nervous Iranians released the hostages one hour after Ronald Reagan was inaugurated, on January 20, 1981.

Some say the hostages were released because Carter had brokered a deal with the Iranians, in which the United States agreed to unfreeze $8 billion in Iranian assets and swore never to intervene in Iranian affairs. In a 2001 retrospective, CBS News sneered that it was Reagan's "Lucky Day." [125]

But an examination of Reagan's campaign speeches and his firm actions as governor shows clearly that the *mullahs* had something to fear from a Reagan administration. In Reagan's acceptance speech for the Republican nomination, he declared:

> *Adversaries large and small test our will and seek to confound our resolve, but we are given weakness when we need strength, vacillation when the times demand firmness. The Carter Administration lives in a world of make-believe, every day, drawing up a response to that day's problems [and] troubles, regardless of what happened yesterday and what'll happen tomorrow. But you and I live in a real world, where disasters are overtaking our nation without any real response from Washington. This is make-believe, self-deceit and, above all, transparent hypocrisy.* [126]

That Reagan's assertions were accurate was confirmed, even at the time, by political adversaries who agreed with him. For example, Democrat Senator Patrick Moynihan of New York stated that Carter was "unable to distinguish between our friends and our enemies, he has essentially adopted our enemies' view of the world." [127]

Reagan was able to distinguish friend from foe, but unfortunately, while he performed well in fostering the collapse of the Soviet Union, his record against radical Islam was, in many ways, as unsatisfactory as Carter's. His troubles started with the American involvement in the Lebanese Civil War in 1982, after he ordered U.S. Marines to Beirut to help the multinational force quell the conflict. The decision proved disastrous. On April 18, 1983, the U.S. embassy in Beirut was destroyed by a suicide bomber, killing 57. [128]

Only after five months – the same interval required for Jimmy Carter to mount a response to the Tehran embassy takeover – did Ronald Reagan finally order a military action, with the battleship U.S.S. New Jersey lobbing automobile-sized shells at rebel positions. [129] A few days after that, on October 23, a truck bomber rolled past a guard post and detonated his explosives outside a barracks housing hundreds of U.S. Marines, killing 241. A similar attack that day on a French military barracks killed 58 more. [130] The terrorist group Islamic Jihad [131] took credit, and significantly this particular attack was backed by Iran. In a telephone interview, the group claimed:

> *This is part of the Iranian revolution's campaign against imperialist targets throughout the world. We shall keep striking at any imperialist presence in Lebanon, including the international force.* [132]

The Free Islamic Revolutionary Movement was able to identify the bombers, but later investigations suggested that another organization backed by Iran was responsible: Hezbollah ("Party of God"). After some indecision about how to respond, the multinational force, including American troops, withdrew entirely from Lebanon. The Reagan administration had left the attacks on the embassy and the Marine barracks unpunished, giving the jihadists another unmistakable impression that they could act with impunity.

A second American administration had accomplished nothing and made the problem of Islamism much worse. In December 1983, the Islamic Dawa Party, an Iraqi terrorist organization also known as al-Dawa, in conjunction with Islamic Jihad set off a series of bombs in Kuwait that foreshadowed the modus operandi of al-Qaeda: simultaneity and close coordination. The terrorists hit the American and French embassies and attempted to attack Kuwait International Airport as well as an oil refinery, an electric plant and a U.S. corporation. There were only six fatalities, resulting from the driver of a truck failing to approach the chancellery building. Again, the United States did little to retaliate, while the Kuwaitis commenced a massive roundup of suspects, resulting in the imprisonment of al-Dawa members. [133]

In reaction to this imprisonment, Hezbollah took 30 Westerners hostage in Lebanon, including several Americans.

The terror incidents of 1983 marked the beginning of the Islamists' war against the United States. They also marked a nearly decade-long campaign by Hezbollah and associated groups to take Western hostages, particularly Americans. Those incidents resulted in many deaths and injuries, and the hostage-taking ended only after many Islamist prisoners were exchanged, and Syria and Iran guaranteed Hezbollah's continued existence. More pertinent to this discussion, few if any of the incidents were resolved or punished by American military retaliation. [134]

The list goes on. When civil war broke out in Somalia among Islamic warlords, millions of innocents were caught in the crossfire. Somali agricultural production was destroyed, leading to wholesale starvation. The international community began to send large quantities of food and supplies, but up to 80 percent was stolen by the warring factions. Some 300,000 Somalis lost their lives to famine, and as the humanitarian crisis deepened, a multinational force was sent in to protect the delivery of aid. Inevitably, military operations were directed against the warlords who were interfering with food distribution. [135]

In October 1993, President Bill Clinton sent a coalition force consisting mostly of U.S. troops, but also including Pakistani and Malaysian soldiers, against a Somali militia headed by Mohamed Farrah Aidid in the capital of Mogadishu. In the course of one battle, Aidid's men shot down two Blackhawk helicopters, isolating the men they were carrying and forcing them to fight their way out. In the process, one Pakistani, one Malaysian and 18 Americans were killed among the grounded troops and their rescuers, and 73 were wounded. Estimates vary for Somali casualties, but combined militia and civilian dead and wounded were estimated at as many as 3,000. [136]

Clinton's response, after an uproar at home, was to withdraw U.S. forces by April 1994. Once again, Islamists had won a propaganda victory, and the jihadists saw the American Great Satan as a paper tiger, lacking resolve and staying power. The Somalia episode was particularly damaging, because Osama bin Laden had helped finance and train Aidid's forces. This was confirmed by bin Laden himself during an interview with CNN reporter Peter Arnett in 1997. [137]

Without question, the American withdrawal from Somalia was not only a victory for Islamists but also a triumph for al-Qaeda and bin Laden. Combined with al-Qaeda's first attempt to bring down the World Trade Center towers the previous year, when terrorists parked an explosives-laden truck under the North Tower, killing six and injuring over a thousand, bin Laden's terror group was on a roll. True, four of the bombers were quickly identified, rounded up and convicted, along with two more in 1997. But those arrests occurred, at least in part, because Emad Salem, an Egyptian army colonel, had warned the FBI in 1992 of the impending attack and was able to identify the suspects.[138]

What didn't seem to matter was that al-Qaeda had been directly linked to the attack. Al-Qaeda member Khalid Sheikh Mohammed financed the operation. Further al-Qaeda links were eventually established to Sheikh Omar Abdel-Rahman, aka the Blind Sheikh, who was indicted and convicted of conspiracy to commit terror for the first World Trade Center bombing. [139]

The fateful and terrible mistake was that other than apprehending some of the perpetrators, the Clinton administration took no meaningful action. It chose to treat terrorism as a law-enforcement problem rather than a grave ideological threat that needed to be eradicated. Terrorist organizations and infrastructures did not otherwise suffer, and state sponsors of terror paid no price.

The straw that should have broken the camel's back occurred in 1998, when simultaneous explosions rocked the U.S. embassies in Dar es Salam, Tanzania, and Nairobi, Kenya. The Tanzania attack killed 11 and wounded 85, while the blast in Kenya resulted in 212 dead and more than 4,000 injured. The attacks again were directly linked to al-Qaeda and, for the first time, the FBI placed Osama bin Laden on its Most Wanted list – even though by that time al-Qaeda had been murdering Americans for years and long since should have been confronted. [140]

In all these incidents, spanning nearly two decades, the U.S. response could be described as tepid at best. President Clinton lobbed a few cruise missiles at terrorist training camps in Afghanistan and at a pharmaceutical factory in Sudan. These weak and haphazard actions merely confirmed to jihadists that America posed little threat to their operations. U.S. fecklessness encouraged Osama bin Laden and al-Qaeda to prepare for the 9/11 attacks.

The Product of a Lack of Resolve

America's pitiful response to terrorism in the 1980s and 1990s can be likened to an insufficient use of antibiotics to treat an infection: It will not cure the disease and at the same time allows the emergence of resistant strains. Military responses are no different. You either conduct them in a potent and focused manner or you don't engage an enemy at all. Using insufficient power aggravates the problem, because it reveals to jihadists their enemy's hesitancy and vulnerability to intimidation.

Please understand; jihadists consider limited military responses as weakness, upon which they will seize as motivation to intensify their terrorism efforts. There is no question in my mind that if President Clinton had responded to al-Qaeda's attacks with an iron fist, the probability of 9/11 happening would have been much less. And now as then, preventative military measures are vital to protect the United States from further attacks by al-Qaeda. If not before, then after the Kenya and Tanzania attacks on its embassies – on its sovereign territory – the United States of America should have immediately mounted a relentless campaign to locate and capture or kill Osama bin Laden. It was a national security obligation.

Despite this imperative, in the fall of 2000, an unmanned Predator drone flying over an Afghan landscape snapped photos of someone whom intelligence analysts identified as bin Laden. To this day, it remains unclear why the United States did not act on that intelligence. One CIA officer said the White House wanted to capture bin Laden alive. Others contended that the Clinton administration, weakened by scandal, couldn't muster support for an attack. One general complained that military preparedness was insufficient for such an attack. [141, 142]

Regardless of the reason or who was responsible for the decision, bin Laden survived to perpetrate 9/11.

Since that horrible day, Americans – military and civilian alike – have remained prime targets of Islamic terrorism, both on American soil and abroad. Successful attacks, failed attacks and foiled attacks have been unrelenting and occasionally devastating.

A few well-known examples include:

+   In December 2001, just three months after 9/11, Richard Reid, a British citizen but avowed follower of Osama bin Laden, attempted to detonate an explosive embedded in the sole of his shoe aboard an airliner bound for Miami before he was restrained by irate fellow passengers. [143]

+   In August 2006, U.S. and British counterterrorism officials broke up a suspected al-Qaeda plot to detonate explosives simultaneously aboard 10 airliners bound for the United States. [144]

+   In November 2009, however, the jihadists drew blood. Nidal Hasan, a U.S. Army major, opened fire on his colleagues at Fort Hood, Texas, killing 13 of them and wounding 30 others before being shot himself. Though the Obama administration persisted in calling the incident "workplace violence," witnesses testified that Hasan continually shouted "Allahu Akbar" ("God is great") while mowing down his victims.

Sentenced to death for his crime in 2014, Hasan petitioned the Islamic State for citizenship. [145, 146]

+   Three days before Christmas 2009, a Nigerian named Umar Farouk Abdulmutallab attempted to blow up the airliner on which he was riding as it prepared to land in Detroit. As with Richard Reid, irate passengers subdued him and prevented him from detonating the explosives he had concealed in his underwear. The offshoot group Al-Qaeda in the Arabian Peninsula claimed credit for sponsoring the attack. [147]

+   In May 2010, Pakistan-born Faisal Shahzad parked an explosives-laden sport-utility vehicle in Times Square in New York City in an attempt to cause mass casualties. His plan was thwarted because street vendors noticed smoke coming from the vehicle and notified the police, and demolition experts were able to disable the devices Shahzad had constructed. He later told federal officials he had been trained at a terrorist camp in Pakistan. [148]

+   The worst attack since 9/11 occurred in April 2013 near the finish line of the annual Boston Marathon. There, two Chechen brothers, Dzhokhar and Tamerlan Tsarnaev, placed two bombs encased in pressure cookers. When they exploded, nearly simultaneously, the bombs killed three and injured 264, many of them maimed for life. Tamerlan was killed trying to escape from police and Dzhokhar was found guilty on 30 counts of murder and terror-related charges, and then he was sentenced to death by a jury after a brief deliberation. [149, 150]

This short list of course doesn't include the many terror attacks – against Europeans, Israelis, Africans and non-Muslims and even other Muslims – the world has experienced in the years since 9/11. In particular, it hasn't chronicled the horrific acts by ISIS in Syria and Iraq; by al-Qaeda and its affiliates throughout the Middle East, Europe, Africa and Asia; and by Iran and its puppets around the world (see Appendix 1). But the message from it all should be clear: Peace-loving people across the globe face a grave and growing threat from radical Islam.

The Problem of Moral Relativism

A central obstacle in the battle with jihadism is the West's tendency to engage in moral relativism. By this I mean placing the failings of different cultures or religions on an equal footing – assigning them equal portions of blame.

Moral relativism shows up in many places; for example, the repeated "cycle of violence" metaphor that the media apply to the Arab-Israeli conflict. Here, however, I'm talking about the moral relativism applied to fundamentalist strains of Judaism and Christianity juxtaposed with Salafism. Call it "relative fundamentalism."

As evident from their current behavior in Iraq, Muslim fundamentalist groups such as ISIS take pleasure in burning churches and killing and enslaving non-Muslims with unspeakable brutality. They also will applaud such acts even if they don't commit them, ascribing the viciousness to the glory and power of Islam. Islamic radicals are responsible for vastly higher rates of violence compared to fundamentalists of other faiths.

In contrast, Jewish fundamentalists are observant Jews who strictly follow the laws of their faith. Christian fundamentalists are those who understand the Bible literally. They might express anger or demonstrate against people who violate biblical commands about issues such as abortion or gay marriage, but except for a few notable outliers, they do not practice or accept violence. They do not engage in murdering members of other faiths. And their murder rate for those of their own faiths who lapse or convert to other religions is effectively zero.

Moral relativists argue that calls for violence appear in the Bible as well as the Quran. Yet there is a vast difference. The Old Testament does chronicle stories of wholesale slaughter and warfare against specific groups of people in a particular territory at a precise time in history, but those enjoinders are in no way regarded as calls to action in the modern age, nor were they applicable beyond very specific instructions even at that time. And the New Testament specifically condemns violence of both thought and action.

Traditional Salafi Islamic texts, on the other hand, promote fighting and murdering people at all times, everywhere, solely based on their beliefs. In other words, biblical violence took place in the past for particular motives; Islamic violence continues today, abetted by a still-thriving universal injunction that violence must continue until Islamic texts are reinterpreted.

For example, there is a huge chasm between Israel's wars of retribution against the Amalekites in the Book of Exodus, and Salafist tenets that enjoin violence now and in the future. According to non-Quranic sources of Salafi Islam, Prophet Muhammad said,

I have been ordered by Allah to fight and kill all people (non-Muslims)
until they say, "No God except Allah."
                                        —*Sahih al-Bukhari* and *Sahih Muslim*

This *hadith* explains why Dr. Ayman al-Zawahiri declared on videotape that violence against Americans will cease only when they submit
to Islam. The Amalekite case is merely a historical event that happened
against a specific nation, but the *hadiths* of al-Bukhari enjoin war on all
infidels, for all time, if they do not submit to Islam.

That is a critical distinction in terms of defining religious fundamentalism in the Abrahamic faiths. Current teaching in both Judaism
and Christianity prohibits violence against others, while Salafi Islam
promotes many violent values, including the one mentioned above; a
review of current Islamic Sharia and jurisprudence books clearly shows
this to be the case. Therefore, equating fundamentalism among different
religions is misleading, because it ignores the enormous gulf between
Salafists and Jews and Christians.

How do Christian fundamentalists and Jewish fundamentalists compare with Islamic fundamentalists? Take, for example, the stoning of
women until death as a punishment for adultery.

Despite the fact that stoning is mentioned in the Old Testament,
Jesus was clear in rejecting this practice, and Christianity is clear in its
position not to apply it. Likewise, the mainstream understanding of
Judaism nowadays does not permit the stoning of women.

In contrast, you will not see even a single leading Islamic scholar
or preacher standing against the stoning of women in Sharia-controlled
parts of the world such as Saudi Arabia, where it is the accepted law
of the country. In Iran, stoning is also accepted. In Pakistan, it is practiced by the country's tribes, and in Somalia, it is enforced by al-Shabaab.
Boko Haram perpetrates it in Nigeria, as does ISIS in Syria and Iraq.

Why don't we ever hear Islamic organizations, either in the Muslim
world or the West, demonstrating against such barbaric punishment? If
stoning counters what Islamic fundamentalists believe, why don't we
hear from them?

In contrast, imagine if the rabbis in Jerusalem or the cardinals in the
Vatican suddenly advocated a return to some of the practices mandated
in the Torah/Old Testament such as stoning. No question, such action
would trigger worldwide condemnation.

Yet this day, in Muslim nations across the globe, stoning is not only advocated by Muslim leaders but is also practiced in areas where Sharia law applies.

Yet we hear only a deafening silence from Muslims and little or no protests from Westerners.

What does this – and let's call it what it is: hypocrisy – convey to us?

The danger of a religion's fundamentalism should be defined by the number of terrorists and barbaric acts, such as stoning and beadings, it produces. By that measure, Islamism should be considered by far the most threatening. If fundamentalism is defined by the acceptance of violent precepts, such as killing converts or essentially enslaving women, then Islamism should again be considered a much bigger threat. Don't forget; many so-called moderate Muslims accept the oppressive edicts of Sharia. Given this fact, even a moderate Muslim could be far more dangerous than a fundamentalist Jew or Christian.

Religious fundamentalism should be judged chiefly by its violent tendencies and threats against other faiths and individuals, not by how its practitioners dress or follow rituals.

I know or have met many Orthodox rabbis and devout Christians, and not one of them promotes or accepts the stoning of women for sexual immorality. On the other hand, many – if not most – of those considered moderate Muslims tacitly accept this barbaric concept. Who, then, represents the threat to civilized society?

The silence of the Muslim world about stoning in Saudi Arabia, Iran and other Sharia-governed areas clearly demonstrates a terrible problem that demands special attention. The proliferation of fundamentalist Islam has resulted in uncivilized acts throughout the world and is responsible for grievous friction between societies. Therefore, equating Salafism to Christian or Jewish fundamentalism is inaccurate and distorted. It is a difference of substance, not merely form; a difference that is qualitative rather than quantitative. The inability of multiculturalists to see – let alone comprehend – the difference makes them indirectly dangerous.

Have abortion doctors been murdered by Christians? Yes. Did Baruch Goldstein attack a mosque full of innocent worshippers? Yes. Of course, such acts are deplorable. But murdering abortion doctors, or anyone else for that matter, is universally considered un-Christian behavior. And Baruch Goldstein believed he was fighting to protect the Jewish state, not the Jewish religion. More to the point – and setting aside the issue of motivation for a moment – let's consider the sheer scale. In what reasonable way do these isolated crimes of passion compare to the 3,000 murdered on 9/11 or the thousands of barbaric terror attacks conducted by Islamists around the globe on a near-daily basis? (Appendix 1)

Progressives often object to restrictions placed on Salafist incitement under the banner of freedom of speech. They claim it's impossible to determine which speech should be restricted and which should be permitted. But it isn't impossible; it's only that progressives seem to be unable to recognize a sensible definition of the word "wrong" because of their moral relativism. Any reasonable individual can understand the difference between speech intended to cause physical harm to others and speech that is not. It does no physical harm when someone rejects the existence of God. But when people believe, or teach their children, that nonbelievers must convert, pay the *jizya* or be killed, that's a decidedly dangerous mindset.

Whenever speech advocates physical harm, it should be proscribed.

A Criticism of One Particular Author

Today we constantly hear members of the multicultural Left issue politically correct justifications for Islamic terror. They have often apologized for it, and some even support it, such as the attacks by Hamas on Israel. Today's halls of academia are saturated with such rubbish, and the media promulgate it daily. The battle against Islamism and Islamic terror would be difficult enough if modern, free people united against them. Unfortunately, the statements and actions of large swaths of the Left continue to pave the way for Islamist barbarity.

Examples of what I mean are so numerous, and the problem is so complex, that I can't deal with it in detail in a book of this length. What I can do, however, is analyze one individual whose writings and statements I consider typical of these views: religion writer Karen Armstrong.

Armstrong is, in my opinion, spectacularly representative of the multicultural revisionism and moral backsliding that are helping to cripple efforts at genuine reform of Islam. A former nun who now bills herself as a "freelance monotheist," she writes frequently about Islam and has become a celebrity among multiculturalists and especially the media. Salon.com once hailed her as "arguably the most lucid, wide-ranging and consistently interesting religion writer today." [151]

Ms. Armstrong's positions on radical Islam are longstanding. In a 2002 PBS interview, she acknowledged that Islamic textbooks need improvement but insinuated that Christian Sunday school books were just as bad.

Christians have got to change their textbooks. I'm still shocked by the way the Pharisees are presented in some school textbooks, giving children a very distorted notion of Judaism. [152]

Do Christian textbooks advocate the killing of Jews and the annihilation of Israel? Do they brand Jews the sons of apes and swine? Can Ms. Armstrong differentiate between events that happened in the past and Islamic books that *currently* promote killing Jews and dehumanizing them in our modern times? Apparently not.

In the same PBS interview, she asserted that Islam is "profoundly in tune with the whole American and Western ethos" and that

The heart of Islam beats with the heart of the American people. The passion that Islam has for equality – Islam is one of the most egalitarian religions I know and has always lived out its egalitarianism. It's at its best historically when it has had egalitarian forms of government, and [it is] unhappy with authoritarian forms of government, as it has now. That's one of the reasons Islam is unhappy, because it has a lot of despots and bad government and tyrannical government, some of which are supported by the United States and the West generally. [153]

This is a gross distortion of both history and modern reality. Yes, it is true that Islam, at least in theory, is not supposed to make distinctions among believers in the God of Abraham. But in reality, Islam makes hugely non-egalitarian distinctions between believers in Islam and non-believers, whom in Islamic societies are known as *dhimmis*. They are forced to pay the *jizya* and live as second-class citizens. This form of Islamic teaching is not just a historical reference; it is currently what all Sharia advocates demand.

The egalitarianism of which Ms. Armstrong speaks, if it ever existed, does not explain why *dhimmis* used to live under extreme discrimination during the Islamic Caliphate. The following were the conditions to which non-Muslims were subjected as decreed by the second Islamic Caliph, Umar ibn al-Khattab: [154, 155]

Al-Uhda Al-Umareia

> Christians shall not build, in cities or in their neighborhood, new monasteries, churches, convents, or monks' cells, nor shall they repair, by day or by night, such of them as fall in ruins or are situated in the quarters of the Muslims.
>
> Christians shall keep their gates wide open for passersby and travelers. They shall give board and lodging to all Muslims who pass their way for three days.
>
> Christians shall not give shelter in their churches or in their dwellings to any spy, nor hide him from the Muslims.
>
> Christians shall not teach the Quran to their children. [156]
>
> Christians shall not manifest their religion publicly nor convert any Muslim to it. They shall not prevent any of their kin from entering Islam if they wish it. [157]
>
> Christians shall show respect toward the Muslims, and they shall rise from their seats when Muslims wish to sit on them.
>
> Christians shall not seek to resemble the Muslims by imitating any of their garments such as the qalansuwa (the turban), footwear, or the parting of the hair. They shall not speak as Muslims do, nor shall they adopt their kunyas (nicknames). [158]
>
> Christians shall not mount on saddles, nor shall they gird swords nor bear any kind of arms nor carry them on their persons.
>
> Christians shall not engrave Arabic inscriptions on Muslims' seals.
>
> Christians shall not sell fermented drinks.
>
> Christians shall always dress in the same way wherever they may be, and they shall bind the zunar (kind of belts) round their waists.
>
> Christians shall not display their crosses or their books in the roads or markets of the Muslims. They shall use only clappers in their churches very softly. Christians shall not raise their voices while crying when following their dead. [159]

Is this what Ms. Armstrong calls "egalitarianism?" She continued in the interview:

> People who talk about the need for Islam to have a reformation, as we did in the 16th century, show a great ignorance of Islam and the Protestant Reformation. Islam has had a constant series of reformations; you can trace most of them right back to the 13th, 14th century,

even before. They went back to the basics, got rid of all recent accre-
tions, and tried to get back to the original spirit of Muhammad, just
like Luther and Calvin. [160]

For a moment, let's indulge her assertion that Islam has gone through small reformations. If so, what has been the result? Whatever the reforms, the world has seen an explosion of Salafism and Islamic terror. And if that has happened, shouldn't a far more sweeping reform be necessary?

Generally speaking, the Reformation in Christianity resulted in a religious system that respects human rights. No Christian churches – or Jewish congregations, for that matter – promote killing people for converting, or beating women to discipline them, or stoning them to death for having extramarital sexual relations. In contrast, the outcome of what Ms. Armstrong calls reformation in Islam is a system that condones the killing of apostates, promotes the beating and forced marriage of women, and justifies stoning them to death for sexual immorality.

If this system does not need reformation, what does?

Ms. Armstrong's assertions would be correct only if the majority of Muslims were followers of true Sufi Islam. But in reality, most Islamic educational institutions and mosques promote Salafi Islam, which, as I have illustrated repeatedly, needs significant reformation.

One gets the sense that Ms. Armstrong conceives of Islam almost entirely in terms of the Quran. In the PBS interview, she did not use the word *hadith*, and she claimed that terrorists are "not ordinary Muslims … who hear the basically peaceful message of the Quran." That "bedrock message," she asserted, is equality and sharing of wealth.

I am not suggesting that a non-Muslim cannot write with authority about the Quran. But such statements ignore a critical fact: With the exception of the faith as practiced by a few sects, Islam consists of far, far more than the Quran.

Salafists employ passages in the *hadiths* and the *fiqhs* (Islamic jurisprudence) that are perverted and violent. Moreover, sects that reject the *hadiths* and look only to the Quran are persecuted. I was once a member of such a group. Known as the Quranics, one of its leaders, Dr. Ahmed Subhy Mansour, was expelled from Al-Azhar University for being a Quranic. Another, Mahmoud Muhammad Taha, was judicially murdered in Sudan for his unorthodox Quranic views. Judging Islam solely on the Quran – as Ms. Armstrong appears to do – is an uneducated, primitive and superficial approach; many of the problems in Islam are based on non-Quranic sources such as the Sunnah, the prescribed way of life for Muslims; and the Sira, the biography of Muhammad.

Perhaps most frustrating is Ms. Armstrong's characterization of terrorists:

> *These were odd Muslims, and if they can break a Muslim law like drinking, then they can break other laws, too, like the law against killing innocent people and committing acts of terror. Richard Reid, the British shoe bomber, was a convert to Islam, and his imam in South London said they had to exclude him from the mosque because he came in saying, "Find me a jihad." Here was somebody who joined up because he wanted a fight. Similarly, an Australian boy picked up in Afghanistan at the same time as John Walker Lindh – they were drifters. They went from one group to another and finally ended up in Islam. These are not ordinary Muslims who go regularly to the mosque, who hear the basically peaceful message of the Quran. These are people who are spoiling for a fight, who are angry, who are not living good Muslim lives in other respects and are not characteristic of the Muslim people as a whole.* [161]

To put it bluntly, Ms. Armstrong's presentation of terrorists is rife with flaws. For one thing, she fails to understand the concept of *taqiyya*, or deceiving the enemy. That is why the 9/11 hijackers drank alcohol and went to strip clubs. According to Sharia, such acts did not make them bad Muslims if they did so to mislead unsuspecting communities by masking their true intentions.

Worse, Ms. Armstrong suffers from the common fallacious assumption by the Left that *jihad* proves attractive only to the aimless or the downtrodden. When she called John Walker Lindh, the young American who was captured while fighting for the Taliban in 2001, a "drifter" – apparently a poor, forlorn fellow who had little other choice than to get mixed up with jihadists – her characterization reflected the more recent assertion by a U.S. State Department spokeswoman that ISIS could be dismantled if the West merely found jobs for the vicious group's fighters. [162]

Message to Ms. Armstrong: The jihadists are well funded, both in equipment and personal income, to support their terror campaign around the globe. And they rely on extensive ideological bedrock rooted in Salafism. We can no more generalize about the personal circumstances of jihadists from the pathetic example of Lindh or gauge the pervasiveness of Salafism because an *imam* excluded Richard Reid from his mosque than we can use Ms. Armstrong's spiritual evolution to categorize the nuns of the world.

Islamic terrorist leaders are not – repeat, not – isolated outcasts. For the most part, they are educated, skilled, dedicated men like Ayman al-Zawahiri, the jihadist who recruited me; the medical doctor who successfully built Jamaa Islamiya and now runs al-Qaeda.

What is perhaps most disturbing about Ms. Armstrong's claims is that they are cloaked in proclamations against bigotry – against the popular straw man known as Islamophobia. But it is not bigotry for Westerners to be deeply concerned about Islam as they encounter it today, nor is it bigotry to criticize Islamic teaching. Indeed, without doing so we cannot combat Islamism.

On the contrary, criticism of Salafists is having a positive and demonstrable impact. When British teacher Gilliam Gibbons was released from her Sudanese jail cell in 2007, it was because of Western pressure. [163] When Saudi King Abdullah pardoned the victim of gang rape of a decreed penalty of 200 lashes, he was responding to worldwide outrage. [164] And when Miriam Ibrahim, a Christian and an American citizen, was finally released from Sudan – along with her newborn baby and her older child – that outcome likewise was due to a worldwide demand for her freedom.[165]

Experience has shown that concerted efforts to criticize and publicly embarrass Islamic regimes can curb some of the least-civilized practices of Salafism. But by playing down the widespread nature of those practices or indulging in moral equivalence, Karen Armstrong has made the problem worse. She has made reform more difficult and actually interfered with efforts by Westerners that have yielded results, however small.

Efraim Karsh, head of Mediterranean Studies at King's College, University of London, wrote a scathing review of Armstrong's book, *Muhammad: A Prophet for Our Time*. Among other criticisms, Karsh cited Armstrong's comments after 9/11:

> *Muslims have never nurtured dreams of world conquest ... They had*
> *no designs on Europe, for example, even though Europeans imagined*

that they did. Once Muslim rule had been established in Spain, it
was recognized that the empire could not expand indefinitely. [166]

This is nothing short of an absurd rewriting of history. If Muslims never dreamed of world conquest, what on earth were they doing in Spain, 3,000 miles from Mecca?

Karsh had this to say about Ms. Armstrong's book:

[It is a] thinly veiled hagiography, depicting the prophet as a
quintessential man of peace, "whose aim was peace and practical
compassion" and who "literally sweated with the effort to bring
peace to war-torn Arabia;" an altruistic social reformer of modest
political ambitions, whose life was "a tireless campaign against greed,
injustice, and arrogance" and who founded "a religion and cultural
tradition that was not based on the sword but whose name – 'Islam' –
signified peace and reconciliation." [167]

I might even agree with Ms. Armstrong's characterization of Prophet Muhammad if Islam were reformed, but this is not how Muslims have portrayed the Prophet in non-Quranic sources. In several instances, he is shown to have exterminated the Jewish Qurayza tribe and taken their women as sexual slaves.

Yet Ms. Armstrong claims:

[T]he Qurayza were not killed on religious or racial ground ...
Muhammad had no ideological quarrel with the Jewish people. [168]

It is another example of presenting a false history. Her assertion actually contradicts the traditional Islamic history books, which make it abundantly clear that Umar ibn al-Khattab, the second Islamic Caliph, expelled all Jews from Arabia based on instructions from Muhammad to cleanse the Arabian peninsula of other religions. Notably, Umar was one of only 10 Muslims promised entry into Paradise by the Prophet.

Ms. Armstrong continued:

Later in the Islamic empires, Jews would enjoy full religious liberty
and anti-Semitism would not become a Muslim vice until the Arab-
Israeli conflict became acute in the mid-twentieth century. [169]

It is true that there have been some periods in history when Jews enjoyed more freedom in Muslim lands than in Europe; most notably during the Abbasid Caliphate from the late 8th century until the mid-13th century, a time generally regarded as the Golden Age of Islam. But even during this epoch of relative security, Jews in Muslim lands were always second-class *dhimmis*, living under threat of pogroms and oppression at any moment. Here is a description of typical events from those times:

> The apostle of Allah [Prophet Muhammad] imprisoned the Qurayza
> in Medina while trenches were dug in the market-place. Then he
> sent for the men and had their heads struck off so that they fell in
> the trenches. They were brought out in groups, and among them was
> Kab, the chief of the tribe. In number, they amounted to six or seven
> hundred, although some state it to have been eight or nine hundred.
> All were executed. One man turned to his people and said, 'It matters
> not! By God's will, the children of Israel were destined for this massa-
> cre!' Then he seated himself and his head was struck off. [170]

Accordingly, the notion that anti-Semitism was not a "Muslim vice until the Arab-Israeli conflict" is preposterous.

And a Political Transposition

As we can see, the Left is contributing to the Islamist catastrophe by giving an intolerant ideology the chance to infiltrate the Western world under the banners of cultural tolerance and freedom of religion. These apologists defend the rights of Islamists – and their devotion to Sharia law – despite their disdain for our legal foundations, particularly the U.S. Constitution.

It's puzzling. I would have expected the progressive movement to be the first to stand against Islamic teaching, which promotes polygamy, beating women and stoning them to death, and murdering gays. Instead, I constantly see feminists and gay-rights activists standing against Christians attempting to practice their faith, against Jews fighting to protect their homeland from Islamist attacks and against political conservatives attempting to prevent the spread of Sharia in the West. Meanwhile, the Left is supporting and even blessing the proliferation of mosques, Islamic schools and Islamic libraries in the Western world.

Have these people forgotten that the precious liberal values of freedom and human rights we enjoy today did not result from peace talks or mutual give-and-take with barbarians or monarchs. The Western democracies won and saved their freedom militarily by defeating tyrants. No one could have put a stop to Hitler or the Japanese imperialist ambitions with negotiations or interfaith dialogue. It was the humiliating military defeat of Nazi Germany and Imperial Japan that made room for change in their educational and political systems and thus precipitated their transformation into peace-loving societies.

We have reached such a historic crossroads once again, where we must choose between free societies and Islamism. Hold no illusions; the two systems cannot exist together peacefully. If we permit Sharia law to gain even a toehold within our society, we will be permitting the most repressive system on Earth to thrive.

You might argue that if we limited the freedom of Salafists we would be equally as intolerant. But the difference is vast. Our democratic societies today promote values that respect life and liberty. Salafists promote values of slavery, inequality and hatred of life – indeed, radical Islam as promoted by Salafism extols the glories of martyrdom, particularly of dying while killing the infidel.

This is not rocket science. Progressives in their misguided passion for tolerance are extending that concept to tolerating cultures of brutality while suppressing courageous and righteous anti-Islamist voices. Look at what happens any time Ayaan Hirsi Ali attempts to speak at college campuses, those supposed sanctuaries for freedom of expression and ideas, particularly political ideas. [171, 172]

Such behavior among our intellectual elites betrays a glaring ignorance. As an analogy, tolerance for Islamism – and intolerance for its critics – is the opposite of the body's immune system. The immune system shows tolerance to normal cells in order to preserve the health of the body. That same immune system, however, wages war on cancer and infectious cells. When the immune system wins, the body survives; when it loses, cancer or fatal infections prevail.

Sometimes, tolerance and attempted dialogue are not the proper responses. Both failed to stamp out slavery in America, for example. Tolerance and dialogue likewise failed to contain Hitler's ambitions, let alone produce in him a change of heart. War succeeded in both cases; horrible, all-out war, because there was no alternative. Evil cannot be tolerated if peace is the goal. And today, as throughout history, these acknowledged virtues of tolerance and dialogue are useless against those who have no interest in tolerance or dialogue, such as those fanatically devoted to their Salafist interpretation of Islam. I repeat; tolerance and attempted dialogue are useless where Islamists are concerned. They only promote the slow suicide of free societies.

I am by no means dismissing the goal of reforming Islam and bringing about a true, peaceful understanding of its texts. What I am arguing, based on my long personal experience with this subject, is that progressives who make excuses for Islamists are pursuing a very dangerous course. They claim that Islam is peaceful without providing official Quranic interpretations that stand clearly against the violent edicts of Sharia law. As long as Salafists have progressives in their corner, many Muslims will continue to reject human rights and modernity, and millions of peace-loving people will continue to suffer.

Perhaps most tragic, Islamic writings can be interpreted in a manner that encourages peace and tolerance. But it is untrue to claim that the currently predominant way of teaching Islam promotes these values. Muslims desperately need a theologically rigorous reinterpretation of Islamic texts to bring about reformation. Insisting that there is nothing violent in today's mainstream Islamic teaching will only create more obstacles to reform.

If Westerners think Islam, as it is taught today, is fine, what incentive is there for Muslims to reform their faith?

We now see a transposition of traditional roles, where those typically branded as conservatives have moved to the forefront of the war against Islamism, while those who identify themselves as progressives are enabling the spread of Islamic terror. We must unite to protect ourselves, our freedoms and the next generation of Muslims from the devastating effects of Salafism.

NOTES

81. IslamisPeace.org/uk

82. "Muslim 'peace' adverts launched," BBC News, October 1, 2007.

83. "Boar to be restored to city park," BBC News, July 8, 2004.

84. Mark Steyn, "Making a pig's ear of defending democracy," *The Telegraph*, April 10, 2005.

85. I had tremendous respect for Pope Benedict for showing such genuine desire for peace.

86. Harry de Quetteville, "Statue attack fuels fears of an Islamist Egypt," *The Telegraph*, June 18, 2006.

87. Ahmed Rashid, "After 1700 years Buddhas fall to Taliban dynamite," *The Telegraph*, March 12, 2001.

88. "ISIS burns 1,800-year-old church in Mosul," Al Arabiya News, July 20, 2014.

89. "ISIS destroys 7th-century church, historical mosque in Iraq's Tikrit," RT.com (Russian Television), September 25, 2014.

90. Philip Ross, "ISIS Destroys Christian Churches in Iraq, Replaces Crosses With Islamic State Black Banner," *International Business Times*, March 16, 2015.

91. Muna Fadhil, "Isis destroys thousands of books and manuscripts in Mosul libraries," *The Guardian*, February 26, 2015.

92. Kareem Shaheen, "Isis fighters destroy ancient artefacts at Mosul museum," *The Guardian*, February 26, 2015.

93. "Alabama chief judge ordered to remove ten commandments monument," ACLU news release, November 18, 2002.

94. Robert Spencer, comment on "Minnesota college to install facilities for Muslim daily prayers," DhimmiWatch.org, April 12, 2007.

95. David McCabe, "Indiana's Memories Pizza reopens after gay rights furor," *The Hill*, April 10, 2015.

96. Ethel C. Fenig, "Religious bakery owners refuse to bake a gay wedding cake; liberal media yawns," AmericanThinker.com, April 4, 2015.

97. Neville Chamberlain, "Peace for Our Time," September 30, 1938.

98. National Churchill Museum, "World War II" quotes.

99. Beenish Ahmed, "Attacks in Denmark, France Stoke Fears of Rising Anti-Semitism in Europe," ThinkProgress.org, February 17, 2015.

100. Linton Weeks, "Fonda Reprises a Famous Role at Peace Rally," *The Washington Post*, January 28, 2007.

101. Remarks by the President and First Lady on the End of the War in Iraq, December 14, 2011.

102. "Mosque signals Muslims' return to Spain," BBC News, July 10, 2003.

103. "2004 Madrid train bombings," Wikipedia.org.

104. Giles Tremlett, "Spain arrests eight over plot to bomb court," *The Guardian*, October 20, 2004.

105. "2005 French riots," Wikipedia.org.

106. "Algerian Civil War," Wikipedia.org.

107. "Iran-Iraq War," Wikipedia.org

108. Bat Ye'or, *Eurabia: The Euro-Arab Axis*. New Jersey, Fairleigh Dickinson University Press, 2005.

109. "2006 Ontario terrorism plot," Wikipedia.org.

110. "Oklahoma City bombing," Wikipedia.org.

111. "London bombers: Key facts," BBC News, July 21, 2005.

112. Ray Sanchez, "Radical cleric Abu Hamza al-Masri sentenced to life in prison," CNN, January 9, 2015.

113. Jamie Doward, "Revealed: preachers' messages of hate," *The Observer*, January 7, 2007.

114. "Undercover Mosque," Wikipedia.org.

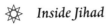

115. Andrew C. McCarthy, "Islamic Supremacism and Rape," *National Review*, October 28, 2014.

116. Mark Steyn, "Battered Westerner Syndrome inflicted by myopic Muslim defenders," *Jewish World Review*, August 23, 2002.

117. Bruce Bawer, "A Problem with Muslim Enclaves," *Christian Science Monitor*, June 30, 2003.

118. Sam Harris and Salman Rushdie, "Ayaan Hirsi Ali: abandoned to fanatics," *Los Angeles Times*, October 9, 2007.

119. Manfred Gerstenfeld, "Radical Islam in The Netherlands: A Case Study of a Failed European Policy," *Jerusalem Issue Brief*, Vol. 4, No. 14, Jerusalem Center for Public Affairs, January 2, 2005.

120. Anna Holligan, "Dutch grapple with jihadist threat," BBC News, August 22, 2014.

121. Slater Bakhtavar, "Jimmy Carter's Human Rights Disaster in Iran," AmericanThinker.com, August 26, 2007.

122. Ibid.

123. "Iran hostage crisis," Wikipedia.org.

124. Amir Taheri, "America can't do a thing," *New York Post*, November 2, 2004.

125. "Reagan's Lucky Day – Iranian Hostage Crisis Helped The Great Communicator to Victory," CBS News, January 21, 2001.

126. Ronald Reagan, "1980 Republican National Convention Address," American Rhetoric.com.

127. Noemie Emery, "The Muse of Malaise," *The Weekly Standard*, July 5, 2004.

128. "1983 United States Embassy bombing," Wikipedia.org.

129. "U.S.S. New Jersey (BB-62)," Wikipedia.org.

130. "1983 Beirut barracks bombing," Wikipedia.org.

131. Here we see the word *jihad* again. The group is not to be confused with the Palestinian and Egyptian radical organizations of the same name; they are Sunni.

132. Maya Shwayden, "U.S. Embassy Attacks and Bombings: A Recent History," *International Business Times*, September 11, 2012.

133. "1983 Kuwait bombings," Wikipedia.org.

134. "Lebanon hostage crisis," Wikipedia.org.

135. "Somalia Civil War," GlobalSecurity.org.

136. "Battle of Mogadishu (1993)," Wikipedia.org.

137. Peter Arnett, interview with Osama bin Laden, CNN, 1997.

138. "1993 World Trade Center bombing," Wikipedia.org.

139. Ibid.

140. "1998 United States embassy bombings," Wikipedia.org.

141. David Ensor, "Drone may have spotted bin Laden in 2000," CNN, March 17, 2004.

142. Lisa Meyers, "Osama bin Laden: missed opportunities," MSNBC Nightly News, March 17, 2004.

143. "2001 shoe bomb plot," Wikipedia.org.

144. John Ward Anderson and Karen De Young, "Plot to Bomb U.S.-Bound Jets is Foiled," *The Washington Post*, August 11, 2006.

145. Ned Berkowitz, "Dem Blames 'Political Correctness' for Fort Hood 'Workplace

Violence' Controversy," ABC News, May 7, 2013.

146. Cheryl K. Chumley, "Fort Hood shooter Nidal Hasan petitions to be 'citizen' of Islamic State," *Washington Times*, August 29, 2014.

147. "Umar Farouk Abdulmutallab," Wikipedia.org.

148. "2010 Times Square car bombing attempt," Wikipedia.org.

149. "Boston Marathon bombings," Wikipedia.org.

150. Milton J. Valencia and Patricia Wen, "Tsarnaev guilty on all counts in Marathon bombings," *Boston Globe*, April 8, 2015.

151. Dave Welch, "Karen Armstrong, Turn, Turn, Turn," Powell's Books Blog, October 10, 2006.

152. "Karen Armstrong Interview," PBS, September 13, 2002.

153. Ibid.

154. For more detail, see "Pact of Umar," Wikipedia.org.

155. See also my posting, "Understanding Radical Islam," at TawfikHamid.com.

156. Because Christians are considered unclean in the view of many Muslims.

157. At the same time, Muslims can convert Christians to Islam and may kill any Muslim who converts to Christianity by Redda (apostasy-related) law.

158. Because Muslims look at Christians as inferior to them so, in their view, the inferior is not allowed to emulate the superior in dress or name. This mirrors the Islamic teaching that slave girls are not allowed to wear the *hijab* while free women must.

159. Raising the voice in a special manner and uttering special expressions to communicate grief are part of Egyptian culture since the time of pharaohs. They are pre-Islamic, as it were.

160. "Karen Armstrong Interview," PBS, op. cit.

161. Ibid.

162. Kendall Breitman, "State Dept. spokeswoman: 'We cannot win this war by killing them,'" Politico.com, February 17, 2015.

163. "'Teddy bear' teacher leaves Sudan after pardon," NBCNEWS.com, December 3, 2007.

164. "Qatif rape case," Wikipedia.org.

165. "Meriam Yahia Ibrahim Ishag," Wikipedia.org.

166. Efraim Karsh, "The Perfect Surrender," *The New York Sun*, September 25, 2006.

167. Ibid.

168. Ibid.

169. Ibid.

170. Ibn Ishaq, *Sirat-a-Rasul* (the earliest biography of Prophet Muhammad), page 84, translated and posted online by USIslam.org.

171. Daniel Gelernter, "Allah and Woman at Yale," *The Weekly Standard*, September 29, 2014.

172. Richard Perez Pena and Tanzina Vega, "Brandeis Cancels Plan to Give Honorary Degree to Ayaan Hirsi Ali, a Critic of Islam," *The New York Times*, April 8, 2014.

CHAPTER 5

Toward Islamic Reformation

Obstacles to Reformation

The Salafists have established a system that suppresses any attempt to reform Islam meaningfully. Those who would change the teachings are threatened with Hell. Those who actually alter Salafist teachings are declared infidels (*kafireen*); they are not only destined for hellfire but also eligible for destruction in this life. Salafists threaten reformers with Redda law – a component of Sharia that justifies killing Muslims who convert or depart from accepted doctrine. Examples of Islamic reformers who were murdered based on Redda law include Dr. Farag Fouda in Egypt, who was killed June 8, 1992, after a *fatwa* of apostasy was issued against him; Dr. Rashad Khalifa in the United States, who was stabbed to death January 31, 1990, at his Tucson, Arizona, mosque; and Muhammad Taha in 1985 in Sudan.

Salafists also teach that violent Islamic texts are fundamental to the religion. Muslims worry that Islam might disintegrate if reformed; they learn to see the religion as a house of cards that can collapse if touched. Thus, resistance to reformation becomes instinctive. Reformers and their families are almost guaranteed to be boycotted or threatened by the local Muslim community, and Salafists have waged unceasing doctrinal warfare on Sufi and secular Muslims.

For example, when Sufis visit shrines to ask for blessings, Salafists proclaim them infidels and idolaters, based on the following verse:

Whereas those whom you invoke instead of Him do not own so much as the husk of a date-stone! If you invoke them, they do not hear your call; and even if they could hear, they would not (be able to) respond

to you. And (withal,) on the Day of Resurrection they will utterly
disown your having associated them with God. And none can make
thee understand [the truth] like the One who is all-aware.

[Quran 35:13-14]

Secular Muslims are branded as infidels as well:

Those who do not judge with Allah's law are Infidels (or Idolaters).

[5:44]

The use of these representative verses by Salafists has deterred many young Muslims from following Sufi or secular paths. Many Muslims have therefore come to believe that Salafist teachings are the only accepted version of Islam. This unmitigated intimidation has paralyzed the thinking process in the Islamic population; Muslims are afraid to challenge Salafism and its violent injunctions.

Information, Transmission, Perception

In the abstract, we can usefully conceptualize the obstacles to reformation on three levels: information, transmission and perception. When we say "information," we mean the ideas and interpretations that are specifically being conveyed. In other words, it is the ammunition, or doctrine of reformation, with which Muslims can arm themselves to make them resistant to violence. But reformation will be obstructed at the information level if it lacks a rigorous theological foundation for true peace and tolerance. Our job is to construct that rigorous foundation.

When we speak of "transmission," we mean the mechanism by which ideas of reformation are conveyed. Even if a reformer possessed a rigorously peaceful interpretation of Islam, he would need to transmit – to convey – that doctrine in order to educate other Muslims. Obstacles to transmission include physical threats from Salafists and the lack of a dedicated medium of communication – for example, a television or radio network, or a publishing company willing to risk capital on the project.

By "perception," we mean the way in which a doctrine of reformation is perceived by the Muslim community. A reformer could have a rigorous doctrine and he could have a well-functioning mechanism of transmission, but he would still face negative perceptions of his new interpretations.

As I stated above, many Muslim communities believe any new approach that contradicts traditional teachings will cause Islam to disintegrate. If they assist the disintegration of their faith, Muslims will face eternal damnation. So, to avoid hellfire they reject any new doctrine. You could use the finest technological tools to transmit information, but the transmission will fail if the receiver is not operating. Merely because a television channel or radio network or printed publication exists does not mean its intended audience will watch or listen or read.

Some years ago, the U.S. government began funding a multimedia effort to win the hearts and minds of Muslims: the Alhurra television network, Radio Sawa and Hi Magazine. The success of the effort is questionable at best. The three media provide information, and for the most part accurate information, but the stigma of Western funding, and the fear of faulty Quranic interpretation, has ensured these initiatives cannot achieve a major perception breakthrough among Muslims around the world.

In order to bring about a reformation of Islam, we need to address all three levels of resistance: perception as well as information and transmission. If we fail to address any one of these components, the attempt will fail.

Inadequate Criteria for Virtue

One obstacle to reform that operates on the perception level is worth singling out for comment: The commonly understood criteria for being a "good Muslim" are based on empty ritual rather than on firm, moral justification.

It's widely believed that a Muslim who fulfills the Five Pillars of Islam is virtuous. The pillars are 1) accept no God but Allah and Muhammad as his Prophet, 2) pray five times each day, 3) fast during Ramadan, 4) give alms to the poor, and 5) perform the *hajj* (pilgrimage to Mecca). Unfortunately, these pillars are mainly rituals.

As a result, Muslims watch jihadists behead someone on videotape and still perceive those jihadists to be good Muslims because they follow the Five Pillars. This inadequate test for goodness explains in part why so many Muslims fail to criticize or demonstrate against Islamism and Islamic terror. Deep in their minds they believe Islamists cannot be bad Muslims because they perform the superficial rituals. It's one reason why we never see truly serious *fatawa* against terrorists by Islamic scholars.

If the moral structure of a Muslim's worldview were built on humane values, rather than on ritual, it would help pave the way to a more peaceful Islam. In itself, the obsession with the Five Pillars is strange, because the concept can be found nowhere in the Quran; it is mentioned only in the *hadiths*. On the other hand, injunctions to virtuous, moral behavior are indeed available in the holy book. But the positive injunctions are not currently considered a main foundation of the religion.

Lack of a Peaceful Theological Foundation

Given the fierce devotion Salafists display toward their faith and the interpretations provided by their *imams*, you might assume that all Muslims possess a strong understanding of the theology of Islam.

But you would be wrong. It pains me to state it, but both Sufi and secular Islam are weak in their theological foundations. When Sufi or secular Muslims are challenged about why they prefer nonviolence, why they recommend a peaceful path, they lack recourse to the doctrinal bedrock in Islam that Salafists enjoy.

The Sufi belief system relies on an individual's spiritual condition rather than a literal understanding of Islamic writings. Sufis believe the Word of God needs no interpreter, and the believer does not require an explanation of Quranic verses. Each believer must endeavor to understand the religion via personal, subjective experience with God. Consequently, Sufi masters do not preoccupy themselves with written explanations (*tafsir*) of the Quran that convey peaceful understanding.

Sufism might be attractive to many, but it suffers from the defect of theological imprecision. The result is that Sufi and secular Muslims find it difficult to resist their Salafist counterparts. For example, a young Muslim could be confused by the following Quranic verse:

Slay the Infidels wherever you may come upon them. [9:5]

If he asks three different Islamic scholars – Sufi, secular and Salafi – to interpret the passage, the Sufi scholar might offer, incredibly, "Love everybody and be kind to all people," essentially saying, "Don't take this literally; behave as a civilized person." Most likely, a young Muslim would find this pronouncement unsatisfying and insist that the verse explicitly enjoins him to kill infidels everywhere.

The Sufi cleric tries again. "You will understand the significance of the verse on the Day of Judgment – Allah wants you to love everyone."

Still dissatisfied, the young Muslim approaches a secular Muslim, who responds, "I'm not sure; my understanding of Islam is that we are a religion of peace."

Next, he approaches a Salafist, who utilizes ample material from authorized Islamic textbooks that justifies – and commands – violence against non-Muslims.

Because the Sufi and secular Muslims lack a powerful theological base, the young Muslim more often than not is attracted to Salafism, because the Salafist can back up his claims with direct quotes from the Quran.

Rigorous Hatred

Because the hatred and violence espoused by Salafism contains a strong supporting body of doctrine, this version of Islam has become mainstream. Salafism is the default doctrine in most if not all Islamic schools, mosques and universities today.

As we mentioned at the start, Islam comprises, from a doctrinal perspective, several components, including:

+ The Quran – the Word of Allah
+ The *hadiths* and the Sunnah – the words and deeds of Prophet Muhammad
+ The exploits of the Sahaba – the disciples of the Prophet
+ The *fiqhs* – the schools of Islamic jurisprudence
+ The *tafsir* – the commentaries on the Quran

You might expect, then, that if a verse in the Quran enjoins violence, other components of Islam would counterbalance it with a peaceful interpretation or limit the scope of the verse to its period of history. The sad reality is non-Quranic components do not properly offset violent verses and, in fact, supplement their violent nature.

Take, for example, the following:

Fight those who believe not in Allah nor the Last Day, nor hold that forbidden which hath been forbidden by Allah and His Messenger (Muhammad), nor acknowledge the religion of Truth (Islam), [even if they are] of the People of the Book (Christians and Jews), until they pay the Jizya (Humiliation Tax) with submission, and feel themselves subdued. [9:29]

The Quranic passage is supported by a *hadith*:

Narrated Ibn Omar, Prophet Muhammad said, "I have been ordered
by Allah to fight and kill all people (non-Muslims) until they say, "No
God except Allah."
　　　　　　　　　　　—*Sahih al-Bukhari* and *Sahih Muslim*

It is also supported by the Sahaba. One such disciple was Umar ibn
al-Kattab. He declared many wars against Jews and Christians in order to
subjugate them to Islam. You might recall Caliph Umar's official decree:

Christians shall not build, in cities or in their neighborhood, new
monasteries, churches, convents, or monks' cells, nor shall they repair,
by day or by night, such of them as fall in ruins or are situated in the
quarters of the Muslims.

This declaration is considered legitimate and valid by most – if not
all – Islamic authorities today.

The problem is not only that various *hadiths* and Sahaba support violent verses in the Quran, but the *tafsir* or commentaries likewise invali-
date the peaceful verses. This technique is called abrogation. It relies on
the fact that Prophet Muhammad, as mentioned in many Islamic books,
revealed verses at different times, and the peaceful verses were revealed
in the earlier Mecca period when Muhammad lacked the strength to
declare war. Later, in Medina, Muhammad gained the power to do so,
and he revealed verses that were violent. Salafists use the chronology to
insist the later, violent verses cancel the earlier, peaceful ones.

In Arabic, "abrogated" is known as *mansukh*. I will never forget
when I presented a peaceful verse of the Quran to my Salafi friend Adel
Seif. I had viewed him as a mentor, but when I showed him a verse that
permitted Muslims to stop hating Jews and Christians, his immediate
comment was that my verse was abrogated by the Sword verse in Quran
9:5. His response was not, strictly speaking, his own; it is the traditional
view of Salafists.

Abrogation allows Salafists to deceive non-Muslims into believing
Islam is a religion of peace. To non-Muslims, Salafists present the peaceful verses. To their own flock, they present the violent verses and teach
that they abrogate the peaceful ones. Therefore, Islam could be the religion of peace only if Muslim scholars provided a theologically rigorous
doctrine that stands unambiguously against violence and hate. Until
such Islamic scholars do so, the problem of violent Islam will remain
with us.

How to Reform Islam

How *do* we reform Islam? Obviously, it won't be easy. Changing the mindset of more than a billion people is a monumental task. But as the ancient Chinese philosopher Lao-tzu once said, in paraphrase, a journey of a thousand miles begins with a single step. To fight and defeat the violence of Salafism, we're going to need a series of steps:

+ *Deemphasize non-Quranic writings.* Many of the violent tenets in Islam are not sourced in the Quran but in secondary writings. These writings are not the Word of God. Therefore, we can ease the task of reforming Islam into a peaceful religion if we rely on the Quran more and deemphasize or even reject many of the non-Quranic texts. For example, Redda law dictates that apostates must be killed. But Redda law is not rooted in the Quran. By objecting to Redda law as an earthly authority, scholars could diminish the theological justification for killing apostates. Other common punishments in Islam, such as stoning women or killing homosexuals, likewise are never mentioned in the Quran. If we jettison or revise Islamic texts that advocate these punishments, Islam will become more humane.

+ *Reexamine the hadiths.* We should also pay special attention to a reconsideration of the *hadiths*. The Sunnah, the deeds of Prophet Muhammad, were written down in the *hadiths* long after his death and therefore must be demoted as an authority. Modern-day scholars are free to reevaluate the *hadiths* for accuracy. We could introduce new evaluations, perhaps calling them the Guaranteed Hadiths, versions that show the peaceful, virtuous words and deeds of Muhammad. Because the *hadiths*, as with other non-Quranic writings, are not the literal Word of Allah, they can be filtered and packaged anew, just as the scholars of old did when they compiled them.

Relying solely on the Quran is not sufficient to make Islam peaceful, however. The Muslim holy book also contains violent passages, so it requires a different technique for interpretation because it is the revealed Word of God. We cannot cancel or jettison a *sura* (chapter) or *ayah* (verse). Abrogation is permissible only because the peaceful verses chronologically precede the violent ones. But first we need to revise and reevaluate the non-Quranic writings to establish a precedent of reform, so new ideas can penetrate the religion more easily. Today, reformers are suppressed; they fear for their lives when they offer an interpretation that departs from traditional tenets, because in doing so they risk being labeled apostates.

+ *Preach the importance of* 'al' *('the')*. Now I'm recalling a line of dialogue in the movie *Lawrence of Arabia*, uttered by the character Dryden, played by Claude Rains: "Big things have small beginnings." In context, Dryden is implying that by commissioning a small Bedouin army to fight the Turks, the course of World War I in the Middle East might be turned. And it was – though repercussions from that conflict are echoing through the region to this day.

For our purposes, there is a small beginning that could have enormous implications in reforming Islam. It's a technique to limit the violent verses that neither cancels nor abrogates them but limits their scope to the historical period within which they were revealed. And we can do it rigorously – it is not a subjective notion. The key is the simple, two-letter Arabic word "*al*," or "the." It might seem like legalese or formal criticism. It isn't; it's legitimate and profoundly important.

"The" is a definite article that refers to something specific. When "the" is absent, the object of a statement is universal; when it is present, it refers to a specific subset of a collection. Here's an analogy: You have dinner in a white house, or you have dinner in *the* White House – two widely different circumstances indeed. Applied to the word "infidel" in the Quran, the definite article "*al*" means specific targets that existed only in Prophet Muhammad's time period and location.

For example, *mn kafar* means "infidels" in the universal sense, while *al-kafireen* means "the infidels" – the specific infidels referred to at the time. Thus, there is a big difference between killing *mn kafar* and killing *al-kafireen*.

The Quran never employs the universal article "*mn*" in reference to wars against non-believers but almost always employs "*al*."

Consider the following verse:

Slay the Infidels wherever you may come upon them. [9:5]

A Muslim who interprets the verse without considering the definite article may join a jihadist organization believing he must kill all infidels. On the other hand, if he had been instructed all along to heed "*al*" strictly in its historical context, he would no longer be permitted to kill nonbelievers. I have explained how these verses played a key role in my indoctrination process as a jihadist. If "*al*" had been universally observed back then, it would have dramatically weakened any injunctions to brutality.

Following are examples of Quranic verses that jihadists employ to incite violence and murder. But as you can see, they all use "the":

The Infidels are your sworn enemies [Quran 4:101]

Make war on the Infidels who dwell around you [9:123]

When you meet the Infidels in the battlefield, strike off their heads
[47:4]
*Muhammad is the Apostle of Allah, and those who are with him are
strong against the unbelievers.* [48:29]

Prophet, make war on the Infidels [66:9]

Never be a helper to the disbelievers [28:86]

Kill the disbelievers wherever we find them [2:191]

*Therefore, when you meet the Infidels (unbelievers), smite their necks
until you overcome them fully, and then tighten their bonds; but
thereafter [set them free,] either by an act of grace or against ransom,
so that the burden of war may be lifted.* [47:4]

It is amazing that this vital emphasis on the word "the" – an emphasis that can mean the difference between life and death – is not available in any approved *tafsir* of the Quran. I am convinced, however, that if Islamic terrorist leaders like Dr. al-Zawahiri or bin Laden had been taught the Quran with this emphasis, they might not have declared war on non-Muslims.

Perhaps Islamic terrorism would not even exist.

Two letters can indeed make a considerable difference – a small beginning leading to a great thing.

+ *Promote the Relativity of the Quran.* In the Quran there are verses that Salafists quote to justify abrogation. Reinterpreting these verses will ease the transition to a non-violent Islam. Doing so will allow young Muslims to contemplate the whole religion in the shadow of the peaceful verses instead of the opposite.

Muslims are permitted by Allah to follow the verses that better suit their point in history and disregard others that do not. When modern laws and Islamic law conflict, as is the case with severe physical punishment, Muslims can apply modern judgments about human rights to resolve the impasse. The Quran permits Muslims to exercise discretion to follow more peaceful verses.

And follow the better of (the Quranic verses) revealed to you from your Lord. [39:55]

We might call this preference for certain verses over others the Relativity of the Quran. It provides essential flexibility to Muslims who practice a peaceful version of the faith, one that lives in harmony with other faiths in civilized societies.

The Relativity of the Quran encourages Muslims to think at the concept level rather than the literal level. For example, a literal understanding of the Quran permits a Muslim to marry more than one wife. At the concept level, Muslims understand that polygamy applied only in the early stages of Islam and that the Quran forbids being unjust to others. Muslims desperately need conceptual thinking where the Quran is concerned as a basis for promoting values of decency.

   +   *Emphasize the humane side of Prophet Muhammad.* When I became a more dedicated Muslim, my dream was to emulate the Prophet in all of his actions. Muslims are encouraged to do so by the following Quranic verse:

Ye have indeed in the Messenger of Allah a beautiful pattern (of conduct) for any one whose hope is in Allah and the Final Day, and who engages much in the Praise of Allah. [33:21]

Following in the footsteps of the Prophet is the ultimate target of most if not all devout Muslim men, and Muhammad can be a positive role model. Many of his traits, as described in numerous verses of the Quran, are worthy of emulation. For example, Muhammad was instructed to assist his enemy during war if the latter became helpless:

If one amongst the Pagans (during the war) ask thee for asylum, grant it to him and give your hand of help to him, so that he may hear the word of God and then assist him to reach where he can feel secure and safe. [9:6]

Other positive aspects include:

But forgive them [the Infidels], and say "Peace! (on you)" But soon shall they know! [43:89]

If then they refused to follow you, we have not sent you as a guard over them. Your duty is (only) but to convey (the Message). [42:48] (Revelation 62)]

If they accuse you of falsehood, say: "Your Lord is full of mercy all-embracing; but from people in guilt never will His wrath be turned back. [6:147 (Revelation 55)]

Say, "The truth (Islam) is from your God": it is up to any person to follow it or not." [18:29 (Revelation 69)]

Imitating these injunctions and patterns in most circumstances produces a virtuous and peaceful outcome. Yet in Salafist books, the following Quranic verse is understood to mean Muhammad was allowed certain privileges above all other Muslims:

The Prophet has a higher claim on the believers than (they have on) their own selves, (seeing that he is as a father to them) and his wives are their mothers (i.e., not allowed to marry any other person). [33:6]

Taking this Quranic verse as a cue, the description of the Prophet in the Sunnah and *hadiths* show a much different side. I mentioned some of them in Chapter 1, but here are more. According to the classical theologian al-Qurtubi, these privileges include:

If (Prophet Muhammad) looked at a woman her husband has to divorce her and Muhammad is allowed to marry her to have sex … if he divorced a woman it is not allowed for anyone to marry her … and he was allowed to take for himself the food from the hungry and the water from the thirsty.—Tafsir al-Qurtubi, Surat al-Azhab

The Prophet married her (Aisha) when she was six years old and he consummated his marriage when she was nine years old, and then she remained with him for nine years.—Sahih al-Bukhari

According to Aisha: The Prophet engaged me when I was a girl of six (years). We went to Medina and stayed at the home of Bani-al-Harith bin Khazraj. Then I got ill and my hair fell down. Later on my hair grew (again) and my mother, Um Ruman, came to me while I was playing in a swing with some of my girlfriends. She called me, and I went to her, not knowing what she wanted to do to me. She caught me by the hand and made me stand at the door of the house. I was breathless then, and when my breathing became all right, she took some water and rubbed my face and head with it. Then

she took me into the house. There in the house I saw some Ansari
women who said, "Best wishes and Allah's Blessing and good luck."
Then she gave me to them and they prepared me (for the marriage).
Unexpectedly Allah's Apostle came to me in the forenoon and my
mother handed me over to him, and at that time I was a girl of nine
years of age.   —Sahih al-Bukhari

Imagine the impact such *hadith* verses can have on a dedicated
Muslim who insists on emulating Muhammad. The relationship of
Muslims to Muhammad and their love for him are extraordinary. This
was exemplified by the violent demonstrations of hundreds of thousands of Muslims in response to the Danish Muhammad cartoons. Their
love and obedience to the Prophet reached such a fever pitch that even
an outstanding, preeminent professor like the late Dr. Aisha Abd al-Rahman (Bint al-Shati) praised Muhammad's marriage to a very young girl
when the Prophet was 50. Here is a passage from her famous book *Nessa*
Allnabi, or *The Women of the Prophet Muhammad*:

> *And He Muhammad, Allah praise him, knew Aisha since she was*
> *in her very early childhood and he put her in the position of his dear*
> *daughter. He observed her growth and her sexual development that*
> *created attractive beauty ... and it is written in the most accurate*
> *books for the Hadith al-Bukhari and Muslim, that Muhammad used*
> *to say to Aisha when she was a child, "I have seen you twice in my*
> *dreams as someone was covered by a white dress made out of silver*
> *and I heard a voice saying to me this is your wife. When I removed*
> *the silver cover I found you, then the voice, a revelation, said to me*
> *this is your wife ... so I said since this is the will of Allah, let it*
> *happen."*

The conversation between Prophet Muhammad and Aisha is supposed to have happened before Aisha was seven. The cultural mind of
Dr. Abdul-Rahman would certainly reject the idea of marriage between
a man of 50 and a girl of seven, but the professor's extreme love of the
Prophet and fear of critiquing him – and the eternal damnation she
would receive if she did – combine to create a religious mind that suppressed her conscience.

The dilemma created by Muhammad would be much less burden-
some if we approached the Prophet in his historical and cultural context.

But that is not the case. In contrast, King David is widely criticized among Jews for his adultery and treatment of Uriah, the Hittite husband of Bathsheba. In fact, it is easy to find many Christian and Jewish writings critical of King David, but it is virtually impossible to find a devout Muslim who is willing to criticize any action of Muhammad. The result is a professor who inexorably finds herself advocating pedophilia [173] – something we hope will never be tolerated in the West under the banner of religious freedom.

The esteem for the Prophet many Muslims feel is, in many situations, even more prominent than their attachment to Allah. For instance, the reaction to the Muhammad cartoons was much more global and violent than reactions have been to acts of Quran desecration. This love for Muhammad could be partially due to the concept of *al-shafaa*, or "the intercession." That is, when some Muslims go to Hell by the order of Allah (on Judgment Day), the Prophet might intercede with Allah on behalf of a sinner so the sinner may enter Paradise. Therefore, in the subconscious of many Muslims, Allah has in fact become an oppressor figure while Muhammad has become their savior.

This conflation of roles has created a form of devotion to the Prophet that can exceed love of Allah. Love of Muhammad is why Muslims praise him with the phrase "peace be upon him" whenever his name is mentioned, while in most cases they fail to use the same phrase in conjunction with Allah. The Quran technically recommends that Muslims use praise in both cases – with Muhammad and Allah [174] – so this selectivity speaks volumes.

If Muslims followed mainly the Quranic verses instead of the *hadiths*, many of the problems related to emulation of Prophet Muhammad could be solved. Most but not all negative examples of Muhammad's conduct are not in the Quran but in books written much later. Islamic sects that reject the *hadiths* are far less conflicted and tortured, because they reject most of the stories about him not found in the Quran. Such rejection has enabled these sects to emphasize the positive aspects of Muhammad's conduct. In the alternative, it is not necessary to reject all of the *hadiths*. We can reclassify the violent *hadiths* as invalid and offer that new category I mentioned – the Guaranteed Hadiths – as peaceful alternatives. [175]

+ *Accept Jews and Judaism.* No doubt this will be a most challenging goal. Many Muslim scholars and clergy promote the notion that Jews are apes and pigs and that Muslims must kill every Jew before the End of Days. These hateful proclamations have created a serious barrier to genuine peace between Arabs and Israel. It is unlikely that any Arab child who has been brainwashed with this Jew-hatred will be able to live in harmony with Israel in the future.

Clerics attempt to justify Jew hatred by employing the Quran and the *hadiths*:

> *Shall I point out to you something much worse than this by the treatment it received from Allah? Those who incurred the curse of Allah and His wrath (the Jews), those of whom He transformed into apes and swine, those who worshipped evil – these are (many times) worse in rank, and far more astray from the even path!* [5:60]

> *The Hour will not come until the Muslims fight the Jews (and the Muslims will kill them), until the Jews hide behind the trees and rocks and the trees and rocks will say, "O Muslim, O Servant of God, Here are the Jews, Come and kill them!"* —Sahih al-Bukhari

How should we approach these two representative passages? The second citation is a *hadith*; it is not the Quran and therefore not the literal Word of God. Therefore, we are justified in calling it invalid because it was compiled and set down by Islamic scholars over 200 years after Muhammad's death.

The first citation is from the Quran, but notice the phrase "the Jews" is in parentheses. That's because the word "Jew" or "Jews" did not originally appear in this particular verse. It was added by later interpreters. So, we can combat this violent interpretation by eliminating any insertion of "Jews" we see that does not appear in the original. In other words, "the Jews" is part of a *tafsir*, a commentary. It is not sacred. Examine the verse without the hateful *tafsir* and it yields an entirely different meaning, one that does not promote Jew hatred.

Indeed, Islamic scholars have intensified hatred of Jews by adding words in parentheses to limit explicitly any instances where the Children of Israel are praised. The Saudis make freely available, to mosques around the world, translations of the Quran with these limiting *tafsir*.

Here is one such example where the clerics have added a parenthesized comment:

> *Children of Israel! Call to mind the favor which I bestowed upon you,*

and that I preferred you to all other nations (of your time period, in
the past). [2:47]

The actual verse is this:

Children of Israel! Call to mind the favor which I bestowed upon you,
and that I preferred you to all other nations. [2:47]

These changes distort the positive references to Jews in the Quran, and they have become common to most approved translations and commentary. It is incredibly hypocritical that Muslim scholars added the word "Jews" to the verse related to "pigs and monkeys," while also adding the phrase "of your time period, in the past" to limit praise for the "Children of Israel." If it is acceptable to historicize the verses, then surely we can do so with "the." If it is acceptable to add commentary, then surely we can add our own or remove existing commentary.

This typical Salafist approach to Islamic writings has amplified Jew hatred in our time to an unprecedented level. But Muslims must seek a new, peaceful relationship with the Jewish people. Most prophets mentioned in the Quran are Jews, so it is unacceptable – according to the Quran – to attack the Jews of today based on the conflicts Muhammad had with them in the 7th century. As Quran 17:15 tells us, no bearer of burdens can bear the burden of another. This is similar to the biblical injunction not to blame the son for the sins of the father.

+   *Justify good values rigorously.* Salafi scholars teach that religious freedom, gender equality and gay rights are not Islamic. Islam as it is taught today promotes killing those who leave the religion and permits beating women, polygamy and murdering gays.

When I was a member of Jamaa Islamiya with Dr. al-Zawahiri, we hated the West mainly because of its freedoms and civil liberties. We believed those fundamentals of democracy violated basic tenets of Sharia law. But looking at the Quran from a rigorous angle can make Quranic teachings compatible with human rights and provide the doctrinal justification for modern values that Muslims need.

The Quran states clearly:

Hold to forgiveness; and command Muslims to follow the "Urf" –
which is commonly accepted among mankind. [7:199]

This verse instructs Muslims to follow what is commonly acceptable among enlightened people. The words easily could be applied to accommodate human rights and the laws of secular societies.

Some Muslims feel uncomfortable applying one verse while ignoring another or rejecting a given Islamic text. But employing the Relativity of the Quran supplies the justification we need, based on the following verses:

And follow the better of what is revealed to you from your Lord.
[39:55]

Say the good news to those who worship me. Those who listen to the
Word, and follow the best meaning (Wherever it is found): those are
the ones whom God has guided, and those are the ones endowed with
understanding. [39:17-18]

They permit Muslims to prefer using certain verses because they are the "best meaning" or the "better of what is revealed" for a given stage of human civilization. They also permit Muslims to learn from other cultures and live at peace with them, minimizing the clash of civilizations.

Speaking the truth, even if it hurts, is essential. It might involve painful critiques of Muslim actions in history, such as the Islamic Conquests. But such critiques can be justified by this verse:

O ye who believe! Stand out firmly for justice, as witnesses to God,
even as against yourselves, or your parents, or your kin. [4:135]

This clearly permits the self-criticism that is a prerequisite for tolerance. And it is essential to promote the value of critical thinking in the Islamic curriculum. Once again, the Quran supports this effort:

Behold, verily in these things there are signs for those who think! [13:4]

Believing that nonbelievers will go to Hell causes Muslims to hate non-Muslim societies and paves the way toward terrorism. But the Quran commands Muslims not to be judgmental:

Then it will be for Us (only God) to call them to account. [88:25]

It is important to promote values of humanity and virtue, and to do so rigorously. The Quran can be cited effectively for this purpose – indeed, it must.

NOTES

173. That Prophet Muhammad married a girl of seven is not mentioned in the Quran itself – it is mentioned in the *hadiths*.

174. [Quran 87:1] Praise the name of your Lord (God) *and* [Quran 33:56] Send your blessings on him (Muhammad).

175. Tactical details of this strategy are beyond the scope of this book, but I would be willing to explain them to appropriate bodies.

CHAPTER 6

A Strategic Plan to Defeat Radical Islam

No single, magical solution exists to combat the problems of Islamism and Islamic terrorism. Military power alone will not solve them, and neither will education alone. Only through an efficient integration of different tactics can we hope to achieve victory in the War on Terrorism. But before we can begin, we must understand this deadly ideology. We must analyze it carefully and objectively and identify its contributing factors.

I hope this book will advance the process.

Violent Islam's proliferation in Islamic societies follows a standard pattern. The process starts with the propagation of Salafist ideology, which can be detected by seeing increasing numbers of women wearing the *hijab*. The *hijab* is both a symptom of Salafi proliferation and a catalyst for Islamism – it helps spread the ideology.

In turn, the proliferation of Salafism and the *hijab* lead to the mentality of passive terrorism. Passive terrorists, as I have mentioned, do not actually perpetrate terror attacks. They do, however, want to implement oppressive Sharia law, and they quietly lend support to active terrorists by failing to denounce them. Passive terrorists support Sharia and do not respect secular rule. They represent a real threat to any free society, because a small but significant fraction of these passive terrorists develop into active terrorists. It follows that if we can discourage passive terrorism we can decrease the number of active terrorists, thereby suppressing the number of attacks.

In addition, Islamists employ anti-American and anti-Western propaganda to incite hatred and fuel Islamization. By carefully observing Islamic communities both in the Muslim world and the West, we find beyond doubt that the production of jihadists follows the pattern illustrated here:

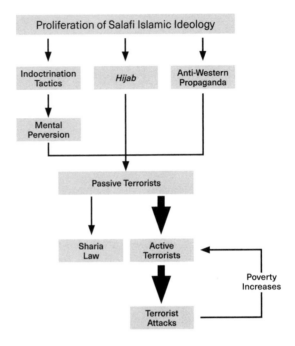

Understanding the Islamization process is the beginning from which we can devise an effective strategy to defeat it. The first step occurs at the ideological level. It involves presenting new interpretations of Islamic texts to counterbalance the violent interpretations Salafists have been promoting.

Simply omitting the violent passages from school curricula and replacing them with peaceful ones is not enough. Muslim children will learn peaceful verses at school during the day and violent passages at mosques in the evening. As we have seen, Salafists utilize abrogation to cancel the peaceful passages in the Quran. A new, rigorously peaceful foundation for Islam would limit the violent verses to their historical context, thereby opening the gate for an enlightened and updated framework.

Furthermore, we Muslims need to teach our children peace. The curricula should promote critical thinking and oppose Salafist indoctrination. Peaceful education must begin at an early age, before jihadists have the chance to reach young minds.

Allow me to speak as an expert in cognitive psychology. Muslim educators should employ proper cognitive methods to prepare the curriculum and promote values of modernity and humanity. Encouraging peaceful sects, such as true Sufis or other genuinely non-jihadist groups, will also help foster change at the ideological and educational levels.

America and the West also must play a critical role. They need to work to improve their image in the Islamic world. They need to wage counterterrorism campaigns to help disrupt the Islamization process. But any program intended to win hearts and minds must be carefully thought out and implemented.

Apologizing for military action, for example, will not do. It will only be perceived as weakness and will aggravate the problem. U.S. and Western foreign policy are not the cause of Islamic terror. But negative images of the West operate at the perception level; any improvement in those images will not stem from drastic changes in policy. Instead, the improvements must consist of sound principles of engagement and a firm, unapologetic defense of universal human rights. These changes will attract members of a culture that is on the one hand steadily self-destructing and on the other hand presenting a potentially lethal threat to the civilized world.

It goes without saying that Western governments must continue to pool information to weaken financial support of Salafi Islam and disrupt communication among Salafi propagandists. Integrating effective intelligence with ideological and psychological tactics will slow down the transformation of passive terrorists into active ones.

Only synchronized efforts on all of these fronts will decrease the frequency of terrorism.

Last, albeit unfortunately, there is little doubt that military force remains crucial to the overall success in the War on Terrorism. The Allies could not combat Nazism without defeating it first at the military level. Hitler was not overcome by peace negotiations or mutual understanding; devastating military power ended his barbaric regime and cleared a path for peace and democracy. Indeed, World War II furnishes an excellent example of the dynamic relationship between military force and ideological transformation. The major Axis partnership of Germany and Japan, which at the beginning of the war threatened global domination, suffered horrible, devastating defeats by the Allies. Yet today both countries are leading members of the family of civilized nations – because their conquerors assisted them afterward.

Hope springs eternal that tyrants will abandon their murderous tendencies through dialogue. That is, essentially, what the Obama administration apparently thinks Iran will do eventually with its nuclear program. The reality is, in the absence of economic collapse or internal revolution, tyrants must be vanquished. Educational, political and social reforms cannot take place otherwise.

Much to my disappointment, it seems the United States and the West presently do not possess sufficient military resolve. Firing cruise missiles or lobbing bombs from drones at a few terrorist targets is like using half a dose of antibiotics to treat an infection. Doing so not only fails to cure the infection but also permits resistant strains of bacteria to arise.

Nearly 20 years ago, the CIA had located Osama bin Laden in Afghanistan. President Bill Clinton had the opportunity to dispatch him, but he balked because he feared collateral civilian casualties. Because of that hesitation, bin Laden was able to plan and order the attacks on 9/11, and thousands more innocents perished than would have died in an attempt to take out al-Qaeda's leader.

Over half a century before Clinton's fateful inaction, President Harry S. Truman made perhaps the most difficult decision in history. He ordered the dropping of atomic bombs on the Japanese cities of Hiroshima and Nagasaki. Those two bombs killed 225,000 people. But because Japan quickly surrendered thereafter, the lives of as many as 1 million American soldiers and perhaps 2 million Japanese were spared – based on estimates of what a full-scale invasion of Honshu would have cost. [176]

Clinton made his decision as well, but he seemed to have forgotten that in war there are no easy moral escapes. Obsessing over the treatment of enemies often jeopardizes more lives.

In the case of jihadists, the West must deal with people who often seek their own deaths, who actually revel in taking as many infidels with them as they can. They hold no hesitation about killing anyone whom they regard as infidels or apostates; about using human shields to discourage attackers; about torturing, enslaving or killing in the most brutal ways imaginable. In dealing with such an enemy, weakness is something the West dare not display.

Where Are We Now and Where Are We Going?

The West has so far failed to defeat radical Islam and its global jihadist movement because we have been fighting the the symptoms (terrorism), not the disease itself (radicalism). In other words, we focus on fighting the Taliban in Afghanistan, for example, while we ought to be fighting radicalism in the region I call "Brainistan." As Major General Michael Nagata, U.S. Special Operations commander in the Middle East, put it:

> [The United States does] not understand the movement, and until we do, we are not going to defeat it ... We have not defeated the idea. We do not even understand the idea. [177]

Radical Islam is spreading because no government or private entity has yet devoted the necessary time and resources to fully understand – let alone counter – the radical ideology that drives worldwide terrorism, civil strife and political unrest.

Fighting Terrorism in 'Brainistan'

For more than a decade, the United States and the West have fought Islamic terrorism predominantly on the military front. Strategists have completely neglected to treat or even address the ideological and psychological foundations in the mind – in "Brainistan."

Human behavior, including acts of terror, is the result of a complex cognitive, psychological and neurological process. Fighting the underlying ideology – in this case the theology of Islam as widely practiced – is key to defeating radicalism.

The critical battlefield in this psychological war is therefore not in Afghanistan, or in Pakistan, Syria, Iraq, Yemen or Nigeria. It is in the minds of Muslims – and their apologists in the Left – throughout the world. Consequently, we must understand the constituents of the battle.

As I mentioned earlier, Islamic law arose from the five sources: the Quran, the *hadiths*, the Sahaba, the schools of Islamic jurisprudence and the interpretations of the Quran.

If we searched those sources as routinely constituted, we would discover something shocking. A literal interpretation of the Quran, along with mainstream teachings of Islam today, can easily be used to justify what ISIS is currently doing. Excusing ISIS as being "un-Islamic" is absurd. It is like calling Islam "a religion of peace" while blithely ignoring the widespread command that Muslims must fight non-Muslims to subjugate them.

The conclusion is inescapable. Current Islamic teaching is hypocritical and counterproductive. It hides the true nature of the problem and impedes efforts to solve it. The key word in the "Islamic State" – whether "in Iraq and Syria," as the group calls itself; or "in the Levant," as some in the West such as President Barack Obama refer to it – is, after all, "Islamic." The fact that IS/ISIS/ISIL commits acts of unspeakable brutality in the name of Islam without receiving universal condemnation by *imams* and Islamic scholars speaks volumes about the current state of the faith.

Yes, there are certainly many moderate Muslims in the world. But until the leading Islamic scholars provide a peaceful theology that forcefully contradicts the violent views of the Islamic State, the existence of moderate Islam must be questioned.

Enter the Campaign for Brainistan, which we also might want to call the War for the Thinking Process. Humans often draw their own distorted conclusions about history, politics and religious faith irrespective of the original intent of the written or spoken words that underpin them. The historical existence of violent radicalism, even among the followers of otherwise peaceful religious texts, points to a thinking process that contributes to this reality.

But what constitutes this process? It's a combination of traits, including absolutism, being judgmental of others, and the suppression of critical, objective thought. In the case of Islamic radicals, you have to add the components I outlined in Chapter 1:

+   Learn hatred
+   Suppress conscience
+   Desensitize violence

Fighting such psychological influences in Brainistan requires the combination of several theological and educational approaches. The media can also play a significant role. All fall under the category of behavioral modification. Decades of research have shown human behavior and actions can be significantly affected by positive and negative reinforcement. For example, when someone kicks a brick wall, the immediate pain in his leg negatively reinforces his urge to kick the wall again.

But the Campaign for Brainistan won't be so simple. Killing jihadists – which under normal circumstances we would assume provides negative reinforcement for other jihadists – is actually positive reinforcement.

To die for Allah is is their ultimate dream; it saves them from Hell and allows them to enter Paradise – and enjoy sex with dozens of beautiful, insatiable virgins.

Additional positive reinforcement was derived from female American soldiers wearing headscarves while serving in Muslim countries. The U.S. military required this in Afghanistan to show respect for the local culture. The Islamic radical mindset regarded this so-called cultural sensitivity as obeisance and a sign of Taliban victory.

We can't keep making these errors if we intend to win the Campaign for Brainistan. Failure to create genuinely effective negative psychological reinforcement for the radicals, particularly following horrific acts, will encourage them to continue their violence. If we want to be effective – and this is something else validated by lengthy research – we must impose negative and positive reinforcement immediately after an act, and that reinforcement must be clearly and unambiguously seen as the direct result of the act. Otherwise, our efforts will continue to fail.

Make no mistake; this is the overriding problem of our age. Over half a century ago, the United States faced a similar challenge fighting the Japanese, whose soldiers with few exceptions thought nothing of dying for their emperor. Imperial Japan was eventually defeated, but only because the U.S. military, after dropping atomic bombs on Hiroshima and Nagasaki – and threatening (through a calculated bluff) to drop more – engendered such primal fear among the Japanese people that Emperor Hirohito at last surrendered.

Radical Islamists represent an enemy every bit as determined as the Japanese of the 1930s and 1940s. Worse, the Islamists regard their current situation as Win-Win-Win. If they are killed, they will become martyrs who will live eternally in Paradise with Prophet Muhammad; if they achieve earthly victory they will impose Sharia law on the rest of us and joyously await the End of Days; and if they are captured by the infidels, they will be treated humanely and will find human-rights activists defending them. This is particularly true of America today, which permits captured jihadists to enjoy the temperate surroundings of incarceration at Guantanamo Bay, Cuba; to be served nutritious, *halal* meals; to pray freely five times each day; to receive legal counsel – even to play soccer on an expensive field built exclusively for their use by U.S. taxpayers.

Knowing what I know about the jihadists and their psyche, I'm sure the West's actions in recent years have provided endless entertainment for them. Do our leaders truly believe that holding news conferences, unaccompanied by powerful and punitive military responses, to denounce the attacks; encouraging weak demonstrations against terrorism; refusing to call radical Islam by its name; and making statements such as "We will bring them to justice" or that ISIS is "un-Islamic," generates any fear or hesitancy among our sworn enemies?

I can only imagine the laughter when President Obama sternly warned, during his comments in September 2014, that the United States would

> *wage a steady, relentless effort to take out ISIL wherever they exist, using our air power and our support for partner forces on the ground. This strategy of taking out terrorists who threaten us, while supporting partners on the front lines, is one that we have successfully pursued in Yemen and Somalia for years.* [178]

At this writing it is six months since the president made that statement, and during that time Yemen has fallen into the hands of Islamic terrorists backed by Iran, [179] and al-Shabaab terrorists in Somalia recently massacred 150 Christian students at Garissa University College in Nairobi, Kenya. [180]

As the Islamists – indeed, as all sane people – are well aware, redoubling the wrong approach will not bring the right results; zero doubled is still zero.

I am more and more persuaded that ultimate victory over these enemies of civilization demands truly effective psychological deterrents as well as military success.

The sad reality is that for the last 10 years Western responses to the problem, which have relied largely on incorrect assumptions, unrealistic perceptions and vain imaginations, have made things worse. Some of the responses have even benefited the radicals. For example, the U.S. government delayed giving the Egyptian army Apache helicopters to fight jihadists in the Sinai Peninsula. [181] As a result, more ISIS fighters received training in Sinai before traveling to Iraq and Syria to wreak havoc.

Another unhelpful action: Efforts by certain U.S. politicians to outlaw enhanced interrogation techniques and punish the CIA officers who conducted them have only emboldened Islamic radicals.

If Not Death, What?

We know death is no hindrance to jihadists, so threatening death is unlikely to bring them to their knees or totally diminish their barbarism. We need to construct alternative deterrents.

If we cannot defeat them just by killing them, we need to create an effective Psychological Operations (PSYOPS) program. This strategy likely has not been used because few people know the possibility even exists. Western so-called experts on Islamism can only recommend solutions they are capable of understanding. And, sadly, these experts seem to lack real insight into the minds of Islamic radicals. Even less do they perceive how the radical psyche can be undermined, manipulated and controlled.

What would an effective PSYOPS strategy look like? What, for instance, needs to be undermined?

Think about the concept of beauty. Remember, an important aspect in the development of a jihadist is suppression of the ability to appreciate beauty. Almost every radical Islamist group prohibits many forms of music and art. Islamists force women to wear bland, shapeless and colorless dresses and forbid any expression of feminine beauty. This degrading of everything lovely eventually kills an individual's ability to recognize, let alone appreciate, beauty. It isn't unlike what happens when a person is served only bland and tasteless food; over time that person loses the ability to distinguish between good and bad tastes. When this phenomenon takes hold in the minds of radicals, they no longer can see differences between beauty and ugliness. Once accomplished, radical demagogues and preachers can spew viciousness and hatred, intolerance and violence, without offending what one might call natural decency, kindness and tolerant behavior.

In the Campaign for Brainistan, the goal of transforming the minds of potential young radicals to appreciate beauty could form the basis of a PSYOPS. It would deter the terrorists from conducting more atrocities and significantly diminish the attraction of jihad in the minds of youthful Muslims. The good news is we have the technology and the capability to engage in a highly successful PSYOPS. Our lack of the willingness to use effective and available methods, however, has given the radicals the upper hand in this war.

In short, a war fought only by military combat is costly and utterly ineffective. But using psychological tactics at the mind level – in Brainistan – would be cheaper, more efficient and essential to defeating the enemy.

The Future of Islam

Since the upheavals beginning in 2010 and collectively called the Arab Spring, new movements and forces have emerged within Islam, some of them hopeful:

+   The Muslim Brotherhood – still seen as the most powerful influence within political Islam – suffered the biggest setback in its history after its miserably incompetent administration in Cairo drove millions of Egyptians into the streets in revolt. Following that defeat, and the rise of President Abdel Fattah el-Sisi, the brotherhood and its now-discredited slogan, "Islam is the Solution," have lost much of their luster.

+   The Salafists have also suffered significantly as a result of the Muslim Brotherhood's failed experiment in Egypt. Exposure by the mainstream Egyptian media of the brotherhood's bizarre teachings – centering on their rumblings about destroying the "pagan idols," aka the Sphinx and the Pyramids [182] – along with their moral corruption, hypocrisy and lack of nationalism, has turned many Muslims against these groups. Salafists are now in a difficult position, because the more they promote or practice violence, the more people will turn against them and their ideology. Some of them will join even more violent groups, but the majority is likely to focus on trying to improve Salafi Islam's image and on making its ideological beliefs more palatable. That creates an opening for the Campaign for Brainistan.

+   Following the brotherhood's political failure and the unprecedented attacks on the Islamist ideology, jihadist groups entered a stage of convulsion that has led many of them to pursue an even darker path of destruction. A last-ditch effort to – as they see it – "save Islam." These groups are still doing significant harm, such as the al-Shabaab massacre in Kenya, the anarchy in Libya, Boko Haram's continuing rampage in Nigeria and the constant flow of atrocities by ISIS. Nevertheless, we can defeat them if we fight them correctly.

One outcome of the Islamists' failure has been the rise of two major anti-Islamist movements: reformation, of which I am a part and which seeks to reinterpret the faith, and atheism, which rejects Islam altogether. The emerging reformation is abundantly evident in the unprecedented explosion of criticism of Islamist ideology. This is happening in the social media, especially on YouTube as well as in the most popular news media in the Arab world. Reformers are producing modern interpretations of the Quran, and those interpretations are spreading rapidly.

Atheism also has begun to captivate a surprising number of Muslims, to the point where some studies estimate that atheists, who previously were extremely rare in the Arab world, now number in the millions. [183, 184]

Let's be clear: There is no middle ground between Islamism and modernity. The former, represented by the Muslim Brotherhood, the Salafists and the jihadists, absolutely cannot coexist with the latter, represented by the reformists and the atheists. It's one or the other. It's this or that. It's a case of zero sum. When two forces are moving forward at different speeds, there can be middle ground. But when one moves forward and the other backward, there is no opportunity for commonality. Islam's future will be determined by which of these forces dominates the Arab street, and several factors are in play.

The first factor is suppression of Islamist activity by the authorities. It's somewhat unfortunate in principle, but history clearly shows that despite its spotty success, suppressing Islamists is far more effective at protecting a society than appeasing them. Consider Nasser's Egypt, Ataturk's Turkey, Assad's Syria or even Hussein's Iraq as distinct from, say, Anwar Sadat, who released the Islamist radicals from prison and was assassinated at their hands for his efforts.

Suppressing Islamists has also been more efficient than implementing democracy. In Afghanistan and Iraq, radical Islam has flourished since the adoption of democracy. In other words, if you hope to protect a society from Islamists, and their inevitable suicide bombers, you had best exclude them from the political process and force secularism on them.

As the record has shown, it's probably not a permanent solution. But it has worked for long periods of time.

The second factor that can affect the balance of power within Islam is the availability of the Internet. Since the Arab Spring, online social media have played a crucial role in spreading criticism of radical Islam. Call it an e-reformation. It ultimately led to the collapse of the Muslim Brotherhood and allowed many anti-Islamist groups to grow. The availability of fast and affordable Internet for young Muslims will be pivotal in shaping the future of Islam and defeating radicalism.

The third factor is the ultimate reaction of the international community to the overthrow of the Muslim Brotherhood in Egypt. So far, that reaction has not boded well. The U.S. government for months withheld aid to the Egyptian military, [185] while the Obama administration pressured Cairo to release Islamists from prison and include them in the political process.

Such behavior is irresponsible and counterproductive. It also is downright dangerous and can only make things worse. Tacit international approval empowers Islamic radicals. Look what happened in May 2015 after an Egyptian three-judge panel condemned former president Mohamed Morsi to death. Within hours of the sentence, three other Egyptian judges were shot dead in their car by unknown assailants near the city of al-Arish, Sinai. [186] Would Islamists have attempted such a terrible deed if the entire international community had united to condemn the Muslim Brotherhood's brief but oppressive rule and hail Egypt's return as a cosmopolitan society?

The fourth factor is something I call the Egypt Model. The defeat of the radical Islamic ideology in Egypt can serve to inspire other Muslim nations, especially in the Middle East and North Africa. Egypt has traditionally played a highly influential role in the Arab drama and media in the region. Egyptian President el-Sisi's unambiguous approach to confronting radical Islam at the ideological level, and his clear and repeated statements in this regard in front of the leading Islamic scholars, gives hope to the idea of reforming Islam. If the world stands with el-Sisi, this evil could end.

The fifth factor is economics. If el-Sisi's government fails to improve the nation's economy, Islamist voices might rise again. They would argue that not adhering to Sharia law caused the failure. It's distorted logic, of course, because many Sharia states have failed. Nevertheless, such claims could resonate with naive and ignorant people. The combination of economic collapse and violent Islamist ideology facilitates the recruitment of more suicide bombers and jihadists. Violence begets economic instability, which leads to poverty, which leads to more violence. Radicalism begets a vicious cycle of violence and poverty, which ends in a death spiral.

Therefore, supporting the economy of Egypt and the government of President el-Sisi at such a critical stage of history – particularly after el-Sisi has expressed such a clear and honest desire for Islamic reformation – is vital. It would ensure the success of this key player in the war against radical Islam. Egypt's leadership in weakening the radical Islamic ideology is essential not only for Egypt but also for the Middle East and the rest of the world.

To understand the delicate balance of current trends in Islam, which sooner or later will impact the entire world, we need to understand Islamic culture and the different types of Muslims.

Here is one way. It's an admittedly simplistic visual analysis of the culture using five concentric circles to represent the various categories.

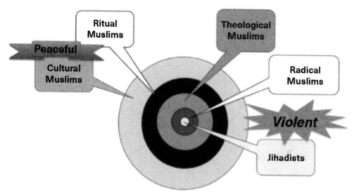

The outer circle, consisting of cultural Muslims, represents those who follow their religion in a somewhat superficial manner. They regard Islam as part of their culture, but they don't necessarily read much about their faith or practice the religion actively. Islam simply forms a framework identity for the social activities in which they engage or with which they identify.

The second circle is occupied by so-called ritual Muslims. They mainly practice the Five Pillars of Islam and oppose the violent edicts of Sharia law, such as stoning adulterers and killing apostates.

The third circle consists of theological Muslims, who study the Islamic texts in depth and are interested in implementing Sharia to replace the secular law of the land. This group can represent a major threat to the values of liberty and the stability of the free world, if their percentage exceeds a certain threshold in society.

The fourth circle comprises radical Muslims, who accept and promote using force to subjugate others to their beliefs.

The innermost and smallest circle contains terrorists, who fortunately still represent a small fraction of Islamic society but who are ready to sacrifice their lives to attack others. Their numbers are few, but they hold the potential to do major harm.

In the last few decades the trend in Islam has favored the center of these circles; i.e., more radicalism. It's probably fair to say the trend is more ambiguous now but perhaps ever so slightly outward bound. After the ascent of the Muslim Brotherhood to power in Egypt – and their rapid failure – and in the wake of ever more barbaric acts by ISIS, we have seen an unprecedented level of criticism of radical Islam and demands for reform in social media and on TV in Muslim nations. The Internet has played a major role in spreading this wave of reform.

I can somewhat illustrate this development. Two years ago, I created a Facebook page called "A Modern Interpretation for the Quran (Commentary on the Verses)" that teaches the religious text in a way that will produce peaceful coexistence between civilizations. [187] If I had created this work prior to the current wave of reform, I would have been surprised if it reached more than few hundred followers. But as of this writing, the page has accumulated more than 2.1 million "likes."

It's been gratifying. When I started my stand against radical Islam and began my attempt at reform over 30 years ago, I had only a few followers. But with the power of the Internet and the exposure of the inhumane features of *jihad* in unprecedented ways in the last few years, that huge group of people is now reading my opinions and studying my interpretation of the Quran. This is – at least in my mind – rather significant; it shows a momentum of reform that needs to be nourished in order to win the ideological battle I have described.

Who Can Solve the Problem of Radical Islam?

To answer this question let's examine the different schools of thought regarding radical Islam. Each group can play an important role in the solution.

+ *The denialists.* The first approach, which is used by many Muslims as a defense mechanism for their faith, is to deny the existence of any ideological or religious role in the problem. Denialists, as I call them, typically and stubbornly promote the view that Islam is a peaceful religion.

This approach cannot solve the problem. Denial clashes with the reality promoted in almost all of the interpretations of Islamic core texts and jurisprudence books in use today. This reality also includes declaring wars to spread the religion, killing apostates, and allowing the beating of women, polygamy and death by stoning for adultery.

In fact, denialists make things worse because Westerners tend to become angry when they recognize the reality of current Islamic teaching. No question, violent teaching exists, and it goes unchallenged by the mainstream clerics.

+   *The bashers.* These individuals see only the violent texts in Islam; its violent practices and its traditional interpretations. They conclude it is impossible to change or reform the religion. The bashers promote the view that peaceful Muslims are peaceful only because they don't follow the mainstream texts of Islam. In other words, they are peaceful *despite* their faith, not because of it.

In important ways, this is true – at least in the present context of Islam. A Muslim man who remains faithful to his wife would take more wives if he became more obedient to the mainstream interpretation of the Quran:

> *And if you fear that you will not deal justly with the orphan girls, then marry those that please you of [other] women, two or three or four. But if you fear that you will not be just, then [marry only] one of those your right hand possesses. That is more suitable that you may not incline [to injustice]. [4:3]*

For the bashers, it is probably impossible to stop their criticism of Islam until the mainstream Islamic jurisprudence and interpretation books clearly stop the discriminatory and inhumane edicts contained in Sharia law.

Bluntly stated, Islamic teaching needs to change first before asking this group to stop their criticism. The main limitation of basher thinking is that by denying any possibility of reform within Islam, they destroy any hope of finding a realistic solution. The bashers expose the problems without offering pragmatic solutions, which makes many Muslims unwilling to accept their views.

+   *The apologists.* This group blames external factors such as socio-economic and political circumstances – e.g., U.S. foreign policy – as the causes of Islamist terrorism, while they completely ignore the role of ideology.

If the apologists' view is correct, critics ask, then why don't non-Muslims who live under similar circumstances become suicide bombers? In other words, why do external factors selectively affect young Muslims and not, say, young Catholics? For that matter, why do Islamists kill, behead and dominate their fellow Muslims because of U.S. foreign policy?

Apologists tend to claim that because most Muslims are moderate people, Islamic ideology cannot be the cause of the problem. It's like saying that because the majority of cigarette smokers do not develop lung cancer, cigarette smoking can't be a significant cause. [188] Even if most Muslims are moderates, it doesn't mean Islamism is not the main cause of terrorism. [189]

+ *The idealists.* They demand that we show tolerance toward any religion for its own sake. This group fails as well, because tolerance for Islamic law means intolerance for its victims. Tolerance of Sharia means extreme and sometimes fatal intolerance for apostates, adulterous women and gays, all of whom would be killed under such law.

Idealists need to clarify their position. They must choose between tolerance for the religious rights of Muslims who practice barbaric Sharia and the religious rights – and lives – of everyone else. It is insane to tolerate both cancer cells and normal cells, because the former will kill the latter. The idealists need to distinguish between tolerating belly-dancing under the banner of cultural relativism and the stoning of women under the same banner.

Accepting the part of Islam that teaches fasting in Ramadan is completely different from accepting the teachings that promote suppression of women and justify killing homosexuals.

+ *The dishonest.* This group selectively chooses information to demonstrate there is no ideological basis for the problem of radical Islam. They use a peaceful but atypical definition of *jihad* and ignore the violent definition of the word. Every sane person who honestly researches Islamic theology and history will recognize that this approach is unscientific and misleading.

Toward a Solution

Despite their shortcomings, each of these groups can contribute to solving the problem of radical Islam. Those who deny the existence of any of its violent teachings must face the unavoidable reality that the teachings do exist, and they remain unchallenged in the mainstream Islamic books. The denialists should provide at least one, mainstream-approved Islamic text that negates and theologically refutes violent Sharia concepts. It has been encouraging to see many Muslims in the last few years beginning to confront this crisis.

As long as such an approved text does not exist, the problem will remain. Claiming Islam is peaceful without changing the violent teachings constitutes unrealistic lip service that aims at deceiving others.

Across the Arabic spectrum of media, more and more commentators are admitting that current radical interpretations in Islamic teaching need to be reformed. In fact, reformers are appearing more frequently on the most popular mainstream Egyptian and Arabic outlets. They include Islam al-Beheiry, Ibrahim Issa, Mokhtar Noah and other prominent figures.

The bashers need to continue exposing the violent teachings and practices in Islam, because exposing such texts and practices is vital to sparking a true reformation. But the bashers can also declare they have no problem with new Islamic teaching that refutes the violent edicts of Sharia and emphasizes the peaceful aspects of the Quran. This will place more responsibility on the shoulders of the Islamic scholars to change the interpretations of the violent texts – if they are truly willing to combat so-called Islamophobia.

Meanwhile, the apologists need to stop the self-flagellation. Ignoring the role of ideology impedes efforts to reform Islam. Muslims will not reform if others are telling them the cause of radicalism is U.S. foreign policy and has nothing to do with Islamic ideology.

The idealists can restrict their tolerance only to Islamic teaching that does not condone harm to other human beings. Such tolerance cannot include religious instruction that discriminates against or threatens the lives of others. The inability to make this distinction could doom any hope of reform.

The dishonest must adopt a frank and scientific approach that addresses the facts without trying to distort or hide them to serve certain agendas. This group can send a better message by acknowledging the existence of the violent interpretations and helping to foster peaceful alternatives until they dominate Islamic jargon and teachings.

Solving the problem of radical Islam requires all of us to cooperate rather than fight against one another. We have a joint responsibility to solve this enormous challenge, a responsibility that demands trust and civility by everyone, not just one of these groups. We will fail tragically if it doesn't happen.

NOTES

176. "Operation Downfall," Wikipedia.org.

177. Eric Schmitt, "In Battle to Defang ISIS, U.S. Targets Its Psychology," *The New York Times*, December 29, 2014.

178. "Statement by the President on ISIL," September 9, 2014.

179. Molly Hunter, "140 Americans Flee Yemen as Country Sinks Deeper Into Chaos," ABC News, April 13, 2015.

180. "Garissa University College attack," Wikipedia.org.

181. Julian Pecquet, "Obama administration holding up Apache helicopters to Egypt," al-Monitor.com, June 3, 2014.

182. "'Destroy the idols,' Egyptian jihadist calls for removal of Sphinx, Pyramids," op. cit.

183. Diaa Hadid, "Arab Muslims-turned-atheists: Out of the shadows and onto the Internet," *Times-Standard*, August 10, 2013.

184. "No God, not even Allah," *The Economist*, November 24, 2012.

185. Talmur Khan, "US posed to lift curbs on $1.5bn aid to Egypt," *The National*, December 13, 2014.

186. Lizzie Dearden, "Egyptian judges shot dead in Sinai hours after former president Mohamed Morsi sentenced to death," *The Independent*, May 17, 2015.

187. Facebook members, please see https://www.facebook.com/ModernQuranInterpretation?ref=hl or go to www.roh-alquran.com.

188. I am only trying to illustrate the point and do not equate Islam with cigarette smoking.

189. I define the word "moderate" here as not being a terrorist or a supporter of it.

Conclusion

As I hope you understand by now, Salafism constitutes the lion's share of mainstream Islamic theology today. It has inspired all of the Islamic violence that has inflicted one atrocity after another for decades on Western and Muslim societies alike. And it will continue to do so if we do not destroy it.

Terrorism is only a symptom, however. Salafism is the abscess afflicting the whole body of the Muslim world. Islam is not sick because of the abscess; the abscess exists because Islam is sick. If we do not understand this distinction, we will continue to treat the symptom and not the disease; the abscess will persist and become more severe. As tragic as events were on 9/11; as horrific as the killing and abduction of innocents by Boko Haram in Nigeria or al-Shabaab in Somalia; as despicable as the *mullahs* of Iran ordering their own people to be mowed down during the Green Revolution; and as heartbreaking as the Christians, Yazidis and Kurds slaughtered by ISIS, all will pale in comparison to what happens if radical Islamists get their hands on a nuclear weapon or engage in widespread chemical or biological warfare. ISIS recently declared it will seek an atom bomb from Pakistan, so at any time this nightmare could become a catastrophic reality. [190]

Though less apocalyptic than Islamic terror, the human-rights disaster represented by Sharia law remains a threat to us all. Sharia has created, in Islamic societies, an environment of constant abuse and oppression. The draconian system treats non-Muslims as second-class citizens, condones the beating and stoning of women, hangs gays from gallows solely because of their orientation, and destroys the lives and futures of young Muslims.

In the past, many in the West took comfort in the false impression that Sharia was a problem strictly for the Middle East. No longer. Muslim populations are exploding in the West, and their leaders predictably are seeking to implement Sharia and overturn the freedoms and constitutional protections of modern, democratic nations, first within Muslim enclaves but eventually and inevitably for everyone else.

Much of this effort, incredibly, is aided by the West because of the currently fashionable phenomenon of political correctness presented as religious tolerance. To put it bluntly, this is madness. It is ignorance. If we do not understand the tactics and strategy behind Islamism, we will never defeat it. We must be forceful and resolute, and we must fight creeping Sharia at every turn. We must lose our fear of offending. We must stop finding unsupportable, external justifications for terror.

The free nations of the world, led by the United States, have become beacons for liberty and civilization because they fought against slavery and discrimination – because they showed intolerance for barbaric values. Those same principles must now be applied to the violent, discriminatory precepts of Sharia.

Religious sensitivity to Muslims is actually harmful to Muslims and non-Muslims alike. Without constructive criticism of Salafist dogma, Muslims will never feel the need to reform or reinterpret it. Excessive hesitancy to expose the tyrannical edicts of Sharia is impeding the process of reformation. And Islamic reformation is needed today more than ever, no less than it was necessary for other faiths at various stages in their respective histories. Take, for example, another poll by Al-Jazeera recently, in which over 80 percent of respondents supported ISIS. [191] What more do we need to see before realizing that a devastating war of civilizations might be in prospect?

The West must stand firm, but we Muslims also have an an important role to play in the war on Islamism. We must condemn terrorists – not just terrorism – by name and oppose the violent teaching that pervades mainstream Islam. Our faith must be reformed in order to shield young Muslims against violent indoctrination. Egyptian President el-Sisi's demand of the leading Islamic scholars to undertake religious reformation has created real hope. [192] It is now possible to see such reformation unfold. Likewise, the availability of the Internet and social media can abet its proliferation.

As for myself, my own thoughts and actions are geared toward saving Islam, not destroying Islam. My goal is, and has always been, to work to save Muslims – and humanity in general – from the catastrophe of Islamism.

     With God's help, it will happen.

NOTE

190. Tom Batchelor, "ISIS in nuke boast: We can get atomic bomb 'within a year' from corrupt officials," Express.co.uk, May 22, 2015.

191. Jordan Schachtel, "Shock Poll: 81% of Al Jazeera Arabic poll respondents support Islamic State," Breitbart.com, May 25, 2015.

192. Egyptian President el-Sisi at Al-Azhar University, via YouTube (with subtitles), December 28, 2014.

GLOSSARY

9 / 11: On the morning of September 11, 2001, the deadliest terror attack in American history took place. Nineteen members of al-Qaeda, the group headed at the time by Osama bin Laden, commandeered four commercial airliners, eventually crashing them all and killing all aboard. The first two aircraft hit, respectively, the North and then the South towers of the World Trade Center in New York City. Both towers eventually collapsed, their structures weakened by the heat of tens of thousands of gallons of burning aviation fuel. Nearly 3,000 died in the towers. Then another fully fueled jetliner crashed into the Pentagon in Washington, killing 184. A fourth plane, also apparently headed to Washington, crashed in a meadow near the hamlet of Shanksville, Pennsylvania, after its passengers revolted against the hijackers. All 44 aboard died instantly when the aircraft smashed to earth at over 500 miles per hour. The Global War on Terrorism, as it came to be called by U.S. President George W. Bush, had begun.

Abbasid Caliphate: The third iteration of Islamic rule after Muhammad and founded by Abbas ibn Abd al-Muttalib – the prophet's uncle – the caliphate established the city of Baghdad in the year 762. Its reign lasted nearly half a millennium and is known as the Golden Age of Islam.

Abdel Fattah el-Sisi: A former military commander and the current president of Egypt, el-Sisi was propelled to power in June 2014 after a tidal wave of an uprising against the Muslim Brotherhood and its leader, Mohamed Morsi. President el-Sisi has since endeavored to return Egyptian society to its non-fundamentalist norm and has even urged Islam's leading clerics to undertake a dramatic reformation, resisting radical Islam and *jihad*, and establishing the faith among the world's peaceful religions.

Abu Bakr: Full name Abdullah ibn Abi Qhuhafah, he was – briefly – the first Islamic caliph. His reign lasted from Muhammad's death in 632 to the year 634, when he died of an unknown illness. Abu Bakr, as he was popularly known, was the father of the prophet's wife Aisha.

Abu Ya'la: Full name Abu Ya'la Muhammad ibn al-Husayn Ibn al-Farra, a 10th century Arab theologian and jurist of the Hanbali *madhahib*, or school of jurisprudence.

Adhab al-Qabr: The "Punishment of the Grave," in which condemned souls are tormented prior to the Day of Judgment. Ahab al-Qabr is not mentioned in the Quran.

Adhan: Meaning "to listen," "to hear" or "to be informed," and derived from the Arabic word for "ear," it is the Islamic call to prayer, issued five times daily from mosques by a *muezzin*.

Ahl al-dhimma: Literally "the people of protection," the Christian and Jewish people living in an Islamic state.

Ahmad al-Nasai: An *imam* of the 9th and early 10 centuries and considered one of the six greatest Islamic scholars, al-Nasai wrote 5,700 *hadiths* collected in 52 books.

Aisha Abd al-Rahman: Widely known in the Arab world by her pen name, Bint al-Shati ("Daughter of the Shore"), Dr. al-Rahman was the preeminent female Muslim scholar of the 20th century. Born in Dumyat, Egypt, she authored 40 books on Islamic teaching and dozens on Arabic literature, as well as novels and biographies about Muslim women.

Al-Azhar University: Located in Cairo, Al-Azhar ("the most resplendent") is considered the most reputable Islamic educational institution in the world.

Al-fikr kufr: The easily remembered (in Arabic) Islamist concept that the mere act of thinking critically (*fikr*) automatically makes one an infidel (*kufr*).

Al-Futuhat al-Islamiyah: The Arabic name for the Islamic Conquests.

Al-murtadeen: Apostates; people who have "turned back" on Islam by rejecting any tenet of the faith or converting to another religion.

Al-Qaeda: The best-known of the radical Islamist terror groups, al-Qaeda, or "the Foundation," was established by Osama bin Laden and others in Afghanistan in the wake of the Russian invasion there from the late 1970s through the late 1980s. Eventually, al-Qaeda turned its wrath against the United States, perpetrating at its height of power the devastating attacks

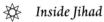

of 9/11. In 2011, American special forces penetrated bin Laden's secret compound in Abbottabad, Pakistan, and killed him. Soon thereafter, Ayman al-Zawahiri, the Egyptian doctor who recruited this author, took over as leader of al-Qaeda's operations.

Al-Qurtubi: Imam Abu Abdullah al-Qurtubi was a 13th century Islamic scholar born in Cordoba, Spain. He is noted for his famous commentary on the Quran, *Tafsir al-Qurtubi*.

Al-Shabaab: The group is not named "the Youth" ironically. Based in Somalia, al-Shabaab comprises a very young membership of indiscriminately murderous jihadists, within which are sprinkled an indeterminate number of foreign fighters, including some among its leadership. For about a decade, al-Shabaab has been wreaking havoc not only in Somalia but often in Kenya and elsewhere in East Africa. Its jihadists sometimes link up with al-Qaeda. For example, at this writing, both are allied and fighting in the civil war in Yemen.

Al-shafaa: The concept that Muhammad might intercede on behalf of a Muslim so he may enter Paradise. But the Quran is ambiguous about *al-shafaa*, as well as *al-Maqam al-Mahmud*, an intercession by a special person – assumed to be the Prophet – on behalf of all Muslims before Allah on Judgment Day.

Al-Tabari: Full name Abu Jafar Muhammad ibn Jarir al-Tabari, a Persian Islamic scholar and historian who lived in the late 9th and early 10th century, and who was also known for his writings on mathematics, medicine and grammar.

Al-takfir wa al-istihlal: A phrase meaning to consider someone and infidel and therefore it is justified for any Muslim to kill or behead that person.

Amir: Also *emir*; in Arabic, "emperor" or "commander," the word's meaning is closer to "prince." One of the titles given to Prophet Muhammad, its root might be in an ancient Sanskrit term for "wise man."

Apostate: *Murtadd* in Arabic, a Muslim who has rejected Islam or has converted to another faith.

Asbab al-nuzul: Reasons for the revelations to Prophet Muhammad by the archangel Gabriel. For example, several *ayat* in the Quran explain specific circumstances that engendered a particular revelation.

Awliya Allah al-Saliheen: Translated as "The Righteous People of Allah," the term refers to the practice by Sufi Muslims of visiting the gravesites of notable, honorable or holy people of all faiths. The visitations, which are considered pilgrimages, are thought to obtain blessings, spiritual guidance and enlightenment from the souls of the dead.

Ayat: The 6,236 poetic verses (singular, *ayah*) contained in the 114 *suras*, or chapters, of the Quran.

Ayman al-Zawahiri: The Egyptian doctor who, as a founding member of Jamaa Islamiya, temporarily recruited the author as a jihadist in the early 1980s. An associate of Osama bin Laden, "Dr. Ayman," as he is known to followers, ascended to leadership of al-Qaeda in 2011, after U.S. Special Forces tracked down and killed bin Laden. The U.S. government has posted a $25 million reward for information leading to his capture.

Baader-Meinhof gang: Also known as the Red Army Faction, this was a West German militant group active from the 1970s to the late 1990s. Collectively, the radicals killed 34 people and injured many more.

Bernard Lewis: A well-known British-American scholar, commentator and Princeton University professor, Lewis is a noted expert on the history of the Middle East and Islam. Born in 1916, he might soon become a centenarian.

Boko Haram: Loosely translated, the name means "Western education is forbidden" – particularly among girls and women. For over a decade, Boko Haram has been making murderous mischief in rural Nigeria and parts of bordering countries. More recently, the radical Islamists have provoked worldwide outrage – though little tangible response – by kidnapping Christian schoolgirls by the hundreds and forcing them either into marriages with Boko Haram members or selling them into slavery.

Burqa: A garment covering a woman's body from head to toe and in some cases even screening her eyes. It is a symbol of oppression and is required of women living in the strictest Islamic societies, such as Afghanistan during the reign of the Taliban.

Caliphate, The: Known as al-Khilafa in Arabic, the Islamic Caliphate originally was the seat of power after Muhammad's death and then the central authority when the Islamic Conquests began in the 7th century. Now, it persists as a concept among jihadists of a return to a worldwide Islamic empire under Sharia law.

Charlie Hebdo: A French satire magazine known for skewering all political and religious points of view. On several occasions, *Charlie Hebdo* printed articles and cartoons deemed offensive by Muslims, and on several occasions the magazine was either sued by Muslim organizations or its offices were ransacked. Then, on January 7, 2015, after the magazine published a cartoon depicting Prophet Muhammad, two heavily armed Algerian jihadists forced their way into the offices and killed 12 members of the magazine's staff, wounding 11 more. Witnesses heard the gunmen shouting *Allahu akbar* ("God is great"). A week later, the magazine was back up and running, and published an issue that sold millions of copies, the profits from which went to aid the families of the dead and wounded.

Dhimmi: In Arabic, "protected person," the term means a non-Muslim in an Islamic country. In the past, residents of conquered lands who would not convert to Islam were permitted to live, essentially, as second-class citizens, but only if they agreed to by the *jizya*, a humiliating tax. As *dhimmis*, non-Muslims could own property and pursue livelihoods, and even practice their faiths, but under the watchful eyes of their Muslim overlords.

Edward Wadie Said: An influential Palestinian-American literary and social theorist who maintained that Western hegemony in the Middle East, Africa and Asia had engendered much of the hatred in those parts of the world, particularly for the former colonial powers. Said was also a powerful advocate for the Palestinian people.

Eid: Either of two traditional Muslim feasts. The first, formally known as Eid al-Fitr, or "Feast of Breaking the Fast," marks the end of Ramadan. The second, Eid al-Adha, or "Feast of the Sacrifice," celebrates the *hajj*. In general, Muslims observe the former by eating sweets and the latter by eating lamb.

End of Days: In Arabic, "Youm ad-Din," or "Day of Judgment," believed by devout Muslims to be the time when all life on Earth will be destroyed and every member of humanity will face Allah's justice. The Quran does not specify when End of Days will occur – only that it will be at a time of Allah's choosing.

ETA: Peripheral to our topic but not entirely unrelated, Euskadi ta Askatasuna ("Basque Country and Freedom") is an ethnic terror organization operating in Spain. Immediately after the 2004 bombings of the Madrid transit system, which turned out to have been perpetrated by al-Qaeda, ETA – whose attacks had killed more than 800 people over the previous three decades – became the prime suspect.

Fatwa: A statement issued by an Islamic scholar to establish an Islamic religious edict or rule (plural: *fatawa*). A *fatwa* can include an order to kill someone for allegedly insulting Islam or Prophet Muhammad.

Fiqh: The jurisprudence of Sharia law.

Fiqh us-Sunnah: Written by Sayyed Sabiq, *Fiqh us-Sunnah* is a four-volume analysis of the four Sunni *madhahib* and is considered the most comprehensive work on this topic. It has been translated into dozens of languages and is used by Muslim scholars and clerics extensively.

Five Pillars: Though not contained in the Quran, observing the traditional Five Pillars of Islam is expected of devout Muslims. They include accepting Allah as the one, true God and Muhammad as his prophet; prostrating oneself to pray five times daily; providing charity to the poor; fasting during the month of Ramadan; and completing the *hajj* at least once in one's lifetime.

Hadiths: The words and deeds of Prophet Muhammad during his lifetime. The *hadiths* do not include the Quran, which is regarded as the literal Word of God.

Halal: In Arabic, "lawful" or "permitted," the term is universal but commonly applied to food or drink that is not forbidden, or *haram*, to Muslims. Common *haram* food includes pork, and forbidden drink includes alcohol.

Hajj: The fifth and final Pillar of Islam, it is the pilgrimage to Mecca required of devout Muslims at least once during their lifetimes if circumstances permit.

Hassan **chain:** In Arab and Islamic oral tradition, a verse, passage or longer message that had been handed down, generation to generation prior to a respected or authoritative person putting it to paper.

Hejaz: An area in the western part of Saudi Arabia encompassing the cities of Mecca and Medina. It is regarded as the most sacred region in Islam because of Muhammad's birth, revelation and reign there.

Hezbollah: Literally, the "Party of Allah," it is a Shia jihadist group and political party based in Lebanon and has been engaging in terror attacks, primarily against Israel, for over three decades. In 2015, for unfathomable reasons, Hezbollah was no longer considered a terrorist organization by the U.S. government.

Hijab: An Islamic head scarf for women worn in several styles and colors, the *hijab* is also a symbol of the onset of Sharia law and potentially of radical Islam's emergence in a Muslim community.

Hur: The collective name for the legendary 72 virgins that will serve each martyred jihadist in Paradise. Curious, but the women are described in certain authoritative writings, such as *Tafsir ibn Kathir*, as having soft, white flesh.

Ibn: A common connective word used in Arabic names, *ibn* and its alternative, *bin*, both mean "son of."

Imam: An Islamic leader of worship at a mosque – a holy man.

Infidel: In Arabic, *kufr*; anyone who will not accept Islam and Prophet Muhammad.

ISIS: The self-proclaimed Islamic State in Iraq and Syria, which has arisen over the past several years as an offshoot of civil war in Syria, now claims a sizable chunk of territory in both countries. Its members impose an extremely brutal form of Sharia law wherever they take power, and they claim to have reestablished the Caliphate in basically the same location as the original. In 2014, the organization declared that their name was IS, meaning they considered the drive toward a global Islamic State begun.

Islamic Conquests: Beginning in the 7th century and lasting over 400 years, the term – in Arabic, al-Futuhat al-Islamiyah – was an era during which Muslims swept across the Middle East, North Africa and parts of Europe and western Asia.

Islamism: The attempted or successful imposition of Sharia law as a society's or nation's sole legal authority. All Islamists are fundamentalists, but not all are jihadists or terrorists.

Jahadu and *jahidhum*: Two variations of the word *jihad*, the first meaning "to strive in our cause," and the second meaning "to strive greatly (or mightily)."

Jahannam: The name for the Islamic concept of Hell, the eternal fire in which those condemned by Allah will suffer.

Jamaa Islamiya: Formal name Al Gamaa al-Islamiyya, or "The Islamic Group," the militant student movement was founded in Egypt in the early 1970s in an attempt to overthrow the country's secular government.

Jannah: "Garden" in Arabic, the Islamic name for Paradise, where all the faithful and the martyrs will enjoy eternity.

Jihad: Literally, "struggle," the word is traditionally and widely understood by Muslims to signify holy war against infidels and apostates.

Jihadist: An individual who will use violent means – including suicide attack – to forward the agenda of radical Islam.

Jizya: In certain Muslim countries in the past, a humiliating tax that was required of non-Muslims who refused to convert to Islam. In exchange, the nonbelievers were allowed to practice their faiths and live in relative safety. Though no longer enforced by Islamic governments, extremist groups such as ISIS reportedly have resurrected the practice in the areas they currently control.

Kaaba: In Arabic, "square building," the structure at the center of the great mosque in Mecca and considered the most sacred site in Islam. Tradition says the Kaaba was built by Abraham (Ibrahim) and his son, Ishmael, about the year 2130 B.C. as the first temple for worshippers of Allah. Before Muhammad conquered Mecca and reconsecrated the Kaaba, it had been appropriated by local tribes for worship of their pagan idols.

Karbala: The first battle in an intermittent, millennia-long clash between the Sunni and Shia sects of Islam. Fought in the year 680 (61 in the 354-day Islamic calendar), a small band led by Hussein ibn Ali – Muhammad's grandson – was wiped out by a larger force sent by Caliph Yazid I. Today, all Muslims regard the battle dead as martyrs, but Shias observe the date (October 10) as an occasion of mourning.

Kiswah: In Arabic, "pall," the large embroidered fabric covering the Kaaba. Once each year, the Kiswah is replaced, and the old fabric is cut into small pieces and given as gifts to prominent Muslims and sold as souvenirs to participants in the *hajj.*

Kitab: The word for "book" in both Arabic and Farsi, as well as other languages in Asia.

Ma malakat aymanukum: Literally, "what your right hands possess." The phrase, which appears in the Quran, has been interpreted even by mainstream *imams* to mean Allah's guidance in the treatment of prisoners of war, slaves and concubines.

Madhahib: The schools of thought within *fiqh,* or Islamic jurisprudence (singular: *madhhab*). Many *madhahib* emerged over Islam's first two centuries, springing forth from the Sahabah – the direct descendants and associates of Muhammad. But eventually four Sunni *madhahib* (the Hanbali, Hanafi, Shafi'i and Maliki), two Shia (Ja'fari and Zaidi) and two independent (Ibadi and Zahiri) emerged as the most widely accepted among Islamic clerics – though the Sunni schools predominate.

Mansukh: The doctrine in Islam that the violent, chronologically later *suras* of the Quran abrogate the earlier, peaceful *suras*.

Maraji: After the Quran, Prophet Muhammad and the *imams*, the collective highest authority among Shia Muslims (singular: *marja*).

Mecca: The city of Muhammad's birth; the holiest place in Islam.

Medina: Originally known as Yathrib, it is the first city that Muhammad ruled. Its full name in Arabic is Medinat un-Nabi; literally, "City of the Prophet."

Mn kafar: Also used incorrectly by some as *mn kafir*, it means "infidels," or people who will not accept Islam and Prophet Muhammad. Alternate plural form: *al-kafireen.*("the infidels") – a critical distinction for purposes of fighting jihadism and reforming Islam.

Muezzin: The person, usually a devout non-cleric, who issues the *adhan*, the Muslim call to prayer, five times daily. In earlier times, the *muezzin* would chant or sing the *adhan* from the top of a mosque's minaret. Today, many *muezzin* employ microphones and public-address systems to transmit their calls to the community.

Minhaj al-Muslim: Translated, *The Way of a Muslim*, another bestselling analysis of Islamic jurisprudence. Written by Abu Bakr Jabir al-Jazairi, a 20th century Algerian scholar, the book has been printed and distributed worldwide.

Muhammad at-Tirmidhi: A Persian of the 9th century and considered one of the six greatest Islamic scholars, he wrote 4,400 *hadiths* in 46 books.

Mujahideen: Originally a term for Muslims engaged in *jihad*, it has come to mean the guerrilla forces in Afghanistan that resisted and, after a decade of occupation, successfully beat back Soviet invading forces in 1989.

Mullah: Derived from a somewhat vague term used in the Quran, it has come to mean an Islamic scholar or leader of a mosque.

Muslim Brotherhood: Founded in 1928 in Egypt by Hassan al-Banna, an Islamic scholar and teacher, the brotherhood is, essentially, the mother of all radical Islamic groups. Its goal is to install Sharia law wherever it gains power. Its motto is, "Allah is our objective; the Quran is the constitution; the Prophet is our leader; *jihad* is our way; death for the sake of Allah is our wish." Ayman al-Zawahiri, also an Egyptian and the current leader of al-Qaeda, traces his radical roots back to the brotherhood. Pounded and persecuted for years by Egyptian leaders from Nasser to Mubarak, the brotherhood managed to gain power in its home country in 2011. But after only two years, the Egyptian people rose up by the millions to oust the brotherhood and its leader, Mohamed Morsi. In that country, at least, radical Islam is currently outlawed and on the run.

Nikah mutah: A verbal or written contract between a man and a woman allowing them to become married for a temporary period, whether years, months, days – or even hours. Though commonly practiced among Shia Muslims, most Sunni clerics refuse to permit it.

Niqab: An Islamic veil for women that covers most of the face and hair but does not conceal the eyes and body to the degree of a *burqa*.

Osama bin Laden: Even in death still the world's most notorious terrorist, bin Laden was the scion of a wealthy Saudi family. He rose to prominence in radical Islam by aiding the Mujahideen in Afghanistan in the late 1970s and 1980s. With Ayman al-Zawahiri, he founded al-Qaeda and began plotting terror attacks against the West, with his triumph the terrorism conducted on 9/11. For a decade, he managed to elude efforts by the United States to track him down. But a team of U.S. Navy SEALs invaded his secret compound in Abbottabad, Pakistan, and killed him on May 2, 2011.

Qalansuwa: The traditional turban of Islam, worn since the beginnings of the faith.

Radical Islam: The term is somewhat misleading, because it implies an abrupt and major change of the Muslim faith. Instead, radical Islam is reactionary, a determined, dangerous movement to impose ancient interpretations of the Quran on the Muslim and non-Muslim worlds alike through terrorism and other brutal force, leading to the universal imposition of Sharia law.

Ramadan: A lunar month – the ninth on the 354-day Muslim calendar – during which devout Muslims, with certain exceptions, are required to refrain from eating, drinking, smoking and engaging in sex during the day. Ramadan commemorates the first month in which Muhammad received the revelations of the Quran from the Angel Gabriel.

Redda law: The tent of Sharia law that mandates the killing of any Muslim who renounces Islam or converts to another faith.

Saad Eddin Ibrahim: An Egyptian-American sociologist, author and outspoken defender of human rights in the Muslim world and elsewhere. He currently runs the Ibn Khaldun Center for Developmental Studies in Cairo, which works to advance the social sciences.

Sahabah: In Arabic, "the companions," the disciples and family of Prophet Muhammad, many of whom testified about his words and deeds after his death.

Sahih: In Arabic, literally, "accurate," referring to the *hadiths* considered the most reliable accounts of Muhammad's life and utterances apart from the Prophet's recitations of the Quran.

Sahih al-Bukhari: Considered the most authentic collection of *hadiths* in Sunni Islam, *Sahih al-Bukhari* contains 7,275 installments in 97 books and was written in the 9th century by Imam Muhammad al-Bukhari.

Sahih Muslim: Likewise considered an authentic collection of *hadiths*, and also written in the 9th century, *Sahih Muslim* contains more than 7,500 installments in 57 books by Imam Muslim ibn al-Hajjaj al-Naysaburi.

Sajjada: The small rug or mat on which a Muslim prays five times each day, positioning it so it is pointed geographically toward Mecca.

Salafism: Literally, "of the ancestors," Salafism is a strict, fundamentalist form of Islam, with roots going back to the earliest days of the religion. Its practitioners believe that the world will remain a domain of evil as long as secular states – particularly the Western democracies – exist, infidels and apostates go unpunished, and Sharia law is not universally applied. By far the largest philosophical sect among Muslims, Salafism is sometimes equated with Wahhabism, although many Salafists consider the comparison derogatory.

Salah: The second of the Five Pillars of Islam, which obligates Muslims to pray each day. Because the Quran does not specify the number of daily prayers, some Islamic sects pray less than the traditional five times, while some do not make daily prayer mandatory.

Sawm: The fourth Pillar of Islam, requiring Muslims to fast and abstain from certain activities during daylight hours for the entire month of Ramadan.

Sayyid Qutb: A noted Egyptian author and Islamic scholar, Qutb also became the leading figure of the Muslim Brotherhood in the 1950s. Executed in 1966 for attempting to assassinate President Gamal Abdel Nassar, Qutb also frequently expressed an extreme opposition to the culture of the West, particularly the culture of the United States.

Shahada: The first of Islam's Five Pillars and the creed of every Muslim: "I testify that there is none worthy of worship except God, and I testify that Muhammad is the Messenger of God."

Sharia law: Based on interpretations of the words and deeds of Prophet Muhammad, Sharia covers every aspect Muslim life. In its most forceful form, Sharia is the basis for the oppression – and frequent abuse and killing – of Muslim women and for *jihad* and the brutality demonstrated by radical Islamists. It is more; Islamists believe that Sharia is the only law – that secular law is of no consequence and should be ignored or conquered.

Sheikh: An Islamic scholar.

Sheikh Omar Abdel-Rahman: Also known as the Blind Sheikh, Abdel-Rahman was convicted of plotting the first terror attack on the World Trade Center in 1993. Prior to the attack, he had been preaching at mosques in New York and elsewhere, inciting Muslims to commit crimes and terror acts against Americans, whom he called a race of "apes and pigs." He is currently serving a life sentence at a maximum-security facility in North Carolina.

Shia: the second-largest sect in Islam. The Shia (or, sometimes, Shiites) believe that Muhammad's cousin Ali was divinely appointed as the only legitimate successor to the Prophet. Though Shia Muslims live throughout the Islamic world, they represent the majority only in Iran, Iraq, Azerbaijan and Bahrain.

Sira: Short for Sirat Rasul Allah, in Islamic tradition the name for the biographies of Prophet Muhammad.

Sufism: a mystical and non-literal sect within Islam, and one whose followers tend to believe in a variety of interpretations of the Quran. Unlike their fundamentalist brethren, Sufi Muslims do not ban music and dancing, or the appreciation of beauty. Throughout their history, Sufis have tended to live in relative accord with Christians and Jews.

Sunnah: The words, deeds and biography of Prophet Muhammad, and the basis for Sharia law.

Sunni: By far the largest sect of Islam, comprising Muslims who follow the Sunnah of Muhammad. Sunnis represent the majority of Muslims in all countries except Iran, Iraq, Azerbaijan and Bahrain.

Sura: A chapter of the Quran. The Quran has 114 *suras*, with each chapter divided into verses, or *ayat*.

Tabaqat: Islamic biographies organized according to the centuries in which their authors lived. Singular: *tabaqah*.

Tafsir: An explanation of the meaning of a verse in the Quran.

Tafsir ibn Kathir: A well-known commentary relating the *hadiths* and *sahabahs* to specific verses in the Quran, written by ibn Kathir, a 14th century Islamic scholar.

Takfir: An accusation of apostasy by one Muslim of a fellow Muslim. The accuser is called a *takfiri*.

Taqiyya: Based on the Arabic word for "fear," it is the practice of deceiving the infidel by engaging in practices that seem to belie devotion to Sharia law and *jihad* in order to advance radical Islam's agenda. *Taqiyya* can also be used if a devout Muslim fears persecution because of his or her religion.

Tarjuman al-Ashwaq: The "Interpreter of Desires," a well-known collection of poems by Ibn al-Arabia, a 13th century Sufi writer who completed more than 150 books.

Ulema: The group of Islamic scholars and clerics responsible for interpreting Sharia law.

Umar ibn al-Kattab: The second caliph of Islam, whose reign lasted from 634 to 644; Umar, as he was called, was a successful warrior, conquering Persia in only two years.

Umma: Used figuratively, the Islamic nation that includes all Muslims worldwide.

Wahhabism: A sect of Islam created and still highly influential in Saudi Arabia. Its practitioners, who call themselves *mawahhidun*, or "unifiers" of Islamic practice, aim to impose Sharia law exclusively in every Muslim country and to expand Sharia across the globe.

World Trade Center bombing 1993: Preceding the 9/11 attacks by eight years, al-Qaeda first attempted to destroy New York City's famous twin towers on February 26, 1993. Terrorists parked a truck containing over 1,300 pounds of urea nitrate in the underground parking garage of the North Tower. Though the blast was far too small to weaken the massive skyscraper, six people were killed and 1,042 were injured, mostly by the enormous amount of smoke that worked its way through the building's stairwells and ventilation system.

Zakah: The Third Pillar of Islam, which calls upon all Muslims to help the poor as much as their individual means allow.

RECOMMENDED BOOKS

Arab Cocoon, The: Progress and Modernity in Arab Societies, by Tarek Heggy. Vallentine Mitchell, 2011.

In this book the author suggests that the systematic rejection of modernity and progress is the direct cause of confrontation between most Arabic-speaking peoples and the West. The idea fits in exactly with the theological basis for Salafism, as I have explained, and how it encourages the backward thinking that Muslims – and the whole world – should live as Muslims lived nearly 1500 years ago. *The Arab Cocoon* addresses Salafism at the cultural level.

Arab Mind Bound, The, by Tarek Heggy. Vallentine Mitchell, 2011.

Dr. Heggy addresses how violence conducted in the name of Islam is connected to specific interpretations of the religion while opening the door to alternative interpretations that can play important roles in solving the phenomenon of *jihad*. He also describes the importance of Quranic education in creating the problem.

Clash of Civilizations and the Remaking of World Order, The, by Samuel P. Huntington. Simon & Schuster, 2011.

The power of this book is that it actually predicted the current clash of civilizations between the West and ISIS, and it correctly assessed the role of religious ideology in that clash. Both Salafism and radical Islam illustrate how Huntington's precise analysis is correct, and how these destructive facets of Islam will persist if they remain unchallenged.

Closing of the Muslim Mind, The, by Robert R. Reilly. Intercollegiate Studies Institute, 2011.

Reilly dissects Islamic culture and ideology from a Western point of view. His observations on how regressive Islamic ideology is a major cause –

rather than an outcome – of socioeconomic failures are completely on target. Reilly also describes in detail what I have covered about the link between suppression of critical thinking and the rise of radical Islam.

Crisis of Islam, The: Holy War and Unholy Terror, by Bernard Lewis. Random House, 2004.

Dr. Lewis provides a thoroughly researched historical dimension to my discussion of the theological, psychological and cognitive roots of radical Islam.

Heretic: Why Islam Needs a Reformation Now, by Ayaan Hirsi Ali. Harper, 2015.

Ms. Hirsi Ali addresses the pivotal need for Islamic reformation in personal terms. Persecuted as a young Muslim woman, threatened as a dissident and frequently criticized for her outspokenness, she nevertheless has courageously persisted in her efforts to fight the oppression of women and minorities in Muslim countries. This book is a testimony both to her own story and to her efforts to bring Islam peacefully into the 21st century in coexistence with the modern world.

In the Path of God: Islam and Political Power, by Daniel Pipes. Transaction Publishers, 2002.

Dr. Pipes provides additional historical perspective on the topic of radical Islam, focusing on such events the Iranian revolution, 19th-century radical awakening and the much-earlier Islamic Conquests. In doing so, he gives readers of *Inside Jihad* an excellent companion analysis of the problem.

Infidel, by Ayaan Hirsi Ali. Atria Books, 2008.

In her first bestselling book, Ms. Hirsi Ali provides a riveting first-person chronicle of the pain and suffering of women in Sharia-dominated societies.

Milestones, by Sayyid Qutb. Dar al-lim, 2007.

I am recommending this book, which was written by one of the leading members of the Muslim Brotherhood, not because I agree with any part of it but rather to illustrate how radical Islamists think – something that is vital to understand if we are to confront radical Islam effectively.

Minhaj al-Muslim (The Way of the Muslim), by Abu Bakr Jabir al-Jazairi (2 volumes). Dar-us-Salam Publications, 2001.

Written by one of the leading Islamic scholars of the 20th century, this book is widely distributed in the Western world. It provides a window on the process by which mainstream, so-called moderate interpretations of Islam can be adapted by radicals to dominate the faith and profoundly affect the thinking of young Muslims.

Princeton Readings in Islamist Thought: Texts and Contexts from al-Banna to Bin Laden (Princeton Studies in Muslim Politics), edited by Roxanne L. Euben and Muhammad Qasim Zaman. Princeton University Press, 2009.

This collection of key primary Islamic texts provides an introduction to Islamist political thought from the early 20th century to the present. Although the book shows a diversity of Islamic thought, it also demonstrates how the vast majority of current leading figures/scholars in the Muslim world promote and accept violent principles – or at least do not stand against them. The text also reveals that the Arab-Israeli conflict is not about land but the mere existence of the state of Israel, and that the desire to kill every Jew is not only the view of Hamas but is also an integral part of the current Islamic teachings.

What Went Wrong?: The Clash Between Islam and Modernity in the Middle East, by Bernard Lewis. Harper Perennial, 2003.

I will always remember the first question Professor Lewis asked me when we met for lunch in Washington, D.C., some years ago: "What went wrong?" Little did I know that his question, and our resulting discussion, would spur me to spend so much time thereafter pondering the answer, an effort that eventually led me to write *Inside Jihad.*

APPENDIX I

LIST OF WORLDWIDE TERROR ATTACKS — MAY 2015

SOURCE: TheReligionofPeace.com

Date	Country	City	Killed	Injured	Description
2015.05.31	Pakistan	Kamoke	3	0	A man and his son are among three election workers machine-gunned by the Tehreek-e-Taliban.
2015.05.31	Libya	Misrata	5	7	An Islamic State suicide car bomber takes the lives of five bystanders at a city entrance.
2015.05.31	Iraq	Baghdad	1	0	Video is released of a man being burned alive by the Shia militia group, Imam Ali.
2015.05.31	Afghanistan	Logar	3	4	A teacher and two students are killed when Muslim extremists fire a rocket into a government school.
2015.05.30	Nigeria	Maiduguri	26	28	Over two dozen worshippers at a mosque are disassembled by a Fedayeen suicide bomber.
2015.05.29	Libya	Benghazi	8	8	Eight people lose their lives to an Islamist rocket attack on their neighborhood.
2015.05.29	Nigeria	Tashan Alade	7	30	Seven people at a wedding are blown to bits by a Shahid suicide bomber.
2015.05.29	Saudi Arabia	Dammam	3	4	At least three others are killed by a suicide bomber outside a Shia mosque..
2015.05.28	Iraq	Baghdad	10	27	ISIS sets off a bomb outside a hotel, killing ten innocents.
2015.05.27	Pakistan	Quetta	2	1	Two Hazara religious minorities are gunned down outside their shop by Sunni radicals.
2015.05.26	Thailand	Pattani	2	0	A teacher is among two people riddled with bullets by militant Muslims.
2015.05.26	Afghanistan	Maidan Wardak	2	3	Two Taliban suicide bombers kill two guards.
2015.05.26	Kenya	Yumbis	25	0	Over two dozen police are murdered by al-Shabaab in a single attack.
2015.05.26	Iraq	Nimrud	1	0	An 80-Year-Old Christian woman is burned alive for failing to comply with Sharia restrictions.
2015.05.25	Nigeria	Gubio	43	50	Children are among dozens killed after Boko Haram briefly takes over a small village.
2015.05.25	India	Kashmir	3	4	Lashkar-e-Islam fire on a patrol of soldiers, killing three.
2015.05.25	Pakistan	Quetta	1	0	A Shiite trader is shot to death on the street by Sunni extremists.
2015.05.25	Pakistan	Quetta	2	9	A female doctor is among two Hazara religious minorities murdered in an attack outside a medical center.
2015.05.25	Tunisia	Tunis	6	10	The Islamic State claims an attack at a barracks in

Date	Country	City			Description
					which an alleged recruit shot six soldiers in the back.
2015.05.25	Afghanistan	Naw Zad	26	3	Over two-dozen defenders lose their lives to a brutal suicide assault by armed fundamentalists on a police compound.
2015.05.25	Afghanistan	Zabul	5	73	Two women are among five killed in a massive suicide truck bombing that leaves over seventy others wounded.
2015.05.25	India	Sopore	1	2	Fundamentalists fire on a mobile shop, killing an employee.
2015.05.25	Afghanistan	Guzara	1	0	A tribal elder is ambushed and killed by the Taliban.
2015.05.25	India	Shyamnagar	1	0	A 19-year-old is 'honor' strangled by her brother after marrying without her conservative family's permission.
2015.05.25	Afghanistan	Shah Wali Kot	6	0	All six people in a civilian vehicle are blown to bits by a Sunni bomb blast.
2015.05.25	Afghanistan	Shaheedan	3	0	Taliban in uniform murder three policemen.
2015.05.24	Syria	Raqqa	1	0	A 20-year-old captive is burned alive for refusing sex with Islamic State members.
2015.05.24	Afghanistan	Jawzjan	2	0	An adulterous couple is shot to death by their families on orders of a religious council.
2015.05.24	Syria	Palmyra	400	0	Women and children comprise the bulk of 400 civilians executed in cold blood by the Islamic State.
2015.05.24	Afghanistan	Sangin	13	24	A Taliban assault on police checkpoints leaves thirteen defenders dead.
2015.05.24	Pakistan	Bolochistan	3	15	The Taliban is suspected of a bomb attack that produces three bodies.
2015.05.24	Nigeria	Benue	96	0	Ninety-six are confirmed dead following a church-burning spree by militant Muslims.
2015.05.24	Iraq	Mosul	2	0	Two men are shot in the back of the head by ISIS.
2015.05.23	Afghanistan	Gilan	4	0	A family of four, including two children, is neatly disassembled by a well-placed Taliban bomb.
2015.05.23	Pakistan	Badrashi	2	2	Islamic militants are thought responsible for a shooting attack that leaves a mother and her son dead.
2015.05.23	Iraq	Baiji	16	0	Caliphate members slit the throats of sixteen traders transporting food into a city.
2015.05.23	Afghanistan	Uruzgan	2	0	Two gentlemen are turned into pulp by Taliban bombers.
2015.05.23	Afghanistan	Bala Boluk	4	1	Four local cops are shot to death by religious radicals.
2015.05.23	Somalia	Mogadishu	1	0	A member of parliament is gunned down by an Islamist group.
2015.05.23	Egypt	Sharqeya	1	8	Islamists detonate a bomb under a bridge, killing a passerby.
2015.05.23	Pakistan	Datta Khel	3	3	Religious extremists are blamed for an ambush that
					leaves three security personnel dead.
2015.05.22	Saudi Arabia	Qadeeh	21	81	An ISIS suicide bomber detonates at a Shia mosque, slaying twenty-one worshippers.
2015.05.22	Syria	Hasakah	2	0	Children watch as two captives are shot in the back of the head by caliphate members.
2015.05.22	Afghanistan	Ankhoy	0	15	Fundamentalists throw a grenade into a wedding party over music.
2015.05.22	Egypt	Sinai	1	0	A local soldier is abducted from an ambulance and executed in cold blood by Ansar Beit al-Maqdis.
2015.05.22	Pakistan	Hayatabad	2	2	Two are killed when Sunni radicals fire on a Shiite family.
2015.05.22	Yemen	Sanaa	0	13	Children are among the casualties when ISIS set off bombs at rival mosques.
2015.05.22	Syria	Palmyra	200	0	Two-hundred more Syrians are rounded up and executed by the Islamic State.
2015.05.22	Somalia	Awdigle	7	17	At least seven others are killed when al-Shabaab members attack a small town.
2015.05.22	Afghanistan	Faryab	2	0	A woman kills herself after the Taliban murder her husband with a roadside bomb.
2015.05.22	Saudi Arabia	Tawal	1	3	A child is dismantled by a Shiite rocket.
2015.05.22	Nigeria	Jwanda-Kobla	10	0	Sharia proponents sneak into a village and slaughter ten residents with knives.
2015.05.22	Somalia	Mogadishu	3	1	Pro-Sharia activists block a transport carrying government workers and machine-gun three point-blank.
2015.05.21	Nigeria	Ropp	9	0	Muslim 'mercenaries' set fire to a house and then surround it to prevent the family from leaving. Nine are burned alive.
2015.05.21	Syria	Palmyra	100	0	ISIS releases pictures of some one-hundred beheading victims shortly after taking a small city.
2015.05.21	Pakistan	Karachi	3	0	A Sunni man and his two sons are murdered in a targeted sectarian attack.
2015.05.21	Iraq	Diyala	2	0	Two civilians lose their lives when suspected ISIS burn five homes.
2015.05.21	Uganda	Kireka Cell	1	0	A cleric is gunned down by Religion of Peace rivals.
2015.05.21	Saudi Arabia	Dhahran	1	3	A civilian bleeds to death after Shia militia fire a rocket across the border.
2015.05.21	Libya	Misrata	2	2	Two people are killed by an ISIS suicide bomber.
2015.05.21	Iraq	Fallujah	1	0	A man is paraded through the streets and then hung from a bridge by the Islamic State.
2015.05.20	Pakistan	Peshawar	1	0	A man is gunned down in front of his daughter by Sharia activists, while taking her to school.
2015.05.20	Syria	Damascus	1	23	Sunnis lob a mortar into a school, killing a teacher and injuring twenty-three students.
2015.05.20	Syria	Deir Ezzor	1	0	Religion of Peace proponents tie a man to a post

(continuation from previous page: "…and then blast him with a bazooka.")

Date	Country	City	Killed	Wounded	Description
2015.05.20	Libya	Hawara	1	0	A Fedayeen suicide bomber kills one other person.
2015.05.20	Saudi Arabia	Najran	18	0	Shiite militias reportedly kill eighteen Saudis with a cross-border rocket barrage.
2015.05.19	Afghanistan	Uruzgan	4	8	Taliban bombers take out four locals.
2015.05.19	Nigeria	Barkin Ladi	27	0	Fulani terrorists massacre twenty-seven residents in overnight attacks on two Christian villages.
2015.05.19	Libya	Qubbah	1	7	A Fedayeen suicide bomber kills one other person.
2015.05.19	Syria	Haqef	6	0	A woman is among those killed during an ISIS attack on a Druze village.
2015.05.19	Afghanistan	Kabul	4	42	Four people, including a woman, bleed out following a suicide bombing in a parking lot.
2015.05.19	Iraq	Mosul	1	0	A journalist is executed for refusing to join the caliphate.
2015.05.19	Nigeria	Garkida	8	14	A Fedayeen suicide bomber takes the lives of eight patrons at a livestock market.
2015.05.18	Yemen	Nassab	10	0	Ten Shiites are killed by al-Qaeda in a roadside attack.
2015.05.18	Iraq	Rashid	5	2	Five civilians are reduced to parts by Mujahid bombers.
2015.05.18	Afghanistan	Ghazni	1	0	The Taliban murder a police chief.
2015.05.18	Iraq	Kirkuk	2	0	Two brothers are kidnapped and tortured to death by sectarian rivals.
2015.05.18	Syria	Palmyra	5	0	Two children are among five residents pulled apart when ISIS fire rockets into their neighborhood.
2015.05.18	Afghanistan	Uruzgan	12	0	A series of attacks on police checkpoints by armed fundamentalists leave a dozen dead.
2015.05.18	Afghanistan	Khas Uruzgan	7	0	Seven Afghans lose their lives when Sunni extremists attack a government building.
2015.05.18	Iraq	Husaybah	10	0	Ten civilians are killed trying to defend their homes from ISIS.
2015.05.18	Afghanistan	Kandahar	0	7	A Fedayeen suicide bomber self-detonates outside a hospital.
2015.05.18	Afghanistan	Janikhil	4	2	Four Afghans are shot to death by Sunni militants.
2015.05.17	Afghanistan	Zankhan	2	3	Two policemen on patrol are laid out by a Taliban bomb.
2015.05.17	Afghanistan	Kabul	4	18	Four innocents, including two women, are disintegrated by a Fedayeen suicide bomber near an airport.
2015.05.17	Iraq	Ramadi	5	12	Five people are blown to bits by a Shahid suicide car bomber.
2015.05.17	Israel	Nes Ziona	1	0	A 68-year-old security guard is brutally stabbed to death by a Palestinian.
2015.05.17	Syria	Palmyra	6	0	Six more people are reported killed by ISIS, including three by beheading.
2015.05.17	Iraq	Ramadi	10	15	A Fedayeen suicide car bomber slaughters ten Iraqis.
2015.05.17	Iraq	Baiji	8	0	Eight refinery guards are blown up by a Shahid suicide bomber.
2015.05.17	Iraq	Shura	3	0	Three civilians are buried alive by the Islamic State after being forced to dig their own graves.
2015.05.17	Yemen	Shabwah	21	0	al-Qaeda claims to have killed twenty-one Shiites with heavy weapons.
2015.05.17	Iraq	Ramadi	500	0	Five hundred civilians and soldiers are butchered when the Islamic State overran a city.
2015.05.16	Nigeria	Madagali	3	20	Boko Haram murder three men and kidnap seven women.
2015.05.16	Iraq	Mahmoudiya	2	9	Two Iraqis are blown to bits by Mujahid bombers.
2015.05.16	Iraq	Baghdad	5	0	Fundamentalists storm a brothel and murder three men and two women.
2015.05.16	Pakistan	Pewar	1	0	A Shiite man is murdered by Sunnis while out collecting firewood.
2015.05.16	Syria	Palmyra	23	0	Twenty-three civilians, including nine children, are massacred by the Islamic State.
2015.05.16	Afghanistan	Karikote	1	5	Fundamentalists shoot a youth to death for celebrating a soccer win.
2015.05.16	Egypt	al-Arish	4	0	Three judges and their driver are machine-gunned by activists fighting for Islamic law.
2015.05.16	Nigeria	Damaturu	7	31	Islamists strap a young girl into an explosives vest and send her into a bus station. At least seven others are massacred, not including the 'suicide' bomber.
2015.05.16	Yemen	Taez	15	100	Shiite radicals capture an artillery battery and turn it on a town, killing at least fifteen civilians.
2015.05.15	Thailand	Narathiwat	1	3	Muslim terrorists ambush and kill security personnel riding past on motorbikes.
2015.05.15	Iraq	Najaf	1	0	A prominent cleric is gunned down by Religion of Peace rivals.
2015.05.15	Iraq	Ramadi	10	7	Three suicide bombers murder ten Iraqis.
2015.05.15	Iraq	Jamiya	27	0	Thirteen people are killed in an ISIS attack. Fourteen others are taken captive and executed.
2015.05.15	Pakistan	Karachi	1	0	A policeman is shot to death by a Taliban on a motorbike.
2015.05.15	Pakistan	Hyderabad	1	1	A Shiite man is killed in front of his wife by Sunni gunmen.
2015.05.15	Somalia	Shabelle	15	0	Islamists pour grenades and machine-gun fire into two towns, killing fifteen.
2015.05.15	Kenya	Garissa	2	0	Islamists ambush and kill two police officers at their station.
2015.05.14	Afghanistan	Kabul	14	7	Nine foreigners are among fourteen people massacred when the Taliban storm a guesthouse.
2015.05.14	Syria	al-Sukhna	1	0	A man is riddled with bullets after identifying

...himself as Shia to Sunnis.

Date	Country	Place			Description
2015.05.14	DRC	Mbau	23	0	Twenty-three more villagers are hacked to death with machetes and hatchets by ADF Islamists.
2015.05.14	Syria	Palmyra	26	0	Twenty-six villagers are butchered by the Islamic State, including ten beheaded.
2015.05.14	Iraq	Baghdad	4	17	Shiite militia burn four Sunnis to death in their homes.
2015.05.14	Thailand	Yala	0	20	Militant Muslims set off twenty-eight bombs within a few hours.
2015.05.14	Libya	Benghazi	8	11	Seven children are among eight killed when the Islamic State fires a rocket into an apartment building.
2015.05.14	Iraq	al-Baghdadi	3	27	ISIS car bombers take out three Iraqis.
2015.05.14	Nigeria	Maiduguri	12	12	At least twelve Nigerians lose their lives to three female suicide bombers.
2015.05.14	Afghanistan	Kabul	1	0	Sharia proponents murder a prosecutor in his home.
2015.05.14	Nigeria	Kojiti	7	0	Boko Haram open fire on families preparing for bed, killing seven members.
2015.05.14	Thailand	Yala	1	0	A 32-year-old security guard loses his life to Muslim terrorists.
2015.05.14	Iraq	Badush	20	0	Twenty captives are executed by the Islamic State.
2015.05.14	Nigeria	Kayamla	30	0	Thirty villagers are massacred by Sharia fanatics.
2015.05.14	Iraq	Mosul	39	0	Thirty-nine Indian hostages are reportedly executed by the Islamic State.
2015.05.13	Syria	al-Sukhna	30	0	Thirty others are killed during an ISIS attack on a small town.
2015.05.13	Afghanistan	Dukon	1	0	A government official is kidnapped from his home and beheaded by Sharia proponents.
2015.05.13	Afghanistan	Lashkar Gah	7	7	Seven people are killed when gunmen attack a rival mosque.
2015.05.13	Thailand	Pattani	1	0	A 35-year-old man dies from injuries after being shot by Muslim 'insurgents'.
2015.05.13	Pakistan	Karachi	47	24	Sunni extremists open fire point-blank on a bus carrying Ismaili minorities, slaughtering fifty.
2015.05.13	Iraq	Nineveh	3	0	Three men are forced to kneel on the street and then beheaded by religious 'fanatics'.
2015.05.13	Nigeria	Baale	29	0	Boko Haram murder twenty-nine people and torch their village.
2015.05.13	Egypt	Rafah	3	0	Islamists kill three civilians with a roadside bomb.
2015.05.13	Pakistan	Mashpangai	3	0	Three security personnel are machine-gunned at point-blank range by the Tehreek-e-Taliban.
2015.05.12	Afghanistan	Kandahar	5	3	The Taliban are thought responsible for the bombing of a car that leave five family members dead.
2015.05.12	Iraq	Baghdad	2	9	Two Shiite pilgrims are sent to Allah by Sunni

...bombers.

Date	Country	Place			Description
2015.05.12	Iraq	Kaziniyah	10	25	The Islamic State bomb a roadside stand serving food to Shiite pilgrims, killing ten.
2015.05.12	Iraq	Mashahidah	3	8	Three pilgrims are laid out by an ISIS roadside bomb.
2015.05.12	Libya	Benghazi	4	0	Four children are exterminated by an Islamic State rocket.
2015.05.12	Syria	Homs	4	17	Four bystanders are blown to bits when terrorists sit off two bombs in a Shiite district.
2015.05.12	Iraq	Bab al-Sham	4	12	Three Islamic State rockets end the lives of four Shiite pilgrims.
2015.05.12	Pakistan	Kot Sabzol	1	0	A teen bride is honor killed by her conservative family over alleged sexual impropriety.
2015.05.12	Bangladesh	Bankalaparha	1	0	Four fundamentalists hack a secular blogger to death with knives on charges of being an atheist.
2015.05.12	Pakistan	Quetta	1	7	An innocent Shiite is gunned down in a targeted attack.
2015.05.12	Kenya	Garissa	1	0	A guard at a refugee camp is cut down by al-Shabaab gunmen.
2015.05.12	Pakistan	Sheikh Otar	4	0	Four people lose their lives when religious radicals fire at random into a construction site.
2015.05.12	Thailand	Pattani	1	0	Muslim terrorists gun down a village elder in his pickup truck.
2015.05.11	DRC	Mavivi	5	7	Five people are hacked to death with machetes by Islamist 'rebels'.
2015.05.11	Pakistan	Rialto Chowk	3	6	Fundamentalists are suspected in a drive-by attack on transgenders that leaves three dead.
2015.05.11	Pakistan	Barkamar	6	0	The lives of six tribesmen are brutally snuffed out by Taliban roadside bombers.
2015.05.11	Yemen	Najran	1	4	One resident is killed when Shiite militia send a rocket into a neighborhood from across the border.
2015.05.11	Iraq	Muqdadiyah	8	0	A father and son are among eight victims of sectarian executions found tortured and shot.
2015.05.11	India	Anantnag	2	0	Muslim terrorists murder two guards at a road construction project.
2015.05.10	Iraq	Taji	3	8	Jihadis set off a bomb at an outdoor market, killing three patrons.
2015.05.10	Iraq	Fallujah	6	11	A suicide bombing and several other blasts claim the lives of six people.
2015.05.10	Macedonia	Kumanovo	8	37	Muslim terrorists wage a running battle with police, killing at least eight.
2015.05.10	Afghanistan	Kabul	3	18	A suicide bomber kills three riders on a bus.
2015.05.10	Iraq	Tarmiyah	5	10	Five innocents are reduced to pulp by a suicide car bomber.
2015.05.10	Cameroon	Zelevet	2	0	Boko Haram ambush and kill two local soldiers.
2015.05.10	Syria	Jisr al-	32	0	Thirty-two others are killed during a massive al-

Date	Country	Location			Description
		Shughur			Qaeda attack on a town that began with a suicide bombing.
2015.05.10	Pakistan	Karachi	2	0	Two friends are gunned down by Ahle Sunnat Wal Jamaat.
2015.05.09	Afghanistan	Paktia	2	5	Fundamentalists attack a cricket tournament and murder two people.
2015.05.09	Iraq	al-Khalis	12	14	Terrorists kill a dozen guards at a prison.
2015.05.09	Iraq	Baghdad	7	20	A bomb targeting Shiite pilgrims takes down seven of them.
2015.05.09	Pakistan	Nazimabad	1	0	Sectarian Jihadis gun down a homeopathic doctor for being Shiite.
2015.05.09	Syria	Aleppo	5	19	Women and children are heavily represented among the casualties of an al-Nusra rocket attack.
2015.05.09	Syria	Raqqa	10	0	Ten hostages are forced to kneel, then executed with gunshots by the Islamic State.
2015.05.09	Pakistan	Lakki Mechankhel	2	1	Mujahideen enter a home and shoot a man and his mother to death.
2015.05.09	Iraq	Nineveh	13	0	Thirteen Kurds are executed by the Islamic State.
2015.05.08	Nigeria	Potiskum	3	10	A suicide bomber detonates at a college.
2015.05.08	Syria	Deir al-Zor	19	0	Nineteen others lose their lives to an ISIS suicide blast and subsequent assault on an airport.
2015.05.08	Iraq	Balad Ruz	18	41	A Sunni suicide bomber massacres eighteen worshippers as they are leaving a Shiite mosque.
2015.05.08	Iraq	Kanaan	4	18	A suicide car bomber plows into a crowd of Shiite worshippers, killing four.
2015.05.08	Saudi Arabia	Riyadh	1	0	Terrorists gun down a local cop.
2015.05.08	Egypt	al-Arish	2	0	Four guards are shot to death in separate attacks on a school and market.
2015.05.08	Syria	Homs	2	0	Two men are hacked to death for 'insulting Allah'.
2015.05.08	DRC	Matembo	7	4	Islamists hack seven villagers to death with machetes, including two women.
2015.05.07	Somalia	Galkayo	1	0	Religious extremists shoot an 'apostate' to death.
2015.05.07	Syria	Aleppo	4	0	Three children and a woman bleed to death when militant Sunnis send rockets into a neighborhood.
2015.05.07	Pakistan	Alingar	1	0	A peace committee member is laid out by a Jihadi bomb blast.
2015.05.07	Egypt	Rafah	2	0	Religious extremists roll up on and gun down two guards.
2015.05.07	Syria	Aleppo	2	0	Two men are paraded by the Islamic State, then shot in the back of the head.
2015.05.07	Libya	Benghazi	2	5	Two civilians are killed when Islamists mortar their neighborhood.
2015.05.07	Syria	Deir al-Zor	4	0	Four local soldiers are captured and beheaded by the Islamic State.
2015.05.07	Syria	Aleppo	2	0	A father and son are picked off by Islamist snipers.

Date	Country	Location			Description
2015.05.07	Iraq	Shajarat al-Dur	4	16	Four Iraqis are soundly eliminated by a suicide bomber.
2015.05.07	Iraq	Allas	2	0	A Fedayeen suicide bomber takes two victims with him.
2015.05.07	Cameroon	Mayo-Tsanaga	7	0	Seven people are brutally killed during a Boko Haram rampage through their village.
2015.05.07	Iraq	Hamrin	22	34	Shahid suicide bombers take out twenty-two Iraqis.
2015.05.06	Syria	Hassakeh	16	0	An ISIS suicide assault produces sixteen dead Kurds.
2015.05.06	Saudi Arabia	Najran	5	11	Shiite radicals shell a small town, killing five residents.
2015.05.06	Somalia	Mogadishu	1	0	A politician is assassinated by Sharia activists.
2015.05.06	Pakistan	Lower Kurram	1	3	A botched suicide attack on a school kills one innocent.
2015.05.06	Syria	Hasaka	3	0	A suicide bombing by the Islamic State kills three people in a neighborhood.
2015.05.06	Afghanistan	Sulaimanzai	2	4	Two children are reduced to pulp by a Taliban bomb blast.
2015.05.06	Iraq	Khanaqin	3	0	ISIS members murder three oil tank drivers in cold blood along a highway.
2015.05.06	Yemen	Tawahi	50	100	Women and children are heavily represented in the casualties of an hours long rocket barrage of a refugee camp by Shiite radicals.
2015.05.06	Nigeria	Ngulde	8	8	An 80-year-old man is among eight villagers slaughtered by Boko Haram.
2015.05.06	Niger	Koukodou	5	0	Boko Haram members burn houses and murder five villagers.
2015.05.06	Thailand	Yala	2	0	A Buddhist couple is shot and then burned by Muslim terrorists.
2015.05.05	Iraq	Baghdad	6	11	An ISIS car bomb in front of a hotel kills six civilians.
2015.05.05	Saudi Arabia	Najran	2	5	Shiite militia in Yemen shell a town across the border, killing two residents.
2015.05.05	Yemen	Aden	6	0	Shiite radicals kill one man with a mortar and then six of this rescuers.
2015.05.05	Afghanistan	Kandahar	1	3	Hardliners shoot a scrap dealer to death then plant a bomb that injures responders.
2015.05.05	India	Nadia	3	8	Three Hindu pilgrims are killed when a Muslim mob attack their procession.
2015.05.05	Syria	Sweida	2	23	Two civilians are killed during a series of mortar barrages by al-Nusra on a neighborhood.
2015.05.05	DRC	Kikiki	2	2	Two UN peacekeepers are ambushed and murdered by Islamists.
2015.05.05	Afghanistan	Jalriz	1	1	A child is pulled into pieces by a Taliban bomb blast.
2015.05.04	Syria	Homs	2	0	Two older gentlemen are tied up and shot in the

Date	Country	City	Killed	Injured	Description
2015.05.04	Libya	Derna	3	0	back of the head by Islamic State members.
2015.05.04	Pakistan	Deri Ghazi Khan	1	0	Three brothers are crucified by the Islamic State.
2015.05.04	Syria	Damascus	1	3	One person is killed when Islamic militants attack a school.
2015.05.04	Afghanistan	Kabul	1	15	A Fedayeen suicide bomber takes one other soul with him.
2015.05.04	Somalia	Yatho	3	0	One other person is killed when a Shahid suicide bomber attacks a civilian bus.
2015.05.04	Iraq	Rashad	2	6	Islamists storm a police station and murder three cops.
2015.05.04	Iraq	Baiji	3	5	Jihadi bombers target a displaced family, killing two female members.
2015.05.04	Somalia	Bosasso	1	2	Three Iraqis are blown to bits by a Fedayeen suicide bomber.
2015.05.03	Iraq	Baghdad	6	9	A civilian is killed when al-Shabaab militants toss a grenade into the street.
2015.05.03	Thailand	Yala	1	1	Six Iraqis are sent to Allah by a Shahid suicide bomber.
2015.05.03	Iraq	Baqubah	5	6	A man his killed and his wife wounded when Muslim insurgents' fire into his truck.
2015.05.03	USA	Garland, TX	0	1	Five Iraqis are laid out by an ISIS bomb.
2015.05.03	Afghanistan	Badakhshan	17	20	Two Muslims stage a suicide assault on a conference critical of Islam.
2015.05.03	Syria	Aleppo	2	36	Religious extremists pour machine-gun fire into a checkpoint, killing seventeen.
2015.05.02	Nigeria	Vat	17	0	A woman and child bleed out following a rocket attack by Sunni militants.
2015.05.02	Iraq	Karrada	9	20	Muslim terrorists shoot seventeen Christians to death.
2015.05.02	Iraq	Karrada	10	31	Caliphate members set off a bomb blast in a shopping district, killing seven patrons.
2015.05.02	Iraq	Diyala	7	0	A second bomb blast kills ten first responders at the site of an earlier blast.
2015.05.02	Iraq	Garma	12	0	Five women are among seven passengers torn to shreds by a Mujahid blast on a bus.
2015.05.02	Nigeria	Barkin Ladi	27	0	Suicide bombers at a train station take out a dozen Iraqis.
2015.05.02	Nigeria	Zakupang	13	0	Twenty-seven Christians are slaughtered by Muslim raiders.
2015.05.02	Iraq	Mosul	20	0	Women and children comprise the bulk of thirteen Christians cut down by Muslim militants.
2015.05.02	Nigeria	Foron	2	0	Twenty people associated with a travel agency are executed by the Islamic State for helping other people escape the city.
					Militant Muslims gun down a pastor and a female member of his congregation.

Date	Country	City	Killed	Injured	Description
2015.05.02	Syria	Aleppo	22	45	al-Nusra members send shells into residential neighborhoods, killing twenty-two.
2015.05.01	Afghanistan	Farah	1	0	A man is shot to death in his home by the Taliban.
2015.05.01	Iraq	Tal Afar	300	0	At least 300 Yazidi captives are reportedly executed by the Islamic State, including former sex slaves.
2015.05.01	Pakistan	Karachi	4	0	Four locals are murdered by the Tehreek-e-Taliban drive-by.
2015.05.01	Iraq	Baiji	16	10	Sixteen Iraqis are blown to bits by a Shahid suicide bomber.
2015.05.01	Libya	Benghazi	3	7	Three medics are exterminated by a suspected Ansar al-Sharia mortar round.
2015.05.01	Pakistan	Nawagi Khas	1	0	The Tehreek-i-Taliban murder a peace committee member with a roadside bomb.
2015.05.01	Nigeria	Adamawa	10	0	Ten captured women are stoned to death by Boko Haram to keep them from being rescued.
2015.05.01	Egypt	Sohag	1	0	A Coptic man is abducted and murdered by Muslims.
2015.05.01	Pakistan	Mangah	2	0	A father and son are pulled into pieces by a an Islamic bomb blast.

APPENDIX 2

SELECTED MUSLIM OPINION POLL RESULTS

SOURCE: TheReligionofPeace.com

I. Terrorism

BBC Radio (2015): 45% of British Muslims agreed that clerics preaching violence against the West represent "mainstream Islam"

Federation of Student Islamic Societies (2005): About 1 in 5 Muslim students in Britain (18%) would not report a fellow Muslim planning a terror attack

ICM (2006): 20% of British Muslims sympathized with 7/7 bombers

ICM (2005): 5% of Muslims in Britain told pollsters they would not report a planned Islamic terror attack to authorities; 27% did not support the deportation of Islamic extremists preaching violence and hate

ICM (2005): 25% of British Muslims disagreed that a Muslim has an obligation to report terrorists to police

NOP Research (2006): 1 in 4 British Muslims said 7/7 bombings were justified

Palestinian Center for Political Research (2015): 74% of Palestinians supported Hamas terror attacks

Palestinian Center for Public Opinion (2014): 89% of Palestinians supported Hamas and other terrorists firing rockets at Israeli civilians

People-Press (2004): 31% of Turks supported suicide attacks against Westerners in Iraq; 12% of young Muslims in Britain (and 12% overall) believed suicide attacks against civilians in Britain can be justified, and 1 in 4 supported suicide attacks against British troops

Pew Research (2014): 47% of Bangladeshi Muslims said suicide bombings and violence are justified to "defend Islam," 1 in 4 believed the same in Tanzania and Egypt, and 1 in 5 Muslims in Turkey and Malaysia

Pew Research (2013): 57% of Muslims worldwide disapproved of al-Qaeda, 51% disapproved of the Taliban, 13% supported both groups and 1 in 4 refused to say

Pew Research (2013): At least 1 in 4 Muslims did not reject violence against civilians (study did not distinguish between those who believed it is partially justified or never justified)

Pew Research (2013): 15% of Muslims in Turkey supported suicide bombings (also 11% in Kosovo, 26% in Malaysia and 26% in Bangladesh)

Pew Research (2011): 8% of Muslims in America believed suicide bombings are often or sometimes justified (81% never); 28% of Egyptian Muslims believed suicide bombings are often or sometimes justified (38% never)

Pew Research (2010): 55% of Jordanians gave a positive view of Hezbollah; 30% of Egyptians agreed; 45% of Nigerian Muslims (26% negative); 43% of Indonesians (30% negative)

Pew Research (2010): 60% of Jordanians gave a positive view of Hamas (34% negative); 49% of Egyptians agreed (48% negative); 49% of Nigerian Muslims (25% negative); 39% of Indonesians (33% negative)

Pew Research (2010): 15% of Indonesians believed suicide bombings are often or sometimes justified; 34% of Nigerian Muslims agreed

Pew Research (2007): 26% of younger Muslims in America believed suicide bombings are justified; 35% of young Muslims in Britain agreed (24% overall); 42% of young Muslims in France (35% overall); 22% of young Muslims in Germany (13% overall); 29% of young Muslims in Spain (25% overall)

Pew Research (2007): Muslim-Americans who identified more strongly with their religion were three times more likely to consider suicide bombings justified

Pew Research (2006): 12% of young Muslims in Britain (and 12% overall) believed that suicide attacks against civilians in Britain can be justified, while 1 in 4 supported suicide attacks against British troops

Populus (2006): 16% of British Muslims believed suicide attacks against Israelis are justified and 37% believed Jews in Britain are a "legitimate target"

World Public Opinion (2009): 61% of Egyptians approved of attacks on Americans; 32% of Indonesians agreed; 41% of Pakistanis; 38% of Moroccans; 83% of Palestinians approved of some or most groups that attack Americans (only 14% opposed); 62% of Jordanians agreed (21% opposed); 42% of Turks (45% opposed). A minority of Muslims disagreed entirely with terror attacks on Americans: (Egypt 34%; Indonesia 45%; Pakistan 33%) while about half of those opposed to attacking Americans were sympathetic with al-Qaeda's attitude toward the United States

YNet (2011): One third of Palestinians (32%) supported the slaughter of a Jewish family, including the children

II. Al-Qaeda, Osama bin Laden and the Islamic State (ISIS)

Al-Jazeera (2015): 81% of respondents supported the Islamic State (ISIS)

Al-Jazeera (2006): 49.9% of Muslims polled supported Osama bin Laden

Gallup: 51% of Pakistanis grieved Osama bin Laden's death (only 11% happy about death); 44% of Pakistanis viewed Osama bin Laden as a martyr (only 28% as an outlaw)

Hurriyet Daily News/Metropoll (2015): 20% of Turks supported the slaughter of Charlie Hebdo staffers and cartoonists

ICM (2004): 13% of Muslim in Britain supported al-Qaeda attacks on America

MacDonald Laurier Institute (2011): 35% of Canadian Muslims would not repudiate al-Qaeda

Pew Global (2010): 51% of Palestinians supported Osama bin Laden; 54% of Muslim Nigerians supported Osama bin Laden

Pew Research (2011): 22% of Indonesians gave a favorable view of al-Qaeda (21% unfavorable); 5% of American Muslims agreed (14% couldn't make up their minds)

Pew Research (2011): 1 in 10 native-born Muslim-Americans had a favorable view of al-Qaeda

Pew Research (2010): 49% of Nigerian Muslims had a favorable view of al-Qaeda (34% unfavorable); 23% of Indonesians agreed (56% unfavorable); 34% of Jordanians; 25% of Indonesians expressed "confidence" in Osama bin Laden (versus 59% in 2003); 20% of Egyptians agreed

Pew Research (2007): 5% of American Muslims had a favorable view of al-Qaeda (27% couldn't make up their minds) and only 58% rejected al-Qaeda outright

Pew Research: 59% of Indonesians supported Osama bin Laden in 2003 and 41% supported bin Laden in 2007; 56% of Jordanians supported bin Laden in 2003

Policy Exchange (2006): 7% Muslims in Britain admired al-Qaeda and other terrorist groups

Populus Survey (2005): 18% of British Muslims said they would be proud or indifferent if a family member joined al-Qaeda

World Public Opinion (2009): Muslim majorities agreed with the al-Qaeda goal of Islamic law and with al-Qaeda goal of keeping Western values out of Islamic countries; (Egypt: 88%; Indonesia 76%; Pakistan 60%; Morocco 64%)

World Public Opinion (2009): Attitudes toward Osama bin Laden: Egypt: 44% positive, 17% negative and 25% mixed feelings; Indonesia: 14% positive,

26% negative and 21% mixed (39% did not answer); Pakistan: 25% positive, 15% negative and 26% mixed (34% did not answer); Morocco: 27% positive, 21% negative and 26% mixed; Jordanians: 27% positive, 20 percent negative and 27 percent mixed; Palestinians: 56% positive, 20% negative and 22 percent mixed

Zogby International (2011): Majorities in all six countries said they viewed the United States less favorably following the killing of Osama bin Laden in Pakistan

Informal poll of Saudis in August 2014: 92% agreed that Islamic State (ISIS) "conforms to the values of Islam and Islamic law"

III. 9/11 Attacks

Al-Arabiya (2011): 36% of Arabs polled said the 9/11 attacks were morally justified; 38% disagreed; 26% Unsure

Gallup (2008): 38.6% of Muslims believed the 9/11 attacks were justified (7% "fully," 6.5% "mostly" and 23.1% "partially")

Pew Research (2011): Large majorities of Muslims believed in a 9/11 conspiracy

IV. Violence in Defense of Islam

BBC (2015): Following the Charlie Hebdo attacks, 27% of British Muslims openly supported violence against cartoonists. Another 8% would not say, meaning only 2 of 3 surveyed would judge the killings unjustified

Center for Social Cohesion (2010): 1 in 3 British Muslim students supported killing for Islam

Die Presse (2013): 1 in 5 Muslims in Austria believed that anyone wanting to leave Islam should be killed

ICM (2004): 11% of British Muslims considered violence for religious or political ends acceptable

Jakarta Post (2006): 40% of Indonesians approved of violence in defense of Islam

Motivaction Survey (2014): 80% of young Dutch Muslims saw nothing wrong with Holy War against non-believers. Most verbalized support for Islamic State fighters

NOP Research (2006): 78% of British Muslims supported punishing the publishers of Muhammad cartoons

NOP Research (2006): Hardcore Islamists make up 9% of Britain's Muslim population; another 29% said they would "aggressively defend" Islam

Pew Global (2009): 68% of Palestinian Muslims said suicide attacks against civilians in defense of Islam are justified; 43% of Nigerian Muslims agree; 38% of Lebanese Muslims; 15% of Egyptian Muslims; 13% of Indonesian Muslims; 12% of Jordanian Muslims; 7% of Muslim Israelis

Pew Research (2013): 76% of South Asian Muslims and 56% of Egyptians advocated killing anyone who leaves the Islamic religion

Pew Research (2013): 19% of Muslim Americans believed suicide bombings in defense of Islam are at least partially justified (global average is 28% in countries surveyed)

Pew Research (2013): 39% of Muslims in Malaysia said suicide bombings are "justified" in defense of Islam (only 58% said "never")

Pew Research (2010): 84% of Egyptian Muslims supported the death penalty for leaving Islam; 86% of Jordanian Muslims agreed; 30% of Indonesian Muslims; 76% of Pakistanis; 51% of Nigerian Muslims

Policy Exchange (2009): One third of British Muslims believed anyone who leaves Islam should be killed

Terrorism Research Institute (2011): 51% of mosques in the U.S. offered texts on site rated as severely advocating violence; 30% had texts rated as moderately advocating violence; and 19% had no violent texts at all

V. Sharia law

Center for Social Cohesion (2010): 40% of British Muslim students wanted Sharia

Gfk NOP (2009): 28% of British Muslims wanted Britain to be an Islamic state

ICM (2006): 40% of British Muslims wanted Sharia in the UK

MacDonald Laurier Institute (2011): 62% of Muslims wanted Sharia in Canada (15% say make it mandatory)

NOP Research (2006): 68% of British Muslims supported the arrest and prosecution of anyone who insulted Islam

Pew Research (2013): 72% of Indonesians wanted Sharia to be law of the land

Pew Research (2013): 81% of South Asian Muslims and 57% of Egyptians supported amputating limbs for theft

Pew Research (2013): Approximately 45% of Sharia supporters surveyed disagreed with the idea that Islamic law should apply only to Muslims

Pew Research (2013): 74% who favor Islamic law in Egypt said it should apply to non-Muslims as well

Pew Research (2010): 77% of Egyptian Muslims favored floggings and amputation; 58% of Jordanian Muslims agreed; 36% of Indonesian Muslims; 82% of Pakistanis; 65% of Nigerian Muslims

Pew Research (2010): 82% of Egyptian Muslims favored stoning adulterers; 70% of Jordanian Muslims agreed; 42% of Indonesian Muslims; 82% of Pakistanis; 56% of Nigerian Muslims

Responsible for Equality And Liberty (2009): 83% of Pakistanis supported stoning adulterers and 78%

World Public Opinion (2009): 81% of Egyptians wanted strict Sharia imposed in every Islamic country; 76% of Pakistanis agreed; 49% of Indonesians; 76% of Moroccans

World Public Opinion (2009): 64% of Egyptians said it was "very important for the government" to "apply traditional punishments for crimes, such as stoning adulterers"

WZB Berlin Social Science Center (2014): 65% of Muslims in Europe said Sharia is more important than the law of the country they live in

VI. Honor Killings

BBC (2011): 1 in 10 British Muslims supported killing a family member over "dishonor"

Civitas (2009): 1 in 3 Muslims in the UK strongly agreed that a wife should be forced to obey her husband's bidding

Daily Mail (UK) (2012): 1 in 5 young British Muslims agreed that "honor" violence is acceptable

Middle East Quarterly (2011): 91 percent of honor killings were committed by Muslims worldwide

National Post (Canada) (2011): 95% of honor killings in the West were perpetrated by Muslim fathers and brothers or their proxies

Pew Research (2013): Large majorities of Muslims favored Sharia. Among Muslims who did, stoning women for adultery was favored by 89% in Pakistan; 85% in Afghanistan; 81% in Egypt; 67% in Jordan; about 50% in Indonesia, Malaysia and Thailand; 58% in Iraq; 44% in Tunisia; 29% in Turkey and 26% in Russia

Pew Research (2013): Honor killing the woman for sex outside of marriage was favored over honor killing the man in almost every Islamic country. Over half of Muslims surveyed believed that honor killings over sex were at least partially justified

Turkish Ministry of Education (2009): 1 in 4 Turks supported honor killings

VII. Assimilation

Daily Mail (UK) (2010): Muslims had the highest claimed disability rates in the UK (24% of men, 21% of women)

Die Presse (2013): 1 in 3 Muslims in Austria said it is not possible to be a European and a Muslim, and 22% opposed democracy

Die Welt (2012): 46% of Muslims in Germany hoped there would eventually be more Muslims than Christians in Germany

FrontPage Mag (2012): Pakistani Muslims in the UK were three times more likely to be unemployed than Hindus, and Indian Muslims were twice as likely to be unemployed as Indian Hindus

Gatestone Institute (2013): 45% of Muslims in Europe said Jews cannot be trusted

ICM (2004): 11% of British Muslims found violence for political ends acceptable

ICM (2004): 58% of British Muslims believed insulting Islam should result in criminal prosecution

Ipsos MORI (2011): Muslims were 3 times as likely as Christians to believe that their religion is the only way

NOP Research (2006): 62% of British Muslims did not believe in the protection of free speech, and only 3% adopted a "consistently pro-freedom of speech line"

Pew Global (2006): Only 7% of British Muslims thought of themselves as British first (81% said "Muslim" rather than "Briton")

Pew Research (2013): At least half of Muslims surveyed believed polygamy is morally acceptable; Muslims in most countries surveyed said a wife should always obey her husband (including 93% in Indonesia and 65% in Turkey); 32% of Muslims in Indonesia said a woman should have the right to divorce her husband (22% in Egypt, 26% in Pakistan and 60% in Russia)

Pew Research (2011): Muslim-Americans were four times more likely to say that women should not work outside the home

Pew Research (2011): 20% of Muslim-Americans wanted to be distinct (56% supported assimilation)

Pew Research (2011): 49% of Muslim-Americans said they were "Muslim first" (26% American first)

Pew Research (2011): 21% of Muslim-Americans said there was a fair to great amount of support for Islamic extremism in their community

Pew Research (2007): 26% of Muslim-Americans wanted to be distinct (43% supported assimilation)

Policy Exchange (2009): 1 in 4 Muslims in the UK never heard of the Holocaust; only 34% of British Muslims believed the Holocaust ever happened; 51% of British Muslims believed a woman cannot marry a non-Muslim and only 51% believed a Muslim woman may marry without a guardian's consent; Up to 52% of British Muslims believed a Muslim man was entitled to up to four wives; 61% of British Muslims wanted homosexuality punished

Policy Exchange (2006): 31% Muslims in Britain identified more with Muslims in other countries than with non-Muslim Brits

Vancouver Sun (2015): 42% of Canadian Muslims agreed that Islam is "irreconcilable" with the West

Wenzel Strategies (2012): 58% of Muslim-Americans believed criticism of Islam or Muhammad was not protected speech under the First Amendment; 45% believed mockers of Islam should face criminal charges (38% said they should not); 12% of Muslim-Americans believed blaspheming Islam should be punishable by death; 43% of Muslim-Americans believed people of other faiths have no right to evangelize Muslims; 32% of Muslims in America believed Sharia should be the supreme law of the land

APPENDIX 3

THE AMMAN MESSAGE

SOURCE: AmmanMessage.com

In the Name of God, the Merciful, the Compassionate.

Peace and blessings upon His chosen Prophet, and upon his household, his noble blessed companions, and upon all the messengers and prophets.

God Almighty has said:

O humankind! We created you from a male and female, and made you into peoples and tribes that you may know each other. Truly the most honored of "you before God is the most pious of you. [49:13]"

This is a declaration to our brethren in the lands of Islam and throughout the world that Amman, the capital of the Hashemite Kingdom of Jordan, is proud to issue during the blessed month of Ramadan *in which the Qur'an descended as guidance to humankind and as clarifications for guidance and discernment.* (2:185)

In this declaration we speak frankly to the [Islamic] nation, at this difficult juncture in its history, regarding the perils that beset it. We are aware of the challenges confronting the nation, threatening its identity, assailing its tenets (*kalima*), and working to distort its religion and harm what is sacred to it. Today the magnanimous message of Islam faces a vicious attack from those who through distortion and fabrication try to portray Islam as an enemy to them. It is also under attack from some who claim affiliation with Islam and commit irresponsible acts in its name.

This magnanimous message that the Originator—great is His power—revealed to the unlettered Prophet Muhammad—God's blessings and peace upon him, and that was carried by his successors and the members of his household after him, is an address of brotherhood, humanity and a religion that encompasses all human activity. It states the truth directly, commands what is right, forbids what is wrong, honors the human being, and accepts others.

The Hashemite Kingdom of Jordan has embraced the path of promoting the true luminous image of Islam, halting the accusations against it and repelling the attacks upon it. This is in accordance with the inherited spiritual and historical responsibility carried by the Hashemite monarchy, honored as direct descendants of the Prophet, the Messenger of God—peace and blessings upon him—who carried the message. For five decades, his late Majesty King Hussein Bin Talal—God rest his soul—demonstrated this way with the vigorous effort that he exerted. Since the day he took the flag, His Majesty King Abdullah II has continued this effort, with resolution and determination, as a service to Islam, fortifying the solidarity of 1.2 billion Muslims who comprise one fifth of humanity, preventing their marginalization or extrication from the movement of human society, and affirming their role in building human civilization and participating in its progress during our present age.

Islam is founded upon basic principles, the fundamentals are attesting to the unity of God *(tawhid Allah)*; belief in the message of His Prophet; continuous connection with the Creator through ritual prayer *(salat)*; training and rectifying the soul through the fast of Ramadan; safeguarding one another by paying the alms tax *(zakat)*; the unity of the people through the annual pilgrimage *(ihajj)* to God's Sanctified House, [performed] by those who are able; and [observing] His rulings that regulate human behavior in all its dimensions. Over history these [basic principles] have formed a strong and cohesive nation and a great civilization. They bear witness to noble principles and values that verify the good of humanity, whose foundation is the oneness of the human species, and that people are equal in rights and obligations, peace and justice, realizing comprehensive security, mutual social responsibility, being good to one's neighbor, protecting belongings and property, honoring pledges, and more.

Together, these are principles that provide common ground for the followers of religions and [different] groups of people. That is because the origin of divine religions is one, and Muslims believe in all Messengers of God and do not differentiate between any of them. Denying the message of any one of them is a deviation from Islam. This establishes a wide platform for the believers of [different] religions to meet the other upon common ground, for the service of human society, without encroaching upon creedal distinctions or upon intellectual freedom. For all of this we base ourselves upon His saying:

The messenger believes in what has been revealed unto him from his Lord as do the believers. Each one believes in God and His angels and His scriptures and His messengers. We make no distinction between any of His messengers—and they say: 'We hear, and we obey. [Grant us] Your forgiveness, our Lord. Unto You is the journeying,' (2:285)

Islam honors every human being, regardless of his color, race or religion: *We have honored the sons of Adam, provided them transport on land and sea, sustained them with good things, and conferred on them special favors above a great part of our creation. (17:70)*

Islam also affirms that the way of calling [others] to God is founded upon kindness and gentleness: *Call to the path of your Lord with wisdom and a beautiful exhortation, and debate with them in that which is most beautiful (ahsan).* (16:125) Furthermore, it shuns cruelty and violence in how one faces and addresses [others]:

It is by some Mercy of God that you were gentle to them. Were you severe—cruel-hearted—they would have broken away from you. So pardon them and ask forgiveness for them and consult with them in the conduct of affairs. And when you are resolved, put your trust in God; truly God loves those who trust [in Him]. (3:159)

Islam has made clear that the goal of its message is realizing mercy and good for all people. The Transcendent has said, *We did not send you [Muhammad] but out of mercy for all creatures.* (21:107) And the Prophet Muhammad—blessings and peace upon Him—said, 'The Merciful has mercy upon those who are merciful, be merciful to those on earth, He who is in heaven will be merciful unto you.'

Islam calls for treating others as one desires to be treated. It urges the tolerance and forgiveness that express the nobility of the human being: *The recompense for an evil is an evil equal thereto, but who forgives and reconciles, his recompense is from God. (42:40) Good and evil are not equal. Repel with what is most virtuous. Then he between whom and you there is enmity will be as if he were an intimate friend. (41:34)*

Islam confirms the principle of justice in interacting with others, safeguarding their rights, and confirms that one must not deny people their possessions: *And let not the hatred of others make you swerve to wrong and depart from justice. Be just: that is closer to piety; (5:8) God commands you to return trusts to their owners, and if you judge between people, you shall judge with justice; (4:58) So give [full] measure and [full] weight and do not deny the people their goods, and work no corruption in the land, after it has been set right. (7:85)*

Islam requires respect for pledges and covenants, and adhering to what has been specified; and it forbids treachery and treason: *Fulfill the covenant of God when you have entered into it, and break not oaths after they have been confirmed and you have made God your surety; truly God knows what you do. (16:91)*

Islam recognizes the noble station of [human] life, so there is to be no fighting against non-combatants, and no assault upon civilians and their properties, children at their mothers' bosom, students in their schools, nor upon elderly men and women. Assault upon the life of a human being, be it murder, injury or threat, is an assault upon the right to life among all human beings. It is among the gravest of sins; for human life is the basis for the prosperity of humanity: *Whoever kills a soul for other than slaying a soul or corruption upon the earth it is as if he has killed the whole of humanity, and whoever saves a life, it is as if has revived the whole of humanity. (5:32)*

The primordial religion of Islam is founded upon equanimity, balance, moderation, and facilitation: *Thus have we made of you a middle nation that you might be witnesses over the people, and the Messenger a witness over yourselves.* (2:143) The Prophet Muhammad—peace and blessings upon him—said: 'Facilitate and do not make difficult, bear good tidings and do not deter.' Islam has provided the foundation for the knowledge, reflection and contemplation that has enabled the creation of this deep-rooted civilization that was a crucial link by which the West arrived at the gates of modern knowledge, and in whose accomplishments non-Muslims participated, as a consequence of its being a comprehensive human civilization.

No day has passed but that this religion has been at war against extremism, radicalism and fanaticism, for they veil the intellect from foreseeing negative consequences [of one's actions]. Such blind impetuousness falls outside the human regulations pertaining to religion, reason and character. They are not from the true character of the tolerant, accepting Muslim.

Islam rejects extremism, radicalism and fanaticism—just as all noble, heavenly religions reject them—considering them as recalcitrant ways and forms of injustice. Furthermore, it is not a trait that characterizes a particular nation; it is an aberration that has been experienced by all nations, races, and religions. They are not particular to one people; truly they are a phenomenon that every people, every race and every religion has known.

We denounce and condemn extremism, radicalism and fanaticism today, just as our forefathers tirelessly denounced and opposed them throughout Islamic history. They are the ones who affirmed, as do we, the firm and unshakeable understanding that Islam is a religion of [noble] character traits in both its ends and means; a religion that strives for the good of the people, their happiness in this life and the next; and a religion that can only be defended in ways that are ethical; and the ends do not justify the means in this religion.

The source of relations between Muslims and others is peace; for there is no fighting [permitted] when there is no aggression. Even then, [it must be done with] benevolence, justice and virtue: *God does not prevent you, as regards those who do not fight you in religion's [cause], nor drive you from your homes, from dealing kindly and justly with them: truly God loves the just;* (60:8) *Then if they cease, let there be no aggression, save against the oppressors.* (2:193)

On religious and moral grounds, we denounce the contemporary concept of terrorism that is associated with wrongful practices, whatever their source and form may be. Such acts are represented by aggression against human life in an oppressive form that transgresses the rulings of God, frightening those who are secure, violating peaceful civilians, finishing off the wounded, and killing prisoners; and they employ unethical means, such as destroying buildings and ransacking cities: *Do not kill the soul that God has made sacrosanct, save for justice.* (6:151)

We condemn these practices and believe that resisting oppression and con-firming justice should be a legitimate undertaking through legitimate means. We call on the people to take the necessary steps to achieve the strength and steadfastness for building identity and preserving rights.

We realize that over history extremism has been instrumental in destroying noble achievements in great civilizations, and that the tree of civilization withers when malice takes hold and breasts are shut. In all its shapes, extremism is a stranger to Islam, which is founded upon equanimity and tolerance. No human whose heart has been illumined by God could be a radical extremist.

At the same time, we decry the campaign of brazen distortion that portrays Islam as a religion that encourages violence and institutionalizes terrorism. We call upon the international community to work earnestly to implement inter-national laws and honor the international mandates and resolutions issued by the United Nations, ensuring that all parties accept them and that they be enacted without double standards, to guarantee the return of rights to their [rightful] holders and the end of oppression. Achieving this will be a significant contribution to uprooting the causes of violence, fanaticism and extremism.

The way of this great religion that we are honored to belong to calls us to affiliate with and participate in modern society, and to contribute to its elevation and progress, helping one another with every faculty [to achieve] good and to comprehend, desiring justice for all peoples, while faithfully proclaiming the truth [of our religion], and sincerely expressing the soundness of our faith and beliefs—all of which are founded upon God's call for coexistence and piety. [We are called] to work toward renewing our civilization, based upon the guidance of religion, and following upon established practical intellectual policies.

The primary components of these policies comprise developing methods for preparing preachers, with the goal of ensuring that they realize the spirit of Islam and its methodology for structuring human life, as well as providing them with knowledge of contemporary culture, so that they are able to interact with their communities on the basis of awareness and insight: *Say, 'This is my way. I, and those who follow me, call for God with insight.'* (12:108); taking advantage of the communication revolution to refute the doubts that the enemies of Islam are arousing, in a sound, intellectual manner, without weakness or agitation, and with a style that attracts the reader, the listener and the viewer; consolidating the educational structure for individual Muslims, who are confident in their knowledge and abilities, working to form the integral identity that protects against corrupting forces; interest in scientific research and working with the modern sciences upon the basis of the Islamic perspective that distinguishes between creation, life and the human being; benefiting from modern achievements in the fields of science and technology; adopting an Islamic approach for realizing the comprehensive development that is founded upon [maintaining] the delicate balance between the spiritual, economic and social dimensions [of life]; providing for human rights and basic liberties, ensuring life, dignity and security, and guaranteeing basic needs; administering the affairs of society in accordance with the principles of justice and consultation; and benefiting from the goods and mechanisms for adopting democracy that human society has presented.

Hope lies in the scholars of our Nation, that through the reality of Islam and its values they will enlighten the intellects of our youth—the ornament of our present age and the promise of our future. The scholars shield our youth from the danger of sliding down the paths of ignorance, corruption, close-minded-ness and subordination. It is our scholars who illuminate for them the paths of tolerance, moderation, and goodness, and prevent them from [falling] into the abysses of extremism and fanaticism that destroy the spirit and body.

We look to our scholars to lead us in partaking of our role and verifying our priorities, that they maybe exemplars in religion, character, conduct, and discerning enlightened speech, presenting to the nation their noble religion that brings ease [in all matters] and its practical laws in which lie the awakening and joy of the nation. Among the individuals of the nation and throughout the regions of the world, they disseminate good, peace and benevolence, through subtle knowledge, insightful wisdom and political guidance in all matters, uniting and not dividing, appeasing hearts and not deterring them, looking to the horizons of fulfillment to meet the requirements and challenges of the 21st century.

We ask God to prepare for our Islamic Nation the paths of renaissance, prosperity and advancement; to shield it from the evils of extremism and close-mindedness; to preserve its rights, sustain its glory, and uphold its dignity. What an excellent Lord is he, and what an excellent Supporter.

God Almighty says: *This is My straight path, so follow it. And follow not the [other] ways, lest you be parted from His way. This has He ordained for you, that you may he God-fearing.* (6:152-153)

And the last of our supplications *is that praise be to God, Lord of the worlds.* (10:10)

Amman

The Hashemite Kingdom of Jordan

Ramadan 1425 Hijri

November 2004 A.D.

A Poem by Dr. Maha Hamid

Finding excuses and justification for Islamic terrorism has become a fashion these days. We wish to avoid confronting the real problem of Salafism and blame everyone but the Islamists. This has led many to claim that terrorism is an understandable outcome of Muslim rage at perceived mistreatment by non-Muslims. My wife, Dr. Maha Hamid, has written a poem in response to these assertions.

Who should be angry?

Should it be the Muslims who kill innocents everywhere in the name of God?
Or should it be
...the Christians who have seen their churches burnt by Muslims in Iraq and elsewhere?
...the Jews who have seen their kids die in pizza parlors?
...the Buddhists who have seen their ancient statues of Buddha destroyed by Taliban?
...the Hindus who have seen their most holy temple burnt to the ground at the hands of Muslims?
...the Sikhs, who witnessed Muslims burning one of their gurus alive as he preached a message of peace and love?

Who should be angry?
The Muslims who bless such evil terrorism by their deafening silence against it?
Or should it be
...the Russians who lost their kids in the Beslan school massacre?
...the Americans who lost thousands of innocent people on 9/11?
...the British families whose loved ones were murdered by UK-born Muslims?
...the Spanish who lost hundreds of citizens when Muslims blew up their trains?
...the Australians who lost their sons and daughters when jihadists destroyed the Bali nightclubs?

Who should be angry?
The Muslims who never denounced Bin Laden strongly?
Or should it be
...the child who lost his mother when jihadists attacked?
...the daughter who lost her father from jihadist evil?
...the mother who lost her kids in cowardly acts of Islamist terror?
...the grandmother who lost her grandkids to Islamist atrocities?

Who should be angry?
The Muslims who produced terrorism by preaching hate in mosques?
Or should it be…
…the writer who lost his hand in a terrorist explosion?
…the young boy who lost his legs and cannot play football anymore?
…the musician who lost his fingers and can no longer play?
….the teenager whose face was mutilated by the fire of Islamist terror?

Who should be angry?
The Muslims who celebrated 9/11, mutilated dead bodies or beheaded hostages on videotape?
Or should it be…
….the whole world, which suffers from Islamic terror every day?

Who should be angry?

ACKNOWLEDGMENTS

I would like to express my gratitude to my dear friends Susan P., Robie R., and Susan and Bruce H. for their unforgettable assistance in creating this book.

I would like to say a special thank you to Lieutenant General Claude M. "Mick" Kicklighter for his great support and friendship to me and to my family ever since we moved to the United States.

Special thanks, too, to my friends in New Zealand who stood beside me in my fight against the incursions of radical Islam there. They include Joe B., Gail and Graham R., and Joyce B. Likewise, special thanks to Yair S., who was truly fundamental in editing and producing the first edition of this book.

My dear friend Brian Kumnick helped me immensely in the production and editing of the updated version. Phil Berardelli of Mountain Lake Press sought me out to update the book and distribute it widely through the American and the international book trades.

Above all I want to thank my wife Maha, my son Mada and my daughter Mariam for all of their love and support, not only in the production of this book but also in all of my efforts to redeem my faith and oppose those who have sought to appropriate and pervert it.

Last but not least I beg the forgiveness of all those who have been with me over the years and whose names I have failed to mention here.

INDEX

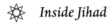

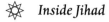

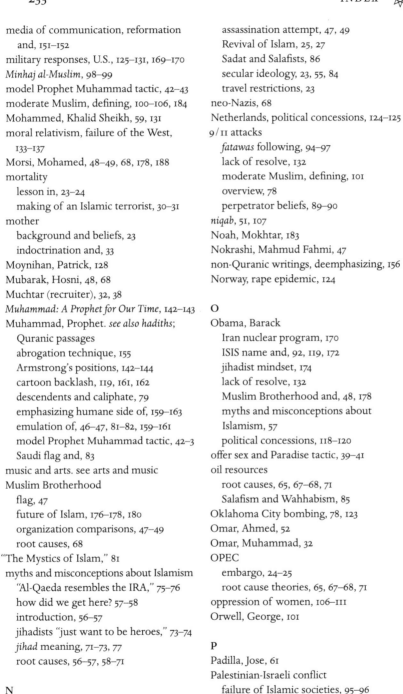

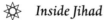